Miranda's Waning Protections

Miranda's Waning Protections

Police Interrogation Practices
after *Dickerson*

WELSH S. WHITE

Ann Arbor
THE UNIVERSITY OF MICHIGAN PRESS

Copyright © by the University of Michigan 2001
All rights reserved
Published in the United States of America by
The University of Michigan Press
Manufactured in the United States of America
⊗ Printed on acid-free paper

2004   2003   2002   2001   4   3   2   1

A CIP catalog record for this book is available from the British Library.

Library of Congress Cataloging-in-Publication Data

White, Welsh S., 1940–
    Miranda's waning protections : police interrogation practices
after Dickerson / Welsh S. White.
        p.   cm.
    Includes index.
    ISBN 0-472-11172-8 (cloth : alk. paper)
    1. Right to counsel—United States.   2. Criminal investigation—
United States.   3. Police questioning—United States.   I. Title.
KF9625 .W48   2001
345.73'056—dc21   2001002078

To Yale Kamisar, whose writings opened the windows of police interrogation rooms and illuminated the legal issues relating to police interrogation and confessions.

Acknowledgments

Although nearly all of the analysis contained in this book is new, I have at various points drawn from my previously published work in presenting accounts of either particular cases or Supreme Court doctrine. I would thus like to thank the following copyright holders for permission to excerpt material from the original sources:

Adapting to Miranda: Modern Interrogators' Strategies for Dealing with the Obstacles Posed by Miranda, 84 Minnesota Law Review 397 (1999) by Richard A. Leo and Welsh S. White. Reprinted with permission of the *Minnesota Law Review* and Richard A. Leo.

What Is an Involuntary Confession Now? 50 Rutgers Law Review 2001 (1998) by Welsh S. White. Reprinted with permission of the *Rutgers Law Review.*

False Confessions and the Constitution: Safeguards against Untrustworthy Confessions, 32 Harvard Civil Rights–Civil Liberties Law Review 105 (1997) by Welsh S. White. Reprinted with permission of the *Harvard Civil Rights–Civil Liberties Law Review.*

Miranda's Failure to Restrain Pernicious Interrogation Practices, 99 Michigan Law Review 701 (2001) by Welsh S. White. Reprinted with permission of the *Michigan Law Review.*

I would also like to thank several people whose assistance enhanced this book's quality. Albert Alschuler's comments on drafts of several of my chapters significantly advanced my understanding of the issues I address. John Parry has contributed valuable critiques of my writing and presentation. Richard Leo has been a constant source of support and assistance not only in helping me collect the material necessary to write this book but also in advising me as to how to deal with empirical issues. And Yale Kamisar, to whom the book is dedicated, has contributed not only through his comments on some of my chapters but also through his own writings, which have illuminated the subject of interrogations and confessions and precipitated my interest in writing a book of this type.

Finally, I would like to express my appreciation to the people who provided indispensable assistance in putting the manuscript together: the members of the Document Technology Center, LuAnn Driscoll, Karen Knochel, Darleen Mocello, Valerie Pompe, and Barbara Salopek, who went to extraordinary efforts to prepare the manuscript; my research assistants, Doug McKechnie and Gary Regan, who assisted in finding difficult sources; and my wife Linda, whose proofreading and other support was invaluable.

Contents

CHAPTER 1

Introduction

In *Miranda v. Arizona*,[1] the Supreme Court's most famous criminal procedure decision,[2] the Court sought to accommodate a fundamental conflict between law enforcement and individual interests. Law enforcement has an interest in obtaining reliable statements that will lead to the solution of crimes. Under our constitutional system, however, individuals must be afforded protection against police interrogation practices that are abusive, overreaching, or otherwise viewed as pernicious by society. In seeking to accommodate these interests, *Miranda*, which was decided by the Warren Court in 1966, adopted a new approach that generated great controversy, especially among those who believed that the decision imposed unnecessary restraints on law enforcement. More than three decades later, when *Miranda*'s most familiar features had become a part of "our national culture,"[3] some people still argued vehemently that the Court's landmark decision should be overruled because of its deleterious effect on law enforcement. In *United States v. Dickerson*,[4] decided in 2000, however, the Rehnquist Court reaffirmed *Miranda*.

Dickerson's holding might seem to suggest that over the past third of a century the Court has not significantly altered its view of how it should accommodate law enforcement and individual interests in police interrogation cases. In fact, however, the Court's efforts to accommodate these interests have been continually changing and evolving. Although the Warren and Rehnquist Courts agreed that the Fourteenth Amendment due process clause and the Fifth Amendment privilege against self-incrimination provide the governing constitutional provisions, in applying these provisions the two Courts would resolve the conflict between law enforcement's interest in obtaining incriminating statements and individuals' interests in being protected from pernicious interrogation practices in significantly different ways.

This conflict existed long before our Constitution, of course. A criminal defendant's confession seems to provide convincing evidence of his guilt.[5] When the government has an interest in establishing a suspect's guilt, it thus has a strong incentive to interrogate the suspect in a way that will produce a confession. Under many early systems of criminal procedure, government agents were permitted to use any means—including torture—to induce a suspect's confession.[6] The justification for allowing the government to employ torture and other abusive interrogation practices was that, at least in certain cases, such practices were necessary to secure the evidence needed for conviction.[7] In continental Europe, where the practices were most widely employed,[8] they were accompanied by two safeguards that were thought to minimize the possibility that false statements would be elicited. First, the practices were permitted only in cases where the evidence strongly tended to establish the suspect's guilt.[9] And, second, the practices were "supposed to be employed in such a way" that a guilty suspect would reveal details corroborating his guilt; through the use of nonsuggestive questioning, the interrogator would establish the suspect's guilt through forcing him to reveal "information which . . . 'no innocent person [could] know.'"[10]

The use of abusive interrogation practices to obtain confessions was much less prevalent in England than it was on the Continent. Indeed, by the sixteenth century, the English common-law courts stated that using torture to obtain a confession was impermissible.[11] As Professor John Langbein has shown, however, during the period from 1540 to 1640, there were "more than eighty cases . . . in which the Privy Council or the monarch ordered torture (or the threat of torture) to be used against criminals or suspected criminals" for the purpose of securing statements that would establish the suspect's guilt or lead to other evidence such as the names of the suspect's accomplices.[12] In many of these cases, interrogators were specifically authorized to employ the rack, manacles, and other excruciatingly painful forms of torture.[13] Even confessions produced by the most blatant forms of torture could be introduced into evidence, moreover, because, during the "early common law, confessions were admissible at trial without restrictions."[14]

As the common law evolved, however, English courts eventually excluded confessions extracted by torture or other abusive interrogation practices.[15] The exclusionary rule was animated by both a skepticism as to coerced statements' reliability and a concern for protecting individual autonomy. By the seventeenth century, it was recognized both in England and on the Continent that, regardless of the safeguards theoretically accompanying abusive interrogation practices, use of those practices was likely to produce false confessions.[16] In England, moreover, it became increasingly accepted that the government should not be permitted to employ certain kinds of coercive pressure against any individual, regardless of the individual's guilt or innocence.[17]

By the latter part of the eighteenth century, these concerns produced two legal doctrines limiting the admissibility of confessions in Anglo-American criminal cases: the common-law rule prohibiting the admission of involuntary confessions[18] and the privilege against self-incrimination.[19] Both of these doctrines played a part in producing the constitutional provisions that the Supreme Court has primarily relied upon in seeking to regulate the admissibility of police-induced confessions.

The Court's efforts to regulate the admissibility of such confessions during the twentieth century may be divided into three stages, each stage covering about a third of a century. During the first third of the century, the Court essentially remained passive. Until 1936, it failed to consider any state cases in which the admissibility of a suspect's confession was at issue. Since the states are primarily responsible for the enforcement of criminal law, the Court's quiescence left the regulation of police interrogation practices largely to state courts, with the result that restrictions on police practices were minimal. By the early 1930s, however, the public's increasing concern about abusive police interrogation practices created a climate that precipitated the Court's effort to regulate interrogation practices through considering the constitutional admissibility of confessions in state criminal cases.

During the second third of the century, from 1936 to 1966, the Court sought to regulate police interrogation practices through application of the due process voluntariness test, which was apparently derived from the common-law rule prohibiting the introduction of involuntary confessions. While the common-law voluntariness test was designed solely to exclude untrustworthy confessions, however, the due process voluntariness test seemed intended to accomplish multiple objectives. At its inception, the due process test was applied to exclude confessions obtained through torture and other practices that seemed apt to produce untrustworthy confessions. In the course of its three decade evolution, however, the test was also applied to exclude confessions resulting from interrogation practices that exerted excessive or unfair pressure on suspects regardless of whether the practices' likely effect would be to produce untrustworthy statements.

In applying the due process test, the Court took account of law enforcement's interest in obtaining confessions. Even at the end of the due process era—when the restrictions imposed on the police were greatest—a pivotal opinion emphasized that police interrogation is "indispensable to law enforcement."[20] While the Court held that confessions produced by particular interrogation practices were involuntary, it never challenged interrogators' right to interrogate suspects at the police station in secret. Moreover, although the Court sometimes referred to interrogated suspects' rights—stating in one case that interrogators must show "full regard for the rights of those being questioned"[21]—it never identified interrogated suspects' rights nor indicated what action, if any, the police should take to protect them.

The third stage in the Court's efforts to regulate police interrogation practices dates from 1966, when the Warren Court decided *Miranda v. Arizona,* to the present. In *Miranda,* the Court broke new constitutional ground by holding that the Fifth Amendment privilege against self-incrimination applied to the pretrial interrogation of suspects in custody. By holding, moreover, that, in the absence of safeguards, custodial interrogation was inherently coercive, *Miranda* set the stage for identifying the rights that must be afforded suspects subjected to custodial interrogation. In the most famous portion of its opinion, the Court provided that, in the absence of other safeguards, confessions obtained through custodial interrogation would be inadmissible unless the police first warned the suspect of four specified rights and the suspect waived those rights.[22] Thus interrogating officers were required to inform suspects in custody of their rights—including the right to remain silent and the right to have an attorney present at questioning—before beginning an interrogation.

By reaffirming *Miranda, Dickerson* indicated that *Miranda's* safeguards continue to apply. Although this indicates that the third stage of the Court's effort to regulate police interrogation practices will continue into the twenty-first century, it does not mean that the constitutional rules governing police interrogation practices have remained static during the *Miranda* era. Like the due process voluntariness test, the protections provided by *Miranda's* safeguards have changed over time. But whereas the Warren Court interpreted the due process test so as to expand protections afforded suspects subjected to police interrogation, the Burger and Rehnquist Courts have interpreted *Miranda* so as to diminish suspects' protections. In assessing the present Court's effort to accommodate the conflicting interests between law enforcement and individual interests in police interrogation cases, it is thus necessary to trace the evolution of the Court's police interrogation decisions in some detail.

In tracing this evolution, I will devote considerable attention to the writings of past and present law professors. Law professors from various eras have played an unusually significant role in shaping the Court's response to interrogation practices. During the early phase of the Court's due process era, John Henry Wigmore, the great evidence scholar, and Fred Inbau, his protégé, were vigorous advocates on behalf of law enforcement. Inbau, the principal author of the most widely used interrogation manual,[23] cogently argued that psychologically oriented interrogation practices were indispensable to effective law enforcement. Specifically, Inbau maintained that the police will often be unable to solve crimes in the absence of a suspect's incriminating statements and that in many cases the police need to employ psychologically oriented interrogation techniques to obtain such statements. In *Miranda*, the Court seemed to disapprove of some of the interrogation techniques described in Inbau's manual. Nevertheless, in both pre- and post-*Miranda* cases, the Court has implicitly accepted Inbau's view that psychologically oriented police interrogation is indispensable to effective law enforcement.

Of the many prominent professors who have argued on behalf of protecting individuals subjected to police interrogation, Yale Kamisar has been the most eloquent and influential. Kamisar, who began writing about police interrogation and confessions in 1963,[24] has not only revealed the nature of police interrogation practices but also meticulously examined Supreme Court cases governing such practices. Through his articles, Kamisar provided a window into the interrogation room, allowing us to obtain a better understanding of the effect that psychologically oriented interrogation techniques are likely to have on a typical suspect. His thorough analysis of the constitutional issues at stake, moreover, not only laid the theoretical groundwork for the *Miranda* decision at the time it was decided but also provided a sound basis for rejecting the constitutional challenge to *Miranda* in *Dickerson* more than a third of a century later.

At least one other law professor deserves mention for the role he has played in shaping the debate on the extent to which constitutional restrictions should be imposed on police interrogation practices. During the past decade, Professor Paul Cassell has spearheaded an assault on *Miranda*, attacking the decision's warning and waiver requirements on both policy and constitutional grounds. In the early 1990s, Cassell wrote a series of articles asserting that the *Miranda* decision has significantly impaired the police's ability to obtain reliable confessions, resulting in innumerable lost convictions. In both scholarly journals and in the media, he has maintained that *Miranda* has been the most harmful decision to law enforcement in the last fifty years.[25] In addition, as the attorney representing the Washington Legal Foundation and the Safe Streets Coalition, Cassell precipitated the constitutional challenge to *Miranda* considered by the Court in *Dickerson*.

In attacking *Miranda*, Cassell's guiding principle has been that the burden *Miranda*'s safeguards impose on law enforcement is not constitutionally justified. Specifically, he has asserted that *Miranda*'s costs should be measured in terms of "confessions . . . not obtained under the *Miranda* rules" that would have been obtained and admissible under the due process voluntariness test.[26] In presenting the issue in this way, Cassell, of course, fails to consider the extent to which *Miranda*'s safeguards may be superior to the due process test in protecting suspects' constitutional rights.[27] In determining whether *Miranda*'s safeguards constitute sound constitutional law or wise public policy, it would seem that the safeguards' efficacy in protecting suspects' constitutional rights as well as their burden on law enforcement should be considered.

Cassell has recognized that, in some contexts, the Court's current constitutional restrictions on police interrogation do not provide sufficient protection for suspects. In particular, he has acknowledged that the present constitutional restrictions sometimes provide inadequate restraints on pernicious interrogation practices because of the difficulty in determining what transpires during police interrogations.[28] In addition, he has indicated that safeguards designed to reduce the likelihood of police-induced false confessions may be appropriate in some situations.[29] To address these problems, however, Cassell has simply proposed that *Miranda*'s safeguards be replaced by alternative safeguards that include mandatory electronic recording of police interrogations.[30] In making this proposal, he has emphasized not only the value of mandating recording of confessions but also the benefits of dropping *Miranda*'s most significant requirements. Indeed, he has proclaimed that *Miranda*'s warning and waiver requirements have not only done nothing to protect the innocent but have actually exacerbated the problem of wrongful convictions resulting from false confessions.[31]

Although *Dickerson* rejected Cassell's constitutional assault on *Miranda*, Cassell's assertions relating to *Miranda*'s burden on law enforcement and *Miranda*'s adverse effect on innocent suspects are likely to precipitate further debate relating to the efficacy of the present Court's constitutional restrictions on police interrogation practices. Accordingly, this is an appropriate time to assess the Court's efforts to address this conflict. In making such an assessment, it is important to consider not only the extent to which *Miranda*'s safeguards have imposed costs on law enforcement but also whether the constitutional restrictions imposed on law enforcement during the post-*Miranda* era have been successful in protecting suspects from pernicious interrogation practices.

In this book, I will attempt to make this assessment. In making it, I will focus not only on *Miranda* but also on the post-*Miranda* Court's total effort to regulate interrogation practices. Although a great deal of attention has been directed toward the *Miranda* decision, *Miranda* has been modified by significant post-*Miranda* decisions. In addition, the due process voluntariness test continues to play a vital role in regulating police interrogation practices. In order to assess the post-*Miranda* Court's efforts to regulate interrogation practices, it is therefore necessary to consider all of the relevant constitutional doctrine, not simply *Miranda* alone.

As Kamisar has pointed out, moreover, in order to assess the Court's decisions relating to police questioning, it is essential to have some understanding of "what such questioning is really like."[32] In order to provide that understanding, I will present material from police interrogation manuals and transcripts of suspects' interrogations. In addition to providing the reader with a richer understanding of the nature of police interrogation, this material will show some of the ways in which Supreme Court doctrine has shaped interrogation techniques and, concomitantly, how modern interrogators have adapted their techniques so as to enable them to obtain confessions despite the obstacles presented by Supreme Court decisions.

In assessing the Court's efforts to regulate interrogation practices, it is obviously necessary to have a clear understanding of the significance of the due process clause of the Fourteenth Amendment and the Fifth Amendment privilege against self-incrimination, the two primary constitutional provisions that the Court has interpreted during the course of its efforts to impose constitutional restrictions on police interrogation.[33] During the latter half of the twentieth century, the due process clause has been interpreted to bar the government from seeking to convict a criminal defendant through means that violate basic notions of fairness.[34] According to this rule, police interrogators should be prohibited from employing interrogation methods that offend contemporary standards of fairness, a principle that has essentially been adopted by the post-*Miranda* Court.[35]

Applying the Fifth Amendment privilege to pretrial interrogation is more difficult. As Professor Albert Alschuler has said, "Nothing closely resembling stationhouse interrogation occurred at the time of the Fifth Amendment's framing."[36] Alschuler's research provides convincing evidence, however, that the privilege was "not intended to prohibit the forceful pretrial interrogation of suspects . . . so long as the suspects remained unsworn."[37] In determining what limits the privilege would impose on pretrial interrogation, the historical evidence is less clear.

Observing that the common-law "requirement that confessions be voluntary antedated the Fifth Amendment," Alschuler asserts that "[t]he Framers of the Fifth Amendment might well have assumed that their prohibition of 'compulsion' to incriminate oneself included a requirement that confessions be 'uncompelled' or voluntary."[38]

Although it has not explicitly relied on historical evidence, the post-*Miranda* Court has adopted a very similar view of the Fifth Amendment's application to pretrial interrogation. In dicta, the Court has stated that confessions produced by pretrial police interrogation will be compelled within the meaning of the Fifth Amendment privilege when they would be involuntary under the due process voluntariness test.[39] Thus confessions that are involuntary under the due process test are also compelled within the meaning of the Fifth Amendment privilege.

In assessing the Court's effort to regulate police interrogation practices, I will accept the Court's interpretations of both of the relevant constitutional provisions. The Court's interpretations, of course, provide substantial leeway for normative choices and policy judgments. In making those choices and judgments, I will be guided to some extent, as I believe the Court should be also, by pragmatic assessments as to the effect that the application of constitutional principles is likely to have in practice.

Broadly stated, my thesis is that during the post-*Miranda* era, the Court has not struck an appropriate balance between protecting the interests of law enforcement and safeguarding the constitutional rights of criminal suspects. Contrary to Cassell and other conservative scholars who have criticized *Miranda*, however, my position is not that *Miranda* has unnecessarily impaired law enforcement's ability to obtain confessions. Rather, I believe that, during the post-*Miranda* era, the Court has provided suspects with insufficient protection against pernicious interrogation practices.

In theory, the *Miranda* warnings provide suspects with ample protection against such practices. The warnings not only provide a suspect with the possibility of eliminating interrogation—through responding to the warnings by invoking his right to remain silent—but also with assurance that the police will respect his rights throughout the interrogation. But because the police have the sole responsibility for implementing *Miranda*'s safeguards, the protections provided by the *Miranda* warnings have often been illusory. During the post-*Miranda* era, the police have sometimes totally avoided the Court's efforts to regulate interrogation practices through lying about their interactions with suspects. And even when police interrogation of suspects has been accurately reported (or even recorded), there is substantial evidence that standard interrogation methods have been abusive not only in the sense that they have improperly interfered with suspects' autonomy but also because they have precipitated a significant number of false confessions, which in turn have contributed to a disturbingly high number of wrongful convictions.

In assessing whether the Court's constitutional restrictions on police interrogation practices have struck an appropriate balance between accommodating law enforcement and individual interests, the constitutional restrictions should not be considered in a vacuum. In order to understand the effect of the restrictions on interrogation practices imposed by the post-*Miranda* due process test, it is important to trace the evolution of that test, showing how the Court developed and refined that test during the pre-*Miranda* era. Similarly, in evaluating *Miranda* from either a constitutional or a policy perspective, it is important to examine both *Miranda*'s historical evolution—tracing the social and doctrinal developments that led the Warren Court to adopt *Miranda*'s requirements—and the effect that its core requirements have had on interrogation practices—exploring the ways in which modern interrogators have adapted their techniques to deal with the problems presented by *Miranda*.

The first part of this book undertakes these inquiries. Chapters 2 through 4 trace the historical evolution of the current constitutional restrictions on interrogation practices, examining the interrogation practices and doctrinal developments that led the Court to attempt to regulate police interrogation practices first through the due process voluntariness test and then through *Miranda*.

The next five chapters consider various aspects of the *Miranda* decision: Chapter 5 explains *Miranda*'s constitutional holding and the immediate reaction to it; chapter 6 delineates *Miranda*'s subsequent history, showing how the Burger and Rehnquist Courts' interpretations of *Miranda* first weakened and then revived the decision; chapter 7 shows how modern interrogators have adapted to *Miranda*, identifying some of the strategies interrogators employ to surmount the obstacles *Miranda* presents; chapter 8 deals with the *Dickerson* decision, explaining the Court's basis for that decision and its effect on *Miranda*; and chapter 9 assesses *Miranda*'s limitations, explaining why *Miranda*, as interpreted by the Burger and Rehnquist Courts, does not provide sufficient protection for suspects subjected to police interrogation.

The following three chapters give examples of situations in which the present constitutional restrictions on police interrogation practices provide insufficient protection against pernicious interrogation practices. Chapter 10 examines evidence showing that a small group of police interrogators have systematically extracted confessions through torture. In analyzing this phenomenon, I do not mean to suggest that police interrogators frequently employ brutality to obtain confessions, a proposition that seems demonstrably false. My point, rather, is that the small group of interrogators' pattern of behavior over a prolonged period—not only extracting confessions through torture, but also having considerable success in admitting these confessions at trial—provides tangible evidence that one of *Miranda's* most fundamental weaknesses is its failure to address the problem of fact-finding in police interrogation cases. In the absence of some mechanism for providing at least a reasonably reliable determination of what transpires during a police interrogation, safeguards designed to protect suspects from pernicious interrogation practices can never be fully effective.

Chapters 11 and 12 address the problem of false confessions resulting from standard interrogation techniques. In recent years, the problem of police-induced false confessions and wrongful convictions resulting from such confessions has received substantial media attention. There have been some celebrated cases in which suspects have plausibly claimed that false confessions produced by standard interrogation methods have either resulted in their wrongful convictions[40] or at least produced trauma for them[41] and interfered with law enforcement's efforts to protect the public.[42] Nevertheless, some readers will undoubtedly remain skeptical, believing that, in the absence of torture, no innocent person "would confess to a crime that he did not commit."[43] Chapter 11 assesses the magnitude of the phenomenon, concluding that the problems of both police-induced false confessions and wrongful convictions resulting from such confessions are sufficiently serious to demand attention. Chapter 12, which examines specific examples of false confessions, then seeks to draw conclusions as to the combination of circumstances likely to produce either police-induced false confessions or wrongful convictions resulting from such confessions.

Through documenting examples of situations in which police employ interrogation practices likely to produce untrustworthy confessions, the ultimate aim of chapters 10–12 is to provide empirical support for the conclusion I reach in chapter 9: the present Court's constitutional restrictions provide insufficient protection for suspects subjected to interrogation in a wide range of situations. In chapters 13 and 14, I explain two means through which the Court should address this problem, proposing specific constitutional rules that the Court should adopt to provide adequate protection to suspects subjected to police interrogation. Finally, chapter 15 summarizes some of the book's most important conclusions.

NOTES

1. Miranda v. Arizona, 384 U.S. 436 (1966).
2. Based on a survey of lawyers, judges, and law professors, a 1974 ABA survey concluded that *Miranda* was the third most notable decision of all time, trailing only *Marbury v. Madison* and *United States v. Nixon. See* Jethro K. Lieberman, *Milestones! 200 Years of American Law: Milestones in Our Legal History* vii (1976).
3. United States v. Dickerson, 120 S. Ct. 2326, 2336 (2000).
4. 120 S. Ct. 2326 (2000).
5. As Peter Brooks has said, "Confession has for centuries been regarded as the 'queen of proofs' in the law: it is a statement from the lips of the person who should know best." Peter Brooks, Troubling Confessions: Speaking Guilt in Law and Literature 9 (2000).
6. John H. Langbein, Torture and the Law of Proof 4 (1977); Leonard W. Levy, Origins of the Fifth Amendment 28 (1968).
7. Langbein, *supra* note 6, at 3–9.
8. *Id.* at 9.
9. *Id.* at 4–5.
10. *Id.* at 5.
11. Levy, *supra* note 6, at 34.
12. Langbein, *supra* note 6, at 73.
13. See Langbein, *supra* note 6, at 123.
14. *Developments in the Law—Confessions,* 79 Harv. L. Rev. 938, 955 (1966) (citing 3 John Henry Wigmore, A Treatise on the Anglo-American System of Evidence in Trials at Common Law, vol. 3, § 818, at 235–36 (3d ed. 1940) (hereinafter Wigmore on Evidence). *See also* Langbein, *supra* note 6, at 136 (observing that even decades after the use of torture to obtain confessions was abandoned, confessions were automatically admissible in English courts).
15. According to Langbein, the last case in which officials were authorized to extract a confession through torture was in 1640. Langbein, *supra* note 6, at 135.
16. See Langbein, *supra* note 6, at 9.
17. See Levy, *supra* note 6, at 313 (by the late seventeenth century, the privilege against self-incrimination was a well-established rule of English common law).
18. See *Developments in the Law—Confessions,* 79 Harv. L. Rev. 935, 954–55 (1966).
19. U.S. Const. amend. V.
20. Culombe v. Connecticut, 367 U.S. 568, 579 (1961) (plurality opinion of Frankfurter, J.).
21. *Id.*
22. *See Miranda,* 384 U.S. at 467–76.
23. Fred Inbau, John E. Reid & Joseph P. Buckley, Criminal Interrogation and Confessions (1962) (hereinafter Inbau et al.).
24. See Yale Kamisar, *What Is an Involuntary Confession? Some Com-*

ments on Inbau and Reid's *Criminal Interrogation and Confessions,* 17 RUTGERS L. REV. 728 (1963), *reprinted in* YALE KAMISAR, POLICE INTERROGATION AND CONFESSIONS: ESSAYS IN LAW AND POLICY 1 (1980) (hereinafter KAMISAR, ESSAYS).

25. See *CBS News: 60 Minutes* (CBS television broadcast, May 28, 2000).

26. Paul G. Cassell, *Miranda's Social Costs: An Empirical Reassessment,* 90 NW. U. L. REV. 387, 473 (1996) (hereinafter Cassell, *Miranda's Social Costs*).

27. In his article, Cassell does address the question "whether any significant portion of the drop in the confession rate . . . is attributable to police abandonment of unconstitutionally coercive tactics within a few months or a year after the *Miranda* decision." Cassell, *Miranda's Social Costs, supra* note 26, at 473. After considering various factors, *id.* at 473–78, he concludes that "it seems quite unlikely that a reduction in coercion had much to do with the confession rate drop that forms the basis of the *Miranda* cost estimate." *Id.* at 478.

28. See *id.* at 486–89.

29. See *id.; see also* Paul G. Cassell, *The Guilty and the "Innocent": An Examination of Alleged Cases of Wrongful Conviction from False Confessions,* 22 HARV. J.L. & PUB. POL'Y 523, 586 (1999).

30. See Cassell, *Miranda's Social Costs, supra* note 26, at 486.

31. See Paul G. Cassell, *Protecting the Innocent from False Confessions and Lost Confessions—and from*

Miranda, 88 J. CRIM. L. & CRIMINOLOGY 497 (1998).

32. KAMISAR, ESSAYS, *supra* note 24, at 1, quoting from Weisberg, *Police Interrogation of Arrested Persons: A Skeptical View, in* POLICE POWER AND INDIVIDUAL FREEDOM 155 (C. Sowle ed., 1962).

33. The Court has also interpreted the Sixth Amendment right to the assistance of counsel to impose constitutional restrictions on police interrogation. In a line of cases, it has held that the police are prohibited from deliberately eliciting incriminating statements from a suspect who has been formally charged with a crime. *See, e.g.,* United States v. Henry, 447 U.S. 264 (1980); Massiah v. United States, 377 U.S. 201 (1964). Since police interrogation generally occurs before a suspect is formally charged with an offense, however, the protection provided by the Sixth Amendment cases is of only limited significance.

34. *See, e.g.,* Duncan v. Louisiana, 391 U.S. 145 (1968); Gideon v. Wainwright, 372 U.S. 335 (1962).

35. See Colorado v. Connelly, 479 U.S. 157, 163 (quoting Miller v. Fenton, 474 U.S. 104, 109 (1985)).

36. Albert W. Alschuler, *A Peculiar Privilege in Historical Perspective: The Right to Remain Silent,* 94 MICH. L. REV. 2625, 2669 (1996).

37. *Id.* at 2653.

38. *Id.* at 2652.

39. *See, e.g.,* New York v. Quarles, 467 U.S. 649, 654 n.5 (1984).

40. See Welsh S. White, *False Confessions and the Constitution: Safeguards against Untrustworthy Confessions,* 32 HARV. C.R.-C.L. L. REV. 105, 108–9 n.26 (1997) (here-

inafter White, *False Confessions*) (iterating numerous cases in which suspects claimed to have given police-induced false confessions, many of which resulted in alleged wrongful convictions).

41. *See, e.g.,* discussion of the *Michael Crowe* case *infra* chapter 12.

42. See *infra* chapter 12.

43. See White, *False Confessions, supra* note 40, at 105 (quoting reported statements of jurors who adjudicated Richard LaPointe guilty of the 1989 rape and murder of his wife's grandmother on the basis of his confession).

CHAPTER 2

The Third Degree

The English experience with confessions induced by the rack and other instruments of torture produced the common-law voluntariness test, which was designed to ensure that only trustworthy confessions were introduced into evidence.[1] Although state courts in this country have applied the voluntariness test for at least three centuries,[2] it was not until 1936 that the Supreme Court became involved in regulating the admission of confessions in state criminal cases. It is generally believed that one reason the Court decided to consider these cases was the public's increasing concern with the police's use of the third degree.

The third degree has meant different things to different people. Even the origin of the term is in dispute. Some etymologists trace the term to "Freemasonry . . . in which the rank of the Master Mason, traditionally the highest or third degree, is conferred only after the candidate has undergone a long and arduous examination of his abilities and qualifications."[3] Wigmore, however, quoted an early source suggesting that the term originally pertained to a stage in an officer's processing of a criminal suspect: the "first degree" referred to the officer's arrest of the suspect, the "second degree" to the officer taking the suspect to the "place of confinement," and the "third degree" to interrogating the suspect in private.[4]

Regardless of its origin, the third degree came to connote prolonged interrogation, possibly accompanied by force or threats of force. During the early part of this century, police officers sometimes maintained that people had a mistaken view of how the third degree was employed. To the public, a New York police captain wrote in *Behind the Green Lights,* a book published in 1931, the third degree conjured up "a terrifying picture of secret merciless beating of helpless men in dark cells of the station."[5] "To the detective," the captain explained, the third degree "is a broad phrase without definition. To him it means any trick, idea, ruse, or action to get the truth from a prisoner."[6] Although the "rough stuff" would be used "when required," detectives employing the third degree would typically get statements without violence. Some of the tactics employed—"having shrieks and groans issue from neighboring rooms," for example—involved implicit threats of violence, whereas others— such as "keeping drugs from an addict"—did not.[7]

Commentators' views of the third degree sometimes depended on what they meant by the term. Wigmore observed that the third degree was sometimes "loosely used" to apply to situations that simply involved "a continuous interrogation while under arrest."[8] In this instance, Wigmore said, "Miscalling a thing by a bad name does not make it any worse than it is."[9] In his view, forbidding this form of inter- rogation would "tie the hands of the police."[10] He maintained that "the attitude of some judges towards these necessary police methods is la- mentable."[11] Admittedly, continuous interrogation would sometimes lead to abuses by the police. Nevertheless, Wigmore believed that "it did not follow that a stricter rule of exclusion for confessions [was] the proper remedy."[12] When the third degree was unaccompanied by vio- lence or other abusive police practices, the police should be permitted to employ this practice to obtain useful evidence.

During the twenties, media accounts of abusive police practices either in general or in specific cases generated increasing public concern about the third degree. In 1922, for example, Luther Boddy, a twenty- two-year-old black youth, was charged with shooting two officers to death while they were leading him to the station house for questioning. Boddy's defense was based on his fear of being brutalized by the police. "On a dozen or more previous occasions he had been 'examined' at the station-house and let go."[13] "Repeatedly he had been brought into the same station house, generally when he was neither under arrest nor charged with a crime and pounded—slashed—with blackjacks and rub- ber hoses until his senses fled."[14] At his trial, Boddy testified that once he saw the green lights of the station house, "everything suddenly blurred. I reached for the gun. I wasn't worried about anything except getting beaten up again."[15]

Reformers drew various lessons from the *Boddy* case. The case showed that, as a means of combating crime, the third degree was coun- terproductive. The deaths of the two policemen could be attributed to the "system" of criminal justice that allowed the third degree to exist. In addition, the case showed that the third degree was especially likely to be employed on the weakest members of society. Boddy was described as belonging to that "luckless group of misfits who no longer have any rights that police feel bound to respect, for whom the ordinary police restraints no longer exist."[16]

Accounts of Chicago police's employment of the "goldfish" also generated public concern. The goldfish was a length of rubber hose, which was used to extract information. In appropriate cases, the police took suspects to see the goldfish or to visit the goldfish room. Perhaps the most notorious examples of "goldfishing" occurred in connection with the Frank murder case, which eventually resulted in the conviction of Loeb and Leopold.[17] During an early phase of the investigation, "the police used the rubber hose unmercifully upon . . . two young teachers of one of the most respected schools in Chicago in order to make them confess."[18] One of the teachers was questioned and held incommunicado for seven days without being charged with any crime and was only reluctantly released on a writ of habeas corpus.[19] Following the confessions of Loeb and Leopold, Chicago papers reported the teachers' accounts of the beatings, police denials, and "interviews . . . in which leading club women expressed their sentiments against such third-degree methods and intimated that action should be taken to stop such practice."[20]

Media attention also focused on the third degree during the New York trial of the Oberst gang for assault and robbery. The defendants "pronounced their confessions to the police to be a fabric of lies, which they said they had woven in desperation under continuous beatings by detectives."[21] The defendants alleged that, after unsuccessful efforts to get them to talk, the inspector ordered some officers to "take them down and stick hairpins in them till they're within two inches of their lives, and maybe they'll come through."[22] Each defendant testified to the beatings he had received. During one defendant's testimony, a juror interrupted the proceedings, demanding to be excused from the trial. The juror stated, "The story of police brutality in this case has become so revolting that I cannot stand it any longer."[23] The juror's outburst resulted in a mistrial. Later, the juror precipitated a debate in the editorial pages of the *New York Times* by writing the *Times* a letter in which he declared his intention to start a "movement for the abolition of the third degree in this country."[24]

Reformers who objected to the third degree complained that the practice—in all its forms—violated the law and infringed on individual rights.[25] Police who physically abused or threatened suspects obviously violated the law. In addition, prolonged interrogation of suspects violated state statutes that required the police to bring arrested suspects promptly before a magistrate.[26] Even without such statutes, moreover, some commentators maintained that prolonged interrogation of a suspect at the police station violated the suspect's Fifth Amendment privilege against self-incrimination.[27]

As to whether the Fifth Amendment applied to pretrial police interrogation, there was considerable dispute. By its terms, the Fifth Amendment privilege only prohibited compelling testimony from a criminal defendant at trial.[28] Wigmore maintained that the common-law voluntariness test that governed the admissibility of statements obtained through police interrogation was completely separate from the Fifth Amendment privilege,[29] which in any event had not yet been applied to the states.[30] Other commentators maintained, however, that, in order to serve its intended purpose, the Fifth Amendment privilege should be interpreted so as to prohibit the police from forcing suspects to incriminate themselves during pretrial interrogation.[31]

Although police defended the third degree—maintaining that intensive interrogation of suspects was often the only means of solving serious crimes, efforts to reform the third degree gathered momentum during the 1920s. Grand juries and bar association committees issued reports relating to police abuses.[32] In addition, the American Civil Liberties Union, buoyed by its success in the area of free speech, "played a pivotal role in creating a national debate on the problem of police misconduct."[33]

One of the ACLU's most significant accomplishments was that it was able to affect the makeup of the Wickersham Commission, which was appointed by President Hoover to study the causes of crime, evaluate the criminal justice system, and examine the question of Prohibition.[34] The ACLU "successfully lobbied the commission to hire Walter Pollack, Zechariah Chafee, and Carl Stern to write the report on police practices."[35] Published in 1931, the Wickersham Commission's report, which was entitled *Lawlessness in Law Enforcement*, examined the extent to which American police employed the third degree.

The report defined the third degree as "the employment of methods which inflict suffering, physical or mental, upon a person in order to obtain information about a crime."[36] The commission viewed its primary role as presenting the facts of "existing abuses before the public."[37] It acknowledged the difficulty, however, of obtaining the information necessary to determine the true facts. Police were likely to "close ranks" and deny reports of abuses, and reports from prisoners were viewed as inherently unreliable.[38]

The commission based its findings on appellate court cases and reliable informers.[39] Over a ten-year period, the commission found sixty-seven appellate cases in which evidence of the third degree was accepted as true by a judicial fact-finder, thirty-nine in which evidence of the third degree was offered but not accepted, and innumerable others in which courts referred to coerced confessions.[40] In contrast, the commission found that in England there had not been a single reported case of the third degree during the twenty years prior to the study.[41]

The commission iterated various reasons why appellate courts' consideration of third degree cases represented only a small fraction of such cases: "The third degree may be employed without getting any information"; "[i]t may be used only to get evidence and not a confession"; "the confession may be excluded by the trial court and not [be] an issue on appeal," "the trial may result in an acquittal or plea bargain," or there may be "no appeal."[42] It concluded that for every case involving the third degree "that find[s] a place in the official reports, there are many hundreds, and probably thousands, of instances of the use of the third degree."[43]

Although the commission stated that the appellate court reports constituted the primary basis for its findings, it also relied on other sources, including interviews with present and former judges, prosecutors, and law enforcement officers,[44] and responses from questionnaires sent to prosecutors, police, and bar associations.[45] The commission was particularly struck by the responses an earlier study had received from questionnaires sent to the police. While some police responded and denied that their departments employed the third degree,[46] the great majority declined to respond to the questionnaire at all, thus creating a wall of silence that inevitably strengthened the commission's belief that police frequently employed third degree practices, but were unwilling to admit that they did so.[47]

The Wickersham Commission report's conclusions were unequivocal: "The third degree—the use of physical brutality, or other forms of cruelty, to obtain involuntary confessions or admissions—is widespread."[48] Observing that physical brutality was "extensively practiced,"[49] the commission cited numerous examples from appellate court cases, including some that involved the use of boxing gloves,[50] rubber hoses,[51] telephone books,[52] placing a rope around the suspect's neck,[53] or using the "water cure," which involved slowly pouring water into the nostrils of a suspect who is held down on his back.[54] The commission also referred to other abusive practices, including confronting the suspect with the victim's dead body,[55] stripping the suspect of clothing,[56] placing him in an airless, overcrowded, or unsanitary room,[57] and depriving him of sleep.[58] It observed, however, that the most common form of the third degree simply involved protracted questioning.[59]

The report also found that the third degree was disproportionately applied against the poorer and weaker members of society, including those least likely to be represented by counsel.[60] It found some evidence that the third degree was more likely to be used against blacks and other minorities. In particular, the commission observed that in most of the third degree cases involving blacks, the treatment seemed particularly harsh and that in cases involving the most severe physical brutality—such as whippings—the victims were invariably black.[61]

The commission's view of the third degree was clear. Although it referred to law enforcement arguments maintaining that the third degree was a necessary means of protecting the "community against crime,"[62] it rejected these arguments, finding that there was no correlation between use of the third degree and police efficiency.[63] Indeed, the commission concluded that the third degree impaired police efficiency because it tended to make police less zealous in their search for objective evidence.[64] By quoting from James Fitzjames Stephen's *History of the Criminal Law in England,* the commission emphasized that it viewed officers who employed the third degree as adopting a "lazy" rather than an efficient or effective approach to law enforcement: "There is a great deal of laziness in it. It is far pleasanter to sit comfortably in the shade rubbing red pepper into a poor devil's eyes than to go about in the sun hunting evidence."[65]

The commission concluded that police employment of the third degree was not only unfair to suspects but also created serious problems for the system of criminal justice. It produced a danger of false confessions[66] that in some cases resulted in wrongful convictions.[67] By forcing the courts to focus on issues unrelated to the defendant's guilt—whether the defendant was illegally detained, for example—law enforcement's employment of the third degree impaired the efficient administration of justice. In addition, the prevalence of the third degree corrupted fact-finding, leading the police to commit perjury and making jurors suspicious of police testimony.[68] Moreover, the commission found that the third degree justifiably lowered the public's view of the administration of justice.[69] It concluded that the practice degraded law enforcement almost to the level of a struggle between two lawless gangs and inevitably hardened prisoners against society, thus creating more work for the police in the long run.[70]

In condemning the third degree, the commission did not distinguish between more and less abusive forms of it. Although it provided examples of particularly sadistic practices, it stated, "Attention should not be concentrated upon the abnormal abuses; the usual method of beating with the fist or a rubber hose can be cruel enough."[71] Moreover, "Rigid distinctions between mental and physical suffering" were not appropriate.[72] The most prevalent practice, protracted incommunicado questioning by relays of officers, could brutally accomplish the same results as the more abusive practices. Both practices enabled the police to exploit the suspect's vulnerable position, allowing them to compel him to incriminate himself.[73]

In condemning the third degree, the commission's report provided relatively little discussion relating to the law governing the admissibility of confessions. The report did make it clear, however, that it rejected Wigmore's view as to the Fifth Amendment's privilege's inapplicability to statements obtained during pretrial police interrogation, observing, "Since the privilege exists during the trial in open court of a person who has been formally charged with crime, it seems even more applicable to the preliminary inquisition of a suspect by police or prosecutors before any judicial proceedings or formal charge."[74] Under the commission's view, the Fifth Amendment privilege would bar the admission of incriminating statements produced by coercive pretrial police interrogation.

Although its condemnation of the third degree was unequivocal, the Wickersham Commission did not recommend sweeping changes to eliminate the practice. Instead, the commission stated, "The law as it stands is sufficient. The difficulty is that it is either not enforced or is deliberately disobeyed."[75] From the commission's perspective, the community's response to the information it was providing would be critical: "The real remedy lies in the will of the community. If the community insists upon higher standards in the police, prosecutors, and judges, the third degree will cease to be a systematic practice."[76]

Nevertheless, the commission did recommend some reforms. It suggested that the facts as to the detention and treatment of prisoners should be made a matter of public record: the police should be required to provide documentation as to the time of a suspect's arrest, the places the suspect was taken, the length of interrogation, and the names of those who participated in the interrogation.[77] Moreover, the commission made a cryptic reference to a legal remedy that it viewed as particularly significant. It stated that "the best remedy" for the third degree "would be enforcement of the rule that every person arrested charged with crime should be forthwith taken before a magistrate, advised of the charge against him, given the right to have counsel and then interrogated by the magistrate."[78]

The commission's suggestion that an arrested suspect could be interrogated by the magistrate was puzzling because, as subsequent commentators pointed out,[79] no law authorized magistrates to interrogate arrested suspects. Rather, examination before a magistrate "is not an interrogation of the accused [but] a mere review of the evidence already accumulated against him to see whether it warrants holding him for further proceedings."[80] Even in the few states where the magistrate was authorized to ask the accused questions, the magistrate was required to "first warn the accused of the danger of answering, and must tell him that he need not answer if he does not wish."[81] Thus the commission seemed to be providing magistrates with more authority than they possessed under existing law.

The commission may, of course, have been suggesting that the then-existing law should be changed so that the magistrate rather than the police would be permitted to interrogate arrested suspects.[82] In view of the commission's recommendation that the police be required to provide documentation of the facts pertaining to their detention and interrogation of suspects,[83] however, it seems unlikely that they were proposing such a radical change in the law. In practical terms, the major thrust of the commission's proposal would be to reduce the time available for pre-trial police interrogation. If the law requiring that the police promptly take an arrested suspect before a magistrate were enforced, the police would not have time to employ the third degree.

When it was released, the Wickersham Commission's report *Law-lessness in Law Enforcement* created a media sensation. In response to the report, there was a flurry of articles and heightened media coverage of cases involving the third degree. Moreover, although some law enforcement figures objected to the report's conclusions, maintaining either that its findings as to the prevalence of the third degree were based on an exaggerated view of "isolated incidents"[84] or that its criticism of the practice failed to take account of the difficulty that the police would have in "combating criminal elements . . . if [they] adhered strictly to the letter of the law,"[85] most commentators viewed the report's conclusions as accurate and disturbing. Although the report's immediate impact was unclear, its "impressive documentation galvanized public opinion and gave support to a new generation of reform-minded police chiefs."[86]

Over the next decade, the report played a major part in unleashing two forces that not only played an important role in reducing the prevalence of the third degree but also shaped the nature of modern police interrogation practices and the law governing such practices. First, during the decade following the report, police interrogation manuals recommended that the third degree be replaced by psychologically oriented techniques. As I will explain in the next chapter, the manuals not only advised interrogators to avoid third degree practices, but also explained in detail the interrogation techniques they should use to induce confessions from suspects in various situations. Although they have been refined and developed over the past six decades, the interrogation techniques described in these manuals provide the basis for modern interrogation techniques.

Second, five years after the publication of the Wickersham Commission report, the Supreme Court became involved in regulating the constitutional admissibility of confessions in state criminal cases. In 1936, the Court decided *Brown v. Mississippi*,[87] the first in a line of cases that addressed the question whether a state defendant's confession was admissible under the due process voluntariness test. As I will explain in chapter 4, the due process voluntariness test evolved over time. Even during the earliest phase of the due process era, however, the Court made it clear that confessions induced by third degree practices would be constitutionally inadmissible. As a result, it has generally been assumed that the Court's application of the due process voluntariness test, combined with the advice contained in interrogation manuals, resulted in the virtual elimination of the third degree.[88]

NOTES

1. See 3 WIGMORE ON EVIDENCE, *supra* chapter 1, note 14, § 842.
2. *See id.* at 860. *See also* Yale Kamisar, *On the "Fruits" of Miranda Violations, Coerced Confessions, and Compelled Testimony,* 93 MICH. L. REV. 929, 937 (1995) (tracing the evolution of the voluntariness test).
3. HUGH RAWSON, DEVIOUS DERIVATIONS 199 (1994).
4. See 3 WIGMORE ON EVIDENCE, *supra* chapter 1, note 14, § 851.
5. Wickersham Commission Report: Lawlessness in Law Enforcement 169 (quoting from WILLANSE, BEHIND THE GREEN LIGHTS (1931) (hereinafter Wickersham Report).
6. *Id.*
7. *Id.*
8. JOHN HENRY WIGMORE, THE PRINCIPLES OF JUDICIAL PROOF 509 (2d ed. 1931).
9. *Id.* at 198.
10. *Id.*
11. *Id.*
12. *Id.* at 199.
13. NATION, Jan. 25, 1922, at 86.
14. See Charles J. V. Murphy, *The Third Degree,* OUTLOOK, Apr. 3, 1929, p. 524.
15. *Id.*
16. NATION, Oct. 29, 1924, at 459.
17. See HAL HIGDON, THE CRIME OF THE CENTURY (1975).
18. Oswald Garrison Villard, *Official Lawlessness,* vol. 155, HARPER'S MONTHLY, Oct. 1927, p. 612.
19. N.Y. TIMES, May 25, 1924, p. 1.
20. J. A. Larson, *Present Police and Legal Methods for the Determination of the Innocence or Guilt of the Suspect,* 16 J. CRIM. L. & CRIMINOLOGY 219, 243 (1925–26).
21. N.Y. TIMES, Aug. 10, 1926, p. 1.
22. *Id.*
23. N.Y. TIMES, Aug. 11, 1926, p. 1.
24. N.Y. TIMES, Aug. 12, 1926, p. 21.

25. Robert M. Fogelson, Big City Police 114 (1977).
26. See Wickersham Report, *supra* note 5, at 213–24.
27. *Id.* at 27.
28. "No person . . . shall be compelled in any criminal case to be a witness against himself." U.S. Const. amend. 5.
29. 3 Wigmore on Evidence, *supra* chapter 1, note 14, § 823.
30. *See, e.g.,* Adamson v. California, 332 U.S. 46, 50–51 (1947) (holding that "it is settled that the clause of the Fifth Amendment, protecting a person against being compelled to be a witness against himself, is not made effective by the Fourteenth Amendment as a protection against state action").
31. *See, e.g.,* Ernest Hopkins, *The Lawless Arm of the Law,* Atlantic Monthly, Sept. 1931.
32. See Richard Angelo Leo, Police Interrogation in America: A Study of Violence, Civility, and Social Change 24 (1994) (unpublished PhD dissertation, University of California at Berkeley) (hereinafter Leo, Police Interrogation).
33. Samuel Walker, In Defense of American Liberties 87 (1990).
34. *Id.*
35. *Id.*
36. Wickersham Report, *supra* note 5, at 19.
37. *Id.* at 6.
38. *Id.* at 21.
39. *Id.* at 24.
40. *Id.* at 53 n. 29.
41. *Id.* at 53.
42. *Id.* at 53–54.
43. *Id.* at 48 (quoting the 1930 Committee on Lawless Enforcement of Law for the American Bar Association, Report to Section of Criminal Law and Criminology (1930)).
44. *Id.* at 24.
45. *Id.* at 23.
46. *Id.* at 45.
47. *Id.*
48. *Id.* at 4.
49. *Id.* at 153.
50. *Id.* at 59.
51. *Id.* at 60.
52. *Id.* at 126.
53. *Id.* at 60.
54. *Id.* at 67.
55. *Id.* at 69.
56. *Id.* at 55.
57. *Id.* at 168.
58. *Id.* at 93.
59. *Id.* at 153.
60. *Id.* at 159.
61. *Id.* at 158.
62. Commissioner Austin J. Roche of the Buffalo Police Department, cited in *id.* at 103.
63. *Id.* at 188.
64. *Id.* at 187.
65. *Id.* at 188 (quoting 1 Stephen, A History of the Criminal Law in England 442 n.1 (1883)).
66. *Id.* at 181.
67. *Id.* at 182, citing cases.
68. *Id.* at 190.
69. *Id.*
70. *Id.* at 191.
71. *Id.* at 165.
72. *Id.* at 168.
73. *Id.*
74. *Id.* at 26–27. The report added that a few courts had held that the third degree did not violate the privilege "because the questioning does not involve any kind of judicial process for the taking of testimony," but dismissed these holdings as "a nar-

row limitation of a constitutional right." *Id.* at 27.

75. *Id.* at 191.
76. *Id.* at 191.
77. *Id.* at 191.
78. *Id.* at 5.
79. See KAMISAR, ESSAYS, *supra* chapter 1, note 24, at 80.
80. *Id.*, quoting John Barker Waite, *Report on Lawlessness in Law Enforcement*, 30 MICH. L. REV. 54, 58 (1931).
81. *Id.*
82. As Kamisar observes, Kauper in his article recommending this approach recognized that the commission might be making such a recommendation. See *id.*, commenting on Kauper, *Judicial Examination of the Accused—a Remedy for the Third Degree*, 30 MICH. L. REV. 1224 (1932).
83. *Id.* at 191.
84. Larson, *supra* note 20, at 224.
85. *The Third Degree under Fire*, LITERARY DIGEST, Aug. 22, 1931, quoting Major Lemuel B. Schofield, director of public safety in Philadelphia.
86. WALKER, POPULAR JUSTICE 155 (1998).
87. 297 U.S. 278 (1936).
88. See JEROME H. SKOLNICK & JAMES J. FYFE, ABOVE THE LAW: POLICE AND THE EXCESSIVE USE OF FORCE 49–52 (1993).

CHAPTER 3

The Evolution of Modern Police Interrogation Practices

The first police interrogation manuals were published in the early 1940s.[1] Inspired by the concern for reforming and professionalizing the police, these manuals were directed toward redefining the ideology and practice of custodial interrogation.[2] The manuals instructed the police that, instead of using brutality or other tactics associated with the third degree, they should interrogate in accordance with scientific principles, relying on sophisticated psychological strategies. In employing these strategies, moreover, the interrogators were directed to maintain a professional relationship with the suspect at all times.[3]

Of all the interrogation manuals, the *Inbau Manual*, as it is commonly known, has been the most influential. In 1942, Fred Inbau, a Northwestern University law professor who was a protégé of Wigmore, wrote a police manual entitled *Lie Detection and Criminal Interrogation*.[4] As its title implies, half of this book was devoted to lie detection and half to police interrogation. Twenty years later, Inbau and his coauthor John Reid substantially revised the part of the *Manual* relating to police interrogation and published it separately under the title *Criminal Interrogation and Confessions*.[5] Now in its third edition, *Criminal Interrogation and Confessions*, or the *Inbau Manual*, has played a major role in shaping modern interrogation practices. By the time the 1962 edition of the *Inbau Manual* appeared, the *Manual*'s popularity indicated that it provided guidance for police interrogators throughout the country.[6] Over the past four decades, the *Manual* has remained the predominant interrogation manual, exerting great influence not only in this country but throughout the world.[7]

Like other interrogation manuals, the *Inbau Manual* sought to professionalize the police. Inbau asserted that professionalizing police interrogation practices would not only minimize interrogation abuses[8] but also advance law enforcement's objectives by enhancing interrogators' ability to obtain confessions that would be both trustworthy and admissible in court.[9] Accordingly, the *Manual* recommended that interrogators treat suspects with decency and respect at all times, emphasizing that the interrogator should endeavor to have the suspect view him as a professional who is merely seeking the "truth" rather than as an adversary who is seeking to obtain evidence for a conviction.[10] Moreover, Inbau condemned interrogation techniques associated with the third degree, insisting that he was "unalterably opposed to the use of any interrogation tactic or technique that is apt to make an innocent person confess."[11]

Although he was a reformer—seeking to extirpate unprofessional police practices—Inbau was also a strong advocate on behalf of law enforcement. While he recognized that the practices described in the *Inbau Manual* "involved the use of psychological tactics and tactics that could well be classified as 'unethical,' if we [were] to evaluate them in terms of ordinary, everyday, social behavior,"[12] he fiercely maintained that confessions resulting from these practices should be admissible in court.[13] In supporting this position, he emphasized law enforcement's need for confessions, observing, "In criminal investigations . . . there are many, many instances where physical clues are entirely absent, and the only approach to a possible solution of the crime is the interrogation of the criminal suspect himself as well as others who may possess significant information."[14] He added that in order to be effective, interrogation of suspects must often be conducted in accordance with the practices described in the *Manual*. Interrogators must be permitted to question suspects for lengthy periods in privacy and to employ sophisticated psychological tactics designed to undermine the resistance of guilty suspects who are initially disinclined to confess.

Consistent with its goal of advancing law enforcement's most important interests, the *Inbau Manual* has always been primarily directed toward obtaining truthful confessions from guilty suspects. In recommending interrogation techniques, the *Manual* distinguishes between suspects "whose guilt is definite or reasonably certain"[15] and those "whose guilt is doubtful or uncertain."[16] In dealing with the latter category of suspects, however, the recommended techniques are primarily directed toward eliciting information or behavioral clues that will enable the interrogator to determine whether the suspect should be elevated to the category of those whose guilt is "reasonably certain." Thus the *Manual* instructs an interrogator as to how she can determine whether a suspect is guilty and, once that determination is made, informs her of the interrogation techniques that will assist in eliciting a truthful confession.

When dealing with a suspect who is probably guilty, the *Manual's* guiding principle has consistently been that a guilty "individual will confess . . . when he perceives the consequence of confession as more desirable than the continued anxiety of deception."[17] Thus an interrogator aims to "decrease the suspect's perception of the consequences of confessing, while at the same time increasing the suspect's internal anxiety associated with the deception."[18] In order to accomplish this goal, the 1962 *Inbau Manual* instructed the interrogator as to specific techniques that an interrogator should employ to obtain a confession. The latest edition of the *Inbau Manual* has refined these techniques. In addition to explaining interrogation techniques to be used in various situations, it sets out nine specific steps that an interrogator should employ to obtain a confession from a suspect whose guilt seems reasonably certain.[19] Moreover, it has added strategies that an interrogator should employ for the purpose of establishing his control over the suspect. Nevertheless, the basic advice that the *Inbau Manual* provides to interrogators dealing with such suspects has remained remarkably consistent. In essence, the interrogator is instructed to interrogate the suspect under circumstances where he is in complete control of the situation. Then, he should convince the suspect that the authorities know he is guilty, cut off the suspect's denials of guilt, and supply the suspect with a motive for the crime that will appear to lessen his culpability.[20]

Before explaining the specific interrogation tactics to be used in particular situations, the *Inbau Manual* explains techniques that the interrogator should employ to establish his psychological domination over the suspect. The interrogation should be conducted in private.[21] In order to emphasize his complete control of the situation, the third edition suggests that the interrogator should require the suspect to wait alone in the interrogation room for a brief period before meeting with him.[22] The interrogator then further asserts his control through his interactions with the suspect: he should invade the suspect's body space, direct him to be seated if he attempts to stand, and prohibit him from smoking or fidgeting.[23] In conducting the interrogation, moreover, the first edition emphasized that in appropriate cases, the interrogator should make it clear to the suspect that the interrogator has "all the time in the world,"[24] and is willing and able to continue the interrogation for as long as it takes to get the truth.

In order to enhance the suspect's anxiety of deception, the interrogator should convince the suspect that he has no doubt as to the suspect's guilt.[25] Toward this end, the third edition identifies a new strategy. Before approaching the suspect, the interrogator should prepare a real or simulated folder relating to the suspect's case. At the outset of the interrogation and at appropriate times thereafter, the interrogator should review the folder in a way that will "lead the suspect to believe that it contains information and material of incriminating significance, even though, in fact, the file contains very little."[26] While not recommending this specific strategy, the *Manual's* first edition strongly advised the interrogator to communicate to the suspect that the police have no doubt as to his guilt. Indeed, the interrogator should plainly tell the suspect not only that his "guilt [has] been detected, but also that it can be established by the evidence that is currently available or that will be available before the investigation is completed."[27] If the suspect persists in maintaining his innocence, the interrogator is advised to confront him with incriminating evidence, and without giving him a chance to explain the evidence, reiterate that the evidence establishes his guilt, adding that the only reason for the interrogation is "to give [the suspect] the opportunity to explain any mitigating evidence that [he] thinks might make a difference."[28] Through thus insisting on his absolute confidence in the suspect's guilt, the interrogator communicates to the suspect the futility of maintaining his innocence.

The heart of the *Inbau Manual* is devoted to instructing interrogators as to the "tactics and techniques" to be employed when dealing with both suspects whose guilt is possible and those whose guilt is reasonably certain. The *Manual's* third edition further breaks down these categories, dividing suspects whose guilt is reasonably certain into emotional or unemotional offenders. In dealing with emotional offenders, the interrogator is advised that various themes are likely to be effective. The interrogator may "sympathize with the suspect by saying anyone else under similar conditions or circumstances might have done the same thing."[29] He may "reduce [the] suspect's feeling of guilt by minimizing [the] moral seriousness of [the] offense."[30] Or he may "suggest a less revolting and more morally acceptable motivation . . . for the offense than that which is known or presumed."[31] In dealing with nonemotional offenders, on the other hand, recommended themes include "point[ing] out [the] futility of resistance to telling the truth"[32] and, when two or more offenders are being questioned for the same crime, "play[ing] one against the other."[33]

In elaborating how interrogators should employ these themes, the *Inbau Manual* provides numerous examples, explaining how specific interrogation techniques will prompt particular suspects to confess. In some cases, interrogators are specifically advised to employ deception. Thus in dealing with a possibly guilty suspect against whom there is no forensic evidence, the interrogator is told that it will sometimes be advisable to pose the following questions: "Is there any reason, Joe, why there would be blood on your overcoat which laboratory tests show to be the same as that of this fellow who was stabbed?" "Is there any reason why your fingerprints would be on a beer bottle in this fellow's home?" Or "Is there any reason why the dirt on your shoes should match the dirt outside the window of that house?"[34] According to the *Manual*'s first edition, an innocent person will answer, "No, because I didn't do it," or "No, because I wasn't there," while a guilty person will usually "try to offer a possible explanation" for the evidence or ask for "further information about the matter mentioned by the interrogator."[35]

Similarly, when playing one probably guilty offender against another offender, the *Manual*'s first edition informs interrogators that there are two principal methods to be used: "The interrogator may merely intimate to one offender that the other has confessed, or else he may actually tell him so." The *Manual* then explains specific techniques that the interrogator may use to "intimate" to one offender that his confederate has confessed. For example, after one offender has been questioned, the interrogator may begin the interrogation of the other offender by telling him, "This other fellow is trying to straighten himself out; how about you?" Or, instead of simply suggesting that the suspect's confederate has confessed, the interrogator may conduct an elaborate charade which is designed to mislead the suspect into believing that such a confession has occurred:

> After subject No. 1 has been unsuccessfully interrogated, he is returned to the reception room occupied by a secretary who is engaged in carrying out her usual secretarial duties; then subject No. 2 is taken to the interrogation room. If likewise unsuccessful in this second interrogation, the interrogator returns to the receiving room and instructs the secretary, "Come in the back with your pencil and notebook." This instruction is given within hearing distance of subject No. 1, but in such a natural manner that it does not appear to be an act performed for his benefit. The secretary then proceeds to sharpen her pencils, turn back some pages of her stenographic notebook—all within the observation of subject No. 1—and then departs in the direction of the interrogation room. After thus absenting herself for the period of time that would ordinarily be required for the actual taking of a confession, she returns to the reception room and begins typing what might appear to be shorthand notes taken during the period of her absence.[36]

In other situations, the interrogator may attempt "the more direct bluff," falsely telling the suspect that his co-offender has confessed.

When employing this strategy, the *Manual* cautions the interrogator "not to make any statement, purporting to come from the co-offender, which the person to whom it is related will recognize as an inaccuracy."[37]

In playing one suspect against another, the *Manual* thus advises the interrogator to employ various types of misrepresentation. And the interrogator should be concerned only about ensuring that the suspect does not suspect deception, not about the propriety of the deceptive practices employed.

The *Inbau Manual's* popularity with the police can be easily explained. The *Manual* clearly and vividly explains interrogation techniques that interrogators should employ to induce confessions from the guilty. Moreover, it tells interrogators that if they comply with the *Manual's* advice, they will be able to obtain reliable confessions that will be admissible in court. Thus the *Manual* tells the police what they want to hear in language that is easy to understand.

Nevertheless, when taken as a whole, the *Inbau Manual* presents difficult issues for both interrogators seeking to follow its advice and policymakers seeking to regulate police interrogation practices. The *Manual's* warning that interrogators should not employ techniques that will result in false confessions[38] could prompt an interrogator to ask a number of questions: What techniques will have a tendency to produce false confessions from innocent suspects? Are interrogators permitted to employ some or all of these techniques once they determine that the suspect is definitely guilty? Or should they never employ them? In dealing with particularly vulnerable suspects, are there additional interrogation practices that should not be employed because of their tendency to produce false confessions? If so, will interrogators be prohibited from employing these practices whenever they are interrogating vulnerable suspects? Or may they employ them when they are certain of the vulnerable suspect's guilt?

The *Manual's* first edition did not address these questions; it clearly adopted the view, however, that interrogators will generally be able to determine a suspect's guilt or innocence through evaluating both the evidence against the suspect and the suspect's behavioral clues, with the latter being particularly significant. Thus an interrogator can determine a suspect's truthfulness by evaluating his speech patterns and body language. Whereas "[a]n immediate response is a sign of truthfulness," a "delayed response . . . usually reflects an attempt to contrive a false answer."[39] Similarly, whereas "[t]ruthful suspects . . . can easily maintain eye contact with the interrogator," "[d]eceptive suspects generally do not look directly at the interrogator; they look down at the floor, over to the side, or up at the ceiling as if to beseech some divine guidance."[40] Other behavioral responses provide similar clues to the suspect's candor or deceitfulness.[41] Through evaluating these clues, the interrogator will be able to determine a suspect's probable guilt or innocence.[42]

Although the *Inbau Manual* states these propositions with great confidence, research into human behavior has failed to provide supporting evidence for the *Manual's* conclusions. Empirical studies show that, in most instances, people are not able to detect deception from behavioral clues, and that, with rare exceptions, law enforcement officers have no more skill than others in this area.[43] Moreover, the few people who are expert at detecting deception on the basis of behavioral clues invariably make their determination on the basis of a sophisticated evaluation of the individual's overall response rather than through determining deception solely on the basis of specific behavioral responses, such as whether or not the individual "maintains eye contact."[44]

Moreover, even assuming that an interrogator could sometimes determine that a suspect is being deceptive by examining his behavioral clues, it does not follow that the interrogator could thereby conclude that the suspect is guilty of the crime the interrogator is investigating. The interrogator would still find it difficult to determine whether the suspect's deception related to that crime or some matter that was either related or unrelated to that crime. As the third edition of the *Manual* admitted, a suspect who is being interrogated about a murder might show signs of deception because he did not want to reveal the "he had been in bed with . . . [a] married woman" at the time of the killing.[45]

More significantly, a suspect might reveal signs of anxiety and deception simply because he feels overwhelmed by the dynamics of the interrogation process.[46] When the interrogator employs deceptive strategies to ascertain the suspect's guilt, asking him if he can explain "why his fingerprints would be found" in the victim's home, for example, an innocent suspect might experience anxiety because he believes that the interrogator's question implies that his fingerprints were in fact found in the victim's home, a communication that might create anxiety either because it calls into question his own memory of events or suggests to him that someone is trying to frame him for a crime he did not commit. Since the *Manual* fails to take these possibilities into account, there is some risk that an interrogator guided by the *Manual* will mistakenly believe that once a suspect has revealed the telltale clues of deception, the interrogator's knowledge of the suspect's guilt makes it unnecessary for her to be concerned about avoiding tactics that would tend to produce a false confession.

Inbau himself indicated that he would provide broader protection to the innocent, stating that he was "unalterably opposed to any ... technique that [would be] apt to make an innocent person confess."[47] Based on this principle, he would presumably prohibit interrogators from employing tactics that would tend to produce untrustworthy confessions, regardless of the suspect's apparent guilt. The *Manual,* however, provides little specific advice as to what tactics should be avoided because of a likelihood that they will produce a false confession. In addition, although Inbau was certainly aware that certain categories of suspects are especially vulnerable to police suggestion,[48] the *Manual* provides only very general guidelines for interrogators dealing with suspects whose vulnerability might make them especially likely to give false confessions.[49] Thus, although the *Manual* identifies the goal of protecting the innocent, it does not go far enough in prohibiting interrogation tactics that are likely to produce false confessions.

Moreover, when the *Manual* does prohibit an interrogation tactic that would have a tendency to produce a false confession, the line between permissible and impermissible tactics is sometimes unclear. Interrogators are warned that they must not induce confessions through offering suspects promises of leniency, a tactic that has historically been viewed as likely to induce an untrustworthy confession.[50] At the same time, one of the interrogator's primary objectives is to decrease the suspect's "perception of the consequences of the offense."[51] How will the interrogator lead the suspect to believe that the consequence of the offense will be less severe? Obviously, by leading him to believe that his explanation of why he committed the offense will reduce his punishment. Indeed, as David Simon has said, "The fraud that claims it is somehow in a suspect's interest to talk with the police will forever be the catalyst in any criminal interrogation."[52] Most, if not all, of the tactics designed to decrease the suspect's "perception of the consequences of the offense" are calculated to suggest to the suspect that confessing will improve his chances with the authorities. The *Inbau Manual* thus instructs interrogators to refrain from promises of leniency but to suggest to suspects that confessing will be in their best interest.

Is there a clear line between the promises interrogators are forbidden to make and the suggestions they are directed to offer? If so, interrogators will find it difficult to adhere to that line in practice. Moreover, if a confession induced by a promise of leniency is problematic because the promise holds out too great an inducement to the suspect, it would appear that confessions induced by suggestions that it is in the suspect's interest to admit his guilt to the police are similarly problematic. In both cases, offering the suspect an incentive to confess places pressure on the suspect to tell the interrogator the story the interrogator is seeking. If the inducement is significant enough, it may lead the suspect to tell the interrogator the story she is seeking regardless of the suspect's own belief in that story's truth. In assessing the extent of the pressure, moreover, the nature of the inducement and the skill with which it is offered will generally be more important than whether the inducement should properly be characterized as a promise of leniency as opposed to a suggestion of advantage.*

For policymakers seeking to regulate police conduct, the *Manual*'s recommendations presented the basic question of whether the interrogation tactics described therein should be permitted. As Kamisar's incisive review of the *Inbau Manual* indicated, by the time the first edition of the *Manual* appeared, the law had moved beyond the stage where only interrogation tactics likely to produce false confessions were forbidden.[53] In a line of cases that will be explored in the next chapter, the Court had held that admitting a suspect's involuntary confession violated his right to due process. Although the meaning of an involuntary confession was far from clear, the due process test seemed to indicate that confessions resulting from coercive or reprehensible police conduct were inadmissible, regardless of their probable trustworthiness. Thus from a legal or policy standpoint, one question precipitated by the *Inbau Manual* was whether the interrogation tactics therein described should be impermissible either because they would be likely to exert coercive pressure on suspects or would constitute reprehensible police conduct.

By the time the first edition of the *Inbau Manual* appeared, there was some indication that the Court was ready to move beyond the due process voluntariness test. Although the direction in which the Court's jurisprudence would evolve was unclear, several justices had expressed concern about depriving suspects subjected to interrogation of their right to have an attorney present at interrogation.[54] In addition, scholars had suggested that the Fifth Amendment privilege, which protects criminal defendants against compelled self-incrimination at trial, should also apply to protect a suspect from being compelled to incriminate himself during custodial interrogation.[55] Thus the *Inbau Manual*'s description of interrogation tactics raised questions relating to these possible protec-

---

* For example, an interrogator who, without making explicit promises, employs subtle suggestions to convince the suspect that he will not be charged if he confesses will be more likely to induce a confession than one who promises the suspect that his confession will result in his sentence being reduced by 10 percent.

tions: Did a suspect subjected to police interrogation have a privilege against being compelled to incriminate himself? If so, would any of the tactics described in the *Inbau Manual* result in a violation of that privilege? Did the suspect have the right to have an attorney present at police interrogation? If so, would interrogators complying with the *Manual's* advice deprive a suspect of that right?

The *Inbau Manual* explicitly advised interrogators as to how they should deal with a suspect who expressed a desire to remain silent or asked to have an attorney present during police questioning. In both cases, interrogators were advised to respond with tactics designed to dissuade the suspect from persisting in his request.

When a suspect refused to discuss the matter under investigation, the interrogator was advised "to concede him the right to remain silent,"[56] a tactic that the *Manual* stated would usually have "a very undermining effect."[57] The suspect would be "disappointed in his expectation of an unfavorable reaction on the part of the interrogator."[58] Moreover, he would be impressed by the interrogator's "apparent fairness."[59] After the suspect had been conditioned by this tactic, the interrogator should then point out to the suspect the significance of his refusal to talk:

> Joe, you have a right to remain silent. That's your privilege and I'm the last person in the world who'll try to take it away from you. If that's the way you want to leave this, O.K. But let me ask you this. Suppose you were in my shoes and I were in yours and you called me in to ask me about this and I told you, "I don't want to answer any of your questions." You'd think I had something to hide, and you'd probably be right in thinking that. That's exactly what I'll have to think about you, and so will everybody else. So let's sit here and talk this whole thing over.

After giving the suspect this advice, the interrogator should then "immediately ask [him] some innocuous questions," such as, "How long have you lived in this city?" When the suspect answers those questions, the interrogator should gradually shift his inquiry toward questions that relate to the offense under investigation. The *Manual* stated, "Except for the career criminal, there are very few persons who" when handled in this manner "will persist in their refusal to talk."[60]

If the suspect requested an attorney, the *Inbau Manual* advised the interrogator to adopt a similar approach. He should suggest to the suspect that he can save himself or his family the expense of this professional service, "particularly if he is innocent of the offense under investigation." The interrogator may also add, "Joe, I'm only looking for the truth, and if you're telling the truth, that's it. You can handle this by yourself."[61]

In both situations, the interrogator is advised to respond to the suspect in a way that suggests he recognizes that the suspect does have the right being asserted. Moreover, the interrogator is not advised to coerce the suspect into declining to exercise his rights. Rather, the tactics described represent further variations of the "fraud that it is . . . in the suspect's interests to speak to the police."[62] In these variations, the specific catalyst is the suggestion that the suspect may be able to avoid further problems by convincing the interrogator of his innocence. Thus if the suspect indicates a desire to remain silent, the interrogator tells him that his silence will eliminate the possibility of convincing the police of his innocence. And, if the suspect indicates a desire to have an attorney, the interrogator communicates essentially the same message by telling him that an innocent suspect has no need to have an attorney.*

The interrogator thus dissuades the suspect from asserting his rights by holding out the hope that he will be able to elude the police by convincing them of his innocence. In the great majority of cases, this hope is illusory, however, because the interrogator will have already made up his mind that the suspect is guilty. At best, the suspect's statements in support of his claim of innocence could lead the police to conduct an investigation that could result in a decision not to charge the suspect. But, from the suspect's perspective, there would almost never be any advantage to providing exculpatory information to the police before conferring with counsel. If the suspect could achieve some advantage by making a statement to the police before he conferred with counsel, he would almost certainly be able to achieve at least as much advantage by making the same statement to them after he conferred with counsel. In most situations, moreover, Justice Jackson's statement that "any lawyer worth his salt will tell the suspect . . . to make no statement to police under any circumstances"[63] is correct. Through using the stratagems employed in the *Inbau Manual*, however, interrogators may deceive the suspect into believing that it is in his best interest to deal with the police on his own.

Is it permissible for interrogators to dissuade suspects from asserting their right to remain silent or to have an attorney present through the use

---

* The suspect would thus be led to believe that he may still be able to convince the interrogator of his innocence, but only if he talks to him without an attorney. To the suspect, of course, the significant message will be that he does still have an opportunity to convince the interrogator of his innocence.

of trickery and deceit? To answer this question, a court or policymaker would first have to decide whether a suspect subjected to police interrogation in fact has either of these rights and, if so, under what circumstances the rights come into effect. Moreover, assuming the suspect has one or both of these rights, it would also have to determine what actions the police may properly take to induce suspects to relinquish them. At the time the *Inbau Manual's* first edition appeared, neither the Supreme Court nor any other policymaker had addressed these questions.

NOTES

1. *See* Leo, Police Interrogation, *supra* chapter 2, note 32, at 68.
2. *See id.* at 67.
3. *See* GISLI GUDJONSSON, THE PSYCHOLOGY OF INTERROGATIONS, CONFESSION, AND TESTIMONY 23 (1992) (hereinafter GUDJONSSON, PSYCHOLOGY); INBAU ET AL., *supra* chapter 1, note 23, at 84.
4. FRED EDWARD INBAU, LIE DETECTION AND CRIMINAL INTERROGATION (1942).
5. FRED E. INBAU & JOHN E. REID, CRIMINAL INTERROGATION AND CONFESSIONS (1962).
6. See KAMISAR, ESSAYS, *supra* chapter 1, note 24, at 1 (observing in 1963 that of all the interrogation manuals, Inbau and Reid's "is . . . the best to be found").
7. *See, e.g.,* GUDJONSSON, PSYCHOLOGY, *supra* note 3: "Although many police interrogation manuals have been produced . . ., undoubtedly the most authoritative and influential manual is the one written by Inbau, Reid, and Buckley."
8. Fred E. Inbau, *Police Interrogation—a Practical Necessity,* 52 J. CRIM. L. & CRIMINOLOGY 16, 20 (1961) (hereinafter Inbau, *Practical Necessity*).
9. INBAU & REID, *supra* note 5, at 140.
10. *Id.* at 13.
11. Inbau, *Practical Necessity, supra* note 8, at 16.
12. *Id.*
13. *Id.*
14. *Id.*
15. INBAU & REID, *supra* note 5, at 21.
16. *Id.* at 88.
17. INBAU ET AL., *supra* chapter 1, note 23, at 332.
18. *Id.*
19. *Id.* at 77.
20. See *id.* at 79–80; INBAU & REID, *supra* note 5, at 23–38.
21. INBAU ET AL., *supra* chapter 1, note 23, at 24–28; INBAU & REID, *supra* note 5, at 1.
22. INBAU ET AL., *supra* chapter 1, note 23, at 81.
23. *Id.* at 37–38.
24. INBAU & REID, *supra* note 5, at 109.
25. INBAU ET AL., *supra* chapter 1, note 23, at 81–82.
26. *Id.* at 84.
27. *Id.* at 131.
28. *Id.*
29. *Id.* at 97.

30. *Id.* at 99.

31. *Id.* at 102.

32. *Id.* at 131.

33. *Id.* at 132.

34. INBAU & REID, *supra* note 5, at 100.

35. *Id.*

36. *Id.* at 82–83.

37. *Id.* at 86.

38. *See, e.g.,* INBAU & REID, *supra* note 5, at 203.

39. *Id.* at 46.

40. *Id.* at 51.

41. Among the behavioral clues pointing toward guilt are the following: pulsation of carotid artery, *id.* at 30; excessive activity of adam's apple, *id.;* restlessness (picking at nails or other objects; finger tapping), *id.* at 30–31; dry mouth, *id.;* swearing to truthfulness of assertions ("I swear to God!"), *id.* at 22; and "[n]ot that I [r]emember" explanations, *id.* at 33–34.

42. *Id.* at 29–34.

43. PAUL ECKMAN, TELLING LIES 284–85 (1992).

44. *Id.* at 288.

45. INBAU ET AL., *supra* chapter 1, note 23, at 128–29.

46. As Eckman explains, "Truthful people may be afraid of being disbelieved and their fear might be confused with the liar's detection apprehension." Eckman, *supra* note 43, at 170. Moreover, there are "individuals who are so guilt-ridden that they feel guilty when they are suspected of a wrongdoing they didn't commit." *Id.* at 175.

47. See *supra* text accompanying note 11.

48. Fred E. Inbau, *Miranda's Immunization of Low Intelligence Offend-* *ers,* 24 PROSECUTOR: J. NAT'L DISTRICT ATTY'S, spring 1991, at 9–10.

49. The *Manual's* latest edition does contain a section explaining how interrogators should deal with "[a]n unintelligent, uneducated criminal suspect with a low cultural background." See INBAU ET AL., *supra* chapter 1, note 23, at 199–200. In dealing with such suspects, this section advises interrogators to operate "on a psychological level comparable to that usually employed in the questioning of a child in respect to an act of wrongdoing." *Id.* at 199. It also emphasizes that throughout the interrogation, "the interrogator must maintain a very positive attitude, without ever relenting in the display of a position of certainty regarding the suspect's guilt." *Id.*

50. See The King v. Warickshall, 168 Eng. Rep. 234, 234–35 (K.B. 1783): "[A] confession forced from the mind by the flattery of hope . . . [must be excluded because it] comes in so questionable a shape when it is to be considered of evidence of guilt, that no credit ought to be given to it."

51. INBAU ET AL., *supra* chapter 1, note 23, at 332.

52. DAVID SIMON, HOMICIDE: A YEAR ON THE KILLING STREETS 223 (1991) (hereinafter SIMON, HOMICIDE).

53. KAMISAR, ESSAYS, *supra* chapter 1, note 24, at 5–6.

54. *See, e.g.,* Spano v. New York, 360 U.S. 315, 325, 326 (1959) (four concurring justices arguing that a suspect formally charged with a

criminal offense should have a right to an attorney at pretrial questioning); Crooker v. California, 357 U.S. 433, 444 (1958) (four dissenting justices maintaining that an arrested suspect should have the right to counsel during pretrial interrogation).

55. See KAMISAR, ESSAYS, *supra* chapter 1, note 24, at 36: "If modern police are permitted to interrogate under the coercive influence of arrest and secret detention, then, insists Professor Albert R Beisel, 'they are doing the very same acts which historically the judiciary was doing in the 17th century but which the privilege against self-incrimination abolished'" (quoting from ALBERT BEISEL, CONTROL OVER ILLEGAL ENFORCEMENT OF THE CRIMINAL LAW: ROLE OF THE SUPREME COURT (1955)). *See also* Charles T. McCormick, *Some Problems and Developments in the Admissibility of Confessions*, 24 TEX. L. REV. 239 (1946).

56. INBAU & REID, *supra* note 5, at 111.

57. *Id.*

58. *Id.*

59. *Id.*

60. *Id.* at 112.

61. *Id.*

62. See *supra* note 49.

63. Watts v. Indiana, 338 U.S. 49, 59 (1949) (concurring and dissenting opinion of Jackson, J.).

CHAPTER 4

The Due Process Voluntariness Test

The Supreme Court began its effort to regulate police interrogation practices in 1936, when it considered for the first time whether the admission of a confession in a state criminal case was so contrary to fundamental fairness that it violated the defendant's right to due process.[1] From 1936 to 1966, the Court decided a long line of cases that raised this issue. Although critics of *Miranda* have sometimes referred to the due process voluntariness test as if it were a monolithic test that applied a fixed set of criteria, the test in fact was anything but static; during the thirty-year period between its inception and the Court's decision in *Miranda*, the due process test was constantly shifting and evolving. The premises that undergirded the test, moreover, were never clear. On the contrary, in applying the test, the Court used language that obfuscated its underlying concerns. Analysis of the Court's results indicated, in fact, that a variety of concerns animated the Court's uneven and evolving application of the test.

The roots of the due process voluntariness test can be traced to the common-law voluntariness test, which was originally designed to exclude untrustworthy confessions. During the eighteenth century, English cases established the rule that confessions induced by certain types of pressure should be excluded because they were unreliable. A leading case explained that "a confession forced from the mind by the flattery of hope, or by the torture of fear, comes in so questionable a shape when it is to be considered as the evidence of guilt, that no credit ought to be given to it."[2] During the eighteenth and nineteenth centuries, English and American courts applied this rule, often equating it with the rule that "the [defendant's] confession must be voluntary."[3]

In *Hopt v. Utah*,[4] decided in the late nineteenth century, the Supreme Court ostensibly adopted the common-law voluntariness test as a matter of federal law.[5] But while the prior common-law cases focused almost exclusively on whether the pressures inducing the confession would be likely to render it untrustworthy, *Hopt* explicitly injected notions of free and overborne wills into the concept of voluntariness, stating that a confession was inadmissible "when made in response to threats, promises, or inducements" that deprive the defendant "of that freedom of will or self-control essential to make his confession voluntary within the meaning of the law."[6] Although this language could be interpreted as merely restating the common-law voluntariness test in a modified form, it could also be understood as altering that test so that it reflected an independent concern for protecting suspects from coercive police practices.[7] Thus, when the Court began applying the due process voluntariness test in state cases more than half a century later,[8] the test's underlying purpose was unclear. While Wigmore believed that the test was exclusively concerned with excluding untrustworthy evidence,[9] other commentators believed that it was also designed to protect suspects from compelled self-incrimination[10] or to curb abusive police practices.[11]

The Court's first due process confession case involved extracting a confession by torture, a practice that could be condemned either because it was reprehensible in itself or because it was likely to produce a false confession. In *Brown v. Mississippi*,[12] a white deputy sheriff hung a black suspect by a rope to a limb of a tree, demanding that he confess to a murder; when the suspect failed to confess, the deputy tied him to the tree and whipped him. When this whipping failed to produce a confession, the suspect was released. Two days later, the deputy arrested the suspect and obtained his confession after whipping him again and telling him the whipping would continue until he confessed to a statement dictated by the deputy.[13] The same deputy also arrested two other black suspects and obtained confessions from them by whipping their bare backs with a leather strap and buckle, informing them the whippings would continue until they gave detailed confessions to the crime.[14] In holding that the admission of these confessions violated due process, the Court did not refer to the voluntariness test. It simply stated that a violation of fundamental fairness occurred because "the state authorities . . . contrived a conviction resting solely upon confessions obtained by violence."[15]

The *Brown* case was typical of the Court's early due process cases in that the government conduct seemed to involve Jim Crow justice: white officers coerced black suspects' confessions through torture and threats of continued torture. The *Brown* case was unusual, however, in that the deputy sheriff frankly admitted that he tortured the suspects in order to induce the confessions.[16] In other early due process cases, black suspects claimed that white officers employed violence or threats of violence to obtain confessions; but the officers denied the claims.[17] Moreover, even though the officers' denials often seemed tenuous,[18] the lower courts credited their testimony, invariably rejecting the suspects' claims that their confessions were induced by violence, threats, or other abusive police tactics.[19]

How was the Court to deal with these cases? On the one hand, allowing the police to avoid constitutional prohibitions on abusive interrogation practices by simply lying about whether the practices were employed would negate the effect of the constitutional protections. On the other hand, the Supreme Court's role as a fact-finder is limited; in most instances, it will base its decision on the facts determined by the lower courts. Thus the Court's institutional limitations inevitably impeded its effort to curb abusive interrogation practices.

The Court dealt with this impediment in various ways. One approach related to its standard of review. In its early due process cases, the Court stated that it was basing its decision on the "undisputed facts."[20] If the Court then found that the undisputed facts established a practice that it viewed as improper, it could then conclude that the undisputed facts established that the suspect's confession was obtained in violation of due process. In later due process cases, the Court modified this standard, stating that instead of accepting the lower courts' finding of facts, it was conducting its own "independent review" of the record.[21] In determining whether a particular suspect's confession was involuntary, the Court could discredit testimony that had apparently been accepted by the lower courts;[22] more importantly, it could decide for itself what inferences should be drawn from the admitted facts.[23] As the voluntariness standard evolved into a complex multifactored test, this method of review became increasingly important.

Both methods of review had limitations, however. From the perspective of regulating police interrogation practices, applying a constitutional prohibition on the basis of the "undisputed facts" would only work if the Court was willing to establish a constitutional rule barring the interrogation methods admittedly employed by the police. Although the Court was willing to curb excessively protracted interrogation—holding that thirty-six hours of virtually continuous interrogation was coercive, for example—it was not willing to hold that incommunicado interrogation was in itself an improper practice. Reviewing interrogation practices on the basis of the "undisputed facts" thus had the potential for imposing restraints on an interrogation's duration; but, so long as the facts relating to the interrogation itself were in conflict, this method of review could not effectively regulate police practices that took place during the secrecy of incommunicado interrogation.

The "independent review" methodology also had limitations. When the record reflected a particularly striking fact—such as a notation that the defendant was to be held incommunicado for a period of time[24]—the Court could use that fact in making the voluntariness determination. More often, however, the record would be in hopeless conflict, with the suspect and police providing contradictory versions of the events relating to the interrogation. Even when conducting an "independent review" of the record, the Court was bound to give some deference to the state court's factual determinations.[25] Thus in most cases, this standard of review could not assist in resolving the conflict between the suspect and the officer. To the extent that lower courts refused to accept suspects' truthful testimony relating to abusive interrogation practices, the fact-finding process presented an impenetrable barrier to the goal of regulating such practices.

In addition to dealing with the intractable problems presented by the litigation process, the Court struggled to articulate a rationale for excluding involuntary confessions. Some of the early cases rejecting due process claims seemed to support Wigmore's view that the sole basis for ruling confessions constitutionally inadmissible was to exclude untrustworthy evidence. In *Lyons v. Oklahoma*,[26] a 1944 case in which the Court refused to exclude the defendant's confession despite the fact that the police employed the macabre technique of showing the defendant the bones of the murder victim,[27] the Court seemed to imply that abusive interrogation practices would not give rise to a due process claim unless the defendant could show that the confession resulting from the practice was likely to be untrustworthy. Speaking for the Court, Justice Reed stated that a "coerced confession is offensive to basic standards of justice, not because the victim has a legal grievance against the police, but because declarations procured by torture are not premises from which a civilized forum will infer guilt."[28] And in *Stein v. New York*,[29] a 1953 case that admitted several defendants' confessions,[30] the Court developed this point more fully. In his majority opinion, Justice Jackson stated, "Reliance on a coerced confession . . . vitiates a conviction because such a confession combines the persuasiveness of apparent conclusiveness with what judicial experience shows to be illusive and deceptive evidence."[31] Based on this premise, the majority characterized the rule excluding involuntary confessions as one of the "constitutional doctrines for protecting the innocent."[32]

In cases excluding confessions, however, the Court seemed more concerned with either the police interrogation practices employed or the practices' coercive effect on the suspects. In *Chambers v. Florida*,[33] a case that involved incommunicado interrogation extending intermittently over five days,[34] the Court concluded that the defendants' "confessions were the result of compulsion"[35] because the interrogation of "ignorant young colored tenant farmers" was conducted under "circumstances calculated to break the strongest nerves and the stoutest resistance."[36] The Court, moreover, summarily dismissed the claim that the interrogation practices employed were necessary for effective law enforcement, stating, "The Constitution proscribes such lawless means irrespective of the end."[37]

Similarly, in *Ashcraft v. Tennessee*,[38] the Court held that the admission of a confession obtained after thirty-six hours of virtually continuous interrogation violated due process. Unlike the defendants in *Chambers*, the defendant Ashcraft was a mature white man who apparently had considerable powers of resistance. Ashcraft in fact claimed that despite being subjected to third degree practices, he never confessed.[39] Moreover, the dissent was able to point to evidence showing that Ashcraft was relatively unfazed by the protracted interrogation[40] and that, if he did confess, his confession was probably true.[41] The Court nevertheless concluded that if Ashcraft made a confession, "it was not voluntary but compelled."[42] Rejecting the dissent's argument that the Court should give deference to the lower court's contrary findings of fact, the Court concluded that thirty-six hours of virtually continuous interrogation is "inherently coercive"; confessions obtained through such interrogation practices will automatically be viewed as "irreconcilable with the [suspect's] possession of mental freedom."[43]

By the late 1950s or early 1960s, as the Warren Court came into being, the due process voluntariness test had clearly entered a new phase. First, the Court made it clear that the test was not solely concerned with excluding unreliable evidence. In *Rogers v. Richmond*,[44] a 1961 case, the Court explicitly stated that the truthfulness of the suspect's confession was not relevant to the question whether the confession was voluntary. Instead, *Rogers* and other cases decided during that era focused increasingly on whether the confession was a product of the defendant's free will. Among the tests employed were "whether the behavior of the State's law enforcement officials was such as to overbear [the suspect's] will to resist and bring about confessions not freely self-determined,"[45] and whether the suspect's "will has been overborne and his capacity for self-determination critically impaired."[46]

What did these tests mean? Taken literally, they indicated that the Court was focusing on whether suspects subjected to interrogation retained sufficient freedom of choice. At some point, prolonged interrogation combined with other police practices might exert so much pressure that the suspect would feel he had no choice other than to respond to the police or even to agree to whatever statement they wanted him to make. Determining when the police pressure should be viewed as undermining free choice would inevitably be difficult. In *Blackburn v. Alabama*,[47] the Court indicated that the judgment as to whether the defendant's will was overborne "must by its nature always be one of probabilities."[48] As Professor Joseph Grano has pointed out, moreover, a Court making this judgment must address not only the empirical question relating to the extent to which the police pressure restricted the suspect's freedom of choice but also the normative question of how much freedom of choice should be afforded the individual under interrogation.[49]

The Court's use of such terms as "overborne wills" and "free choice" might have seemed to suggest that the Court was primarily concerned with preventing the admission of confessions obtained through excessive police pressure. If so, the Court's language was misleading. In a trenchant criticism of the Court's due process cases, Kamisar criticized the Court's use of this terminology, suggesting that terms such as "'involuntariness' or 'coercion' or 'breaking the will'" were in fact little more than labels employed to "vilify" certain interrogation methods.[50] Indeed, the Court itself admitted that the due process voluntariness test was not solely designed to preserve suspects "freedom of will."[51] In *Blackburn*, the Court stated that "a complex of values underlies the stricture against use by the state of confessions which, by way of convenient shorthand, this Court terms involuntary."[52] *Blackburn* observed that, in addition to preserving individuals' freedom of choice, the voluntariness test promoted the values of preventing the introduction of unreliable evidence and curbing improper police practices.[53]

Despite the due process test's complexity, some general principles could be extracted from the Court's decisions. Based on his analysis of the cases, Kamisar asserted that "in 99 cases out of 100," a confession's voluntariness would be determined on the basis of whether the "interrogation methods employed . . . create[d] a substantial risk that a person subjected to them will falsely confess—whether or not this person did."[54]

In view of the Court's rhetoric, including *Rogers'* assertion that a confession's voluntariness would be decided without regard to its reliability, this conclusion might have appeared surprising. In fact, however, applying the voluntariness test so as to prohibit the police from employing practices likely to produce an untrustworthy confession is not inconsistent with *Rogers'* assertion. As the Court indicated in *Blackburn*, the due process voluntariness test was designed in part to curb improper police interrogation practices. Based on the Anglo-American system's traditional concern for excluding untrustworthy confessions, assessing interrogation methods' propriety on the basis of their likelihood of producing untrustworthy confessions is clearly appropriate. Thus if an interrogation practice was likely to create a substantial risk of a false confession, confessions resulting from that practice should be excluded regardless of whether the particular confession before the Court appeared to be reliable.

Indeed, the Court's efforts to eliminate interrogation practices that exert coercive pressure could be interpreted as one means of preventing the admission of untrustworthy confessions. As Professor George Thomas has pointed out, a normal suspect—as opposed to one who is psychologically disturbed—would not falsely "admit guilt unless she found the pressure to confess overwhelming."[55] Thus in most instances, prohibiting interrogation practices that exert coercive pressure on suspects would limit the likelihood that interrogation practices would produce untrustworthy confessions.

In regulating coercive interrogation practices, the Court adopted both objective and subjective standards. In *Ashcraft*, for example, it established an objective standard, holding that thirty-six hours of virtually continuous interrogation was "inherently coercive" without regard to the particular suspect's powers of resistance.[56] Thus interrogators would not be permitted to interrogate any suspect for such a protracted period. In other cases, however, the Court employed a subjective standard, considering the suspect's individual characteristics—such as his youth,[57] mental retardation,[58] emotional instability,[59] or insanity[60]—for the purpose of determining whether the particular suspect's will was overborne.[61]

But as Kamisar has pointed out,[62] at least during the Warren Court era, the Court used suspects' individual characteristics only for the purpose of excluding, never for the purpose of admitting. The suspect's subnormal powers of resistance could be used to support a conclusion that the suspect's will was overborne; but if the interrogation practice would overbear the will of a normal person, the suspect's confession would be involuntary regardless of whether the particular suspect might have had extraordinary powers of resistance. Through this means, the Court imposed blanket prohibitions on interrogation practices viewed as coercive and provided special protections for suspects particularly vulnerable to standard interrogation practices.

As the Court stated in *Blackburn*, the due process voluntariness test was also designed to curb improper police practices regardless of the practice's coercive effect. With the exception of some easy cases, however, the Court rarely identified interrogation practices that it viewed as inherently improper. Early on, the Court did impose a flat prohibition on obtaining confessions through physical force. As Justice Jackson stated in his *Ashcraft* dissent: "Violence per se, is an outlaw."[63] If it were shown that the suspect's confession was induced by force or threat of force, the Court would invariably exclude the confession as involuntary without pausing to determine whether the force or threat of force actually overwhelmed the suspect's powers of resistance.[64]

Later cases indicated that promises of leniency, threats of adverse consequences to others, and certain types of deception would also qualify as improper police practices, which, at least in the context of a prolonged interrogation, might be sufficient to render a resulting confession involuntary. In *Leyra v. Denno*,[65] for example, the police employed both deceit and promises of leniency to extract a confession from the defendant. The defendant, Leyra, who had been interrogated for many hours over several days, was suffering from acutely painful sinus headaches. After promising to get a physician to treat his headaches, a police captain introduced Leyra to Dr. Helfand, who was actually a psychiatrist with considerable knowledge of hypnosis. Over the next hour and half, Dr. Helfand employed skillful questioning techniques to induce a confession. In addition to repeatedly assuring Leyra that he would feel better if he confessed, the psychiatrist told the defendant that he "had a much better chance" if he "played ball" (i.e., admitted the crime), whereas if he said he did not remember, the police would "throw the book at him."[66] In response to the psychiatrist's questioning, Leyra eventually confessed.[67] In holding Leyra's confession involuntary, the Court seemed to disapprove of both the government's deception in presenting the psychiatrist to the defendant as a doctor who would alleviate his sinus condition[68] and the psychiatrist's use of "threat[s]" and "promises of leniency" to obtain the confession.[69]

Similarly, in *Spano v. New York*,[70] the Court criticized the deceptive tactics employed by the police. After being indicted for murder, the defendant, Spano, telephoned his childhood friend Bruno, a "fledging police officer,"[71] and communicated his desire to surrender to authorities, which he did the next day. Although the police immediately attempted to interrogate him, Spano, who had been cautioned by his attorney to remain silent, refused to answer their questions for several hours. Following instructions from his superiors, Bruno then falsely told Spano that Spano's phone call had gotten him "in a lot of trouble" and that his job with the police was being jeopardized by Spano's failure to confess, thus creating dire consequences not only for Bruno but also for his pregnant wife and three children.[72] After Bruno repeatedly told this false story to Spano, Spano agreed to make a statement and eventually confessed to the crime.[73] The Court held Spano's confession involuntary on the basis of a "totality of circumstances" test. After iterating factors that exerted coercive pressure on the suspect—including the fact that he was questioned for virtually eight straight hours by many people[74]—the Court added that the government's use of Bruno was "another factor that deserves mention in the totality of the situation."[75] It indicated that using the suspect's "childhood friend" to falsely arouse his sympathy was an improper police practice that, in combination with the other factors, was sufficient to render the suspect's confession involuntary.[76]

The Court's analysis in these cases was intriguing but frustrating. Its apparent condemnation of particular interrogation practices provided potential guidance for the police and lower courts. Grano has suggested that *Leyra*, for example, could be read to mean that the police are prohibited from exploiting an apparent doctor-patient relationship.[77] *Leyra* might also be read as prohibiting interrogators from offering significant promises of leniency.[78] Some lower courts, moreover, have interpreted *Leyra* and *Spano* together as prohibiting interrogators from employing particular types of trickery, especially trickery that is likely to elicit an untrustworthy confession.[79] Based on these interpretations, the cases could provide a starting point for identifying improper police practices.

The cases are not really so far-reaching, however. As Professor Catherine Hancock has pointed out,[80] *Leyra* and *Spano* can more appropriately be explained as cases in which protracted interrogation produced a considerable possibility of coercion, and one or more "plus factors" then tipped the balance in favor of a finding that the defendant's confession was involuntary.[81] Indeed, in *Spano,* the Court emphasized that it was applying a "totality of circumstances" test under which all of the circumstances relating to the interrogation techniques employed and the individual characteristics of the defendant would be relevant. Under this approach, of course, no one interrogation technique would necessarily be sufficient by itself to render a confession involuntary.

As a result, the due process test provided only minimal guidance for the police and lower courts. If a lower court was confronted with a situation in which interrogators employed exactly the same trick that was employed in *Spano,* for example, the court might be able to distinguish *Spano* on the basis of myriad factors, including the length of the interrogation, the number of interrogators, the defendant's background, and whether the defendant had been indicted. Since lower courts were generally reluctant to exclude defendant's confessions, they would be likely to embrace one or more of the available distinctions,[82] thus limiting *Spano*'s precedential value.

By the mid-1960s, it was clear that the due process voluntariness test was not an effective means of regulating the police interrogation practices that concerned the Warren Court. Even if the Court had only been concerned with curbing torture or other forms of extreme abuse, the due process test could not completely eliminate these practices because of difficulties resulting from the fact-finding process. To the extent that lower courts were unwilling to credit suspects' truthful testimony relating to abusive interrogation practices, the Court's institutional limitations presented a nearly insuperable barrier to eliminating such practices.

Moreover, the Warren Court was not merely concerned with curbing the most abusive interrogation practices. As the Court indicated in *Blackburn*, it was also concerned with regulating interrogation practices that exerted unfair or coercive pressure on suspects. As the Court's sensitivity to the psychological impact of custodial interrogation practices expanded, its concern for regulating interrogation tactics that had the potential for generating such pressure on suspects increased.

The due process voluntariness test was not an effective means of addressing these problems. In addition to the problem of accurately determining objective facts, it was difficult for the Court to assess interrogation practices' effect on suspects. Even if the police testified truthfully as to what happened during the interrogation, a court would inevitably find it difficult to assess the interrogation's impact on the suspect. Suppose the officers testified to six hours of continuous police questioning:[83] Would the suspect be able to deal with that length of questioning? Or would it leave him so exhausted that he would be willing to say whatever he thought the police wanted to hear? Suppose an officer testified that he told the suspect that the police "would play ball" with him if he admitted his involvement in the crime:[84] Would a confused or exhausted suspect be able to accurately gauge the nature of that commitment? Or would such a suspect be inclined to admit to facts he was unsure of in the hope that he would thereby obtain assistance from the police? In assessing cases that raised these types of questions, the Court found it increasingly difficult to determine whether the interrogation practices employed by the police should be permissible. As a result of these difficulties, individual justices and, eventually, the Court itself began to look for per se rules that would alleviate the inherent problems with determining the legitimacy of police interrogation practices on a case-by-case basis.

NOTES

1. Brown v. Mississippi, 297 U.S. 278 (1936).
2. The King v. Warickshall, 168 Eng. Rep. 234, 234–35 (K.B. 1783).
3. *See, e.g.,* Campbell, LCJ, in Scott's Case, 1 D&B 47, 58, 169 Eng. Rep. 909, 914 (1956): "It is a trite maxim that the confession of a crime, to be admissible against the party confessing, must be voluntary; but this only means that it shall not be induced by improper threats or promises, because, under such circumstances, the party may have been influenced to say what is not true, and the supposed confession cannot be safely acted upon."
4. 110 U.S. 574 (1884).
5. 110 U.S. at 584.
6. *Id.* at 585.
7. SEE JOSEPH D. GRANO, CONFESSIONS, TRUTH, AND THE LAW 59 (1993) (hereinafter GRANO, CONFESSIONS).
8. Since the voluntariness test articulated in *Hopt* was applied only in federal cases, that test had no application in state courts where the great majority of criminal cases take place.
9. 3 WIGMORE ON EVIDENCE, *supra* chapter 1, note 14, § 822, at 246.
10. See Charles T. McCormick, *Some Problems and Developments in the Admissibility of Confessions,* 24 TEX. L. REV. 239, 277 (1946).
11. See Monrad G. Paulsen, *The Fourteenth Amendment and the Third Degree,* 6 STAN. L. REV. 431, 441 (1954); Francis Allen, *The Wolf Case: Search and Seizure, Federalism, and the Civil Liberties,* 45 ILL.

L. REV. 1, 29 (1950).
12. 297 U.S. 278 (1936).
13. 297 U.S. at 281–82.
14. *Id.* at 282.
15. *Id.* at 286.
16. In commenting on the severity of the whipping, the deputy testified it was "[n]ot too much for a negro; not as much as I would have done if it were left to me." *Id.* at 284.
17. *See, e.g.,* White v. Texas, 310 U.S. 530, 532–33 (1940) (whereas suspect claimed that officers on several occasions took him from the jail to the woods where he was whipped and told to confess, the police admitted taking the suspect out of the jail but denied any use of force).
18. In *White v. Texas,* for example, the police's explanation for taking the suspect from the jail seemed suspect. They stated that they took him out of the jail and drove to a remote location because they wanted to talk to him in private, the jail being too crowded to allow for a proper interrogation. 310 U.S. at 533.
19. *See generally* Anthony G. Amsterdam, *The Supreme Court and the Rights of Suspects in Criminal Cases,* 45 N.Y.U. L. REV. 785, 789 (1970).
20. *See, e.g.,* Gallegos v. Nebraska, 342 U.S. 55, 61 (1951); Chambers v. Florida, 309 U.S. 227, 239 (1940).
21. *See, e.g.,* Davis v. North Carolina, 384 U.S. 737, 742 (1966); Haynes v. Washington, 373 U.S. 503, 515 (1963).
22. In *Spano v. New York,* 360 U.S. 315

(1959), for example, the Court apparently discredited a detective's testimony that he was unable to find the name of the defendant's attorney in the telephone book. See 360 U.S. at 318 n.1.

23. In *Davis v. North Carolina*, 384 U.S. 737 (1966), for example, the arrest sheet included the directive, "DO NOT ALLOW ANYONE TO SEE DAVIS, OR ALLOW HIM TO USE THE TELEPHONE." 384 U.S. at 744. Based on this evidence in the record, the Supreme Court did not explicitly reject the district court's conclusion that the defendant "was not held incommunicado." *Id.* at 745. It concluded, however, that "no one other than the police spoke to [the suspect] during the 16 days of detention and interrogation that preceded his confessions," *id.*, and, based primarily on that finding, determined that the suspect's confession was involuntary. *Id.* at 752.

24. See *supra* note 23.

25. *See* McCormick, *supra* note 10, at 261.

26. 322 U.S. 596 (1944).

27. See 322 U.S. at 599–600.

28. *Id.* at 605.

29. 346 U.S. 156 (1953).

30. See 346 U.S. at 166–70.

31. *Id.* at 192.

32. *Id.* at 196.

33. 309 U.S. 227 (1940).

34. 309 U.S. at 231.

35. *Id.* at 239.

36. *Id.*

37. *Id.* at 240–41.

38. 327 U.S. 274 (1946).

39. 327 U.S. at 276.

40. *Id.* at 166.

41. In particular, the dissent was able to point to the fact that, after the police completed their examination, Dr. McQuiston, who had had both Ashcraft and his wife as patients, physically examined Ashcraft and testified that Ashcraft, who appeared to be in good condition, calmly told him that "he [had] offered this colored man, Ware, a sum of money to make away with his wife." *Id.* at l66.

42. *Id.* at 153.

43. *Id.* at 154.

44. 365 U.S. 534 (1961).

45. 365 U.S. at 544.

46. Culombe v. Connecticut, 367 U.S. 568, 602 (1961) (Frankfurter, J., concurring).

47. 361 U.S. 199 (1960).

48. 361 U.S. at 208.

49. Joseph D. Grano, *Voluntariness, Free Will, and the Law of Confessions*, 65 VA. L. REV. 859, 884 (1979) (hereinafter Grano, *Voluntariness*).

50. KAMISAR, ESSAYS, *supra* chapter 1, note 24, at 14.

51. *Blackburn*, 361 U.S. at 207.

52. *Id.*

53. *Id.* at 206–7.

54. KAMISAR, ESSAYS, *supra* chapter 1, note 24, at 20–21.

55. George C. Thomas III, *Justice O'Connor's Pragmatic View of Coerced Self-Incrimination*, 13 WOMEN'S RTS. L. REP. 117, 124 (1991).

56. For further discussion of the Court's application of an objective standard, see KAMISAR, ESSAYS, *supra* chapter 1, note 24, at 23.

57. *See* Gallegos v. Colorado, 370 U.S. 49 (1962).

58. *See* Culombe v. Connecticut, 367 U.S. 568, 621 (1961).

59. *See* Spano v. New York, 360 U.S. 315, 323 (1959).

60. *See* Blackburn v. Alabama, 408 U.S. 234, 237 (1972).

61. *See* Lynumn v. Illinois, 372 U.S. 528 (1963); Gallegos v. Colorado, 370 U.S. 49 (1962); Culombe v. Connecticut, 367 U.S. 568 (1961); Reck v. Pate, 367 U.S. 433 (1961); Blackburn v. Alabama, 361 U.S. 199 (1960); Spano v. New York, 360 U.S. 315 (1959); Crooker v. California, 357 U.S. 433 (1958); Payne v. Arkansas, 356 U.S. 560 (1958); Fikes v. Alabama, 352 U.S. 191 (1957).

62. See Kamisar, Essays, *supra* chapter 1, note 24, at 24.

63. *Ashcraft*, 322 U.S. at 160 (dissenting opinion of Jackson, J.).

64. *See, e.g.*, Beecher v. Alabama, 408 U.S. 234, 237 (1972); Thomas v. Arizona, 356 U.S. 395–96 (1958); Crooker v. California, 357 U.S. 433, 483 n.3 (1958). *But see* Lisenba v. California, 314 U.S. 219, 230 (1941) (defendant's confession admitted despite undisputed evidence that an officer slapped him during an early phase of the interrogation).

65. 347 U.S. 556 (1954).

66. 347 U.S. at 583.

67. *Id.* at 559–60.

68. *Id.* at 561.

69. *Id.* at 560.

70. 360 U.S. 315 (1959).

71. 360 U.S. at 317. Bruno was referred to as a "fledging" officer because he had "not yet finished attending the police academy." *Id.*

72. *Id.* at 319.

73. *Id.*

74. *Id.* at 322.

75. *Id.* at 323.

76. *Id.* at 323.

77. Grano, Confessions, *supra* note 7, at 111.

78. See Welsh S. White, *What Is an Involuntary Confession Now?* 50 Rutgers L. Rev. 2001, 2051–53 (1998).

79. See Commonwealth v. Hughes, 521 Pa. 423 (1989); Commonwealth v. Jones, 457 Pa. 423 (1974); Commonwealth v. Johnson, 372 Pa. 266 (1953).

80. Catherine Hancock, *Due Process before Miranda,* 70 Tul. L. Rev. 2195, 2227 (1996).

81. See Hancock, *supra* note 80, at 2227.

82. See Amsterdam, *supra* note 19, at 805.

83. For observations relating to the effect of even *listening* to six hours of interrogation, see Kamisar, Essays, *supra* chapter 1, note 24, at 98–99.

84. See *supra* text accompanying notes 65–66.

CHAPTER 5   *Miranda* **and Its**
            Immediate Aftermath

The Court's first steps toward establishing a more effective means of controlling the perceived evils of police interrogation involved interpretations of the Sixth Amendment right to counsel. The Sixth Amendment provides that "in all criminal prosecutions, the accused shall . . . have the right to the assistance of counsel for his defense."[1] In applying the due process voluntariness test, several justices had expressed the opinion that, at some point during the pretrial interrogation process, the suspect should be viewed as the accused and police interrogation of the suspect should be viewed as part of the criminal prosecution.[2] At that point, the Sixth Amendment provision would come into effect, affording the suspect the right to the assistance of counsel.

In two cases decided in 1964, *Massiah v. United States*[3] and *Escobedo v. Illinois*,[4] the Court adopted this view, but only to a limited extent. In *Massiah*, it held that the Sixth Amendment required the exclusion of incriminating statements deliberately elicited from an indicted accused in the absence of counsel.[5] *Massiah*'s effect was limited, however, because the vast majority of police interrogations take place prior to indictment. In *Escobedo*, the Court indicated that the Sixth Amendment also applied to preindictment interrogation. But *Escobedo*'s precise scope was unclear. In its opinion, the Court combined sweeping language relating to suspects' Sixth Amendment protection[6] with a holding limited to the facts of the case before it.[7] *Escobedo*'s ambiguity generated debate and confusion, prompting several articles from commentators.[8]

In one of these articles, entitled "Equal Justice in the Gatehouses and Mansions of American Criminal Procedure,"[9] Kamisar presented a compelling metaphor that illuminated the disparity between the rights afforded suspects during pretrial interrogation and at trial: the courtroom, where a criminal defendant's trial takes place, was the mansion; the police station, where his pretrial interrogation takes place, was the gatehouse. In colorful language, Kamisar vividly described the difference between the rights afforded suspects at these two stages of the proceedings:

> The courtroom is a splendid place where defense attorneys bellow and strut and prosecuting attorneys are hemmed in at many turns. But what happens before an accused reaches the safety and enjoys the comfort of this veritable mansion? Ah, there's the rub. Typically he must pass through a much less pretentious edifice, a police station with bare back rooms and locked doors.
>
> In this "gatehouse" of American criminal procedure . . . the enemy of the state is a depersonalized "subject" to be "sized up" and subjected to "interrogation tactics and techniques most appropriate for the occasion": he is "game" to be stalked and cornered. Here ideals are checked at the door, "realities" faced and the prestige of law enforcement vindicated.[10]

Prior to Kamisar's article, other commentators, including the authors of the Wickersham Commission's report,[11] had argued that the Fifth Amendment privilege should apply to pretrial police interrogation.[12] But Kamisar's powerful exposure of the disparity between the rights afforded suspects during pretrial interrogation and at trial removed this argument from the realm of academic debate, providing it with an immediacy it had previously lacked.

In addition, although Kamisar did not spell out the full implications of holding that the Fifth Amendment privilege would apply to pretrial police interrogation, he did advert to the significance of both warnings and waiver: he stated that "so long as his interrogators neither advise him of his rights nor permit him to consult with a lawyer who will," a typical suspect subjected to interrogation would be likely to assume that answers to the interrogators' questions were legally required, thus making them compelled within the meaning of the Fifth Amendment privilege;[13] with respect to the argument that the privilege could be waived, moreover, he intimated that the definition of waiver articulated in *Johnson v. Zerbst*,[14] requiring "an intelligent relinquishment . . . of a known right," should provide the controlling standard.[15] Kamisar's article thus articulated guidelines that would allow the Court to adopt a new constitutional approach. Instead of refining Sixth Amendment precedents, such as *Escobedo*, the Court could regulate police interrogation practices through providing a new interpretation of the Fifth Amendment privilege.

In 1965, the Court accepted certiorari in four cases, scheduling them for oral argument during the week of February 28, 1966. One of these cases involved Ernesto Miranda, a man with a prior criminal record who had confessed to the rape of a young woman.

When compared to cases the Court had considered under the due process voluntariness test,[16] the circumstances of Miranda's confession did not seem particularly coercive. According to the officers who questioned him, Miranda was taken to the police station on the morning of March 11, 1963.[17] He there appeared in a lineup where the young woman who had been raped failed to identify him.[18] Two detectives then met with him in an interrogation room. Although the detectives did not warn him of any rights, they neither threatened him nor promised him anything in exchange for his statements, but simply questioned him. In response to their questions, he soon admitted that he had raped the young woman, adding details that seemed to corroborate her account of how the rape occurred.[19] In less than two hours, the police reduced Miranda's confession to writing and Miranda signed it.[20]

In view of the Court's concern for clarifying the scope of *Escobedo*, however, *Miranda* was an ideal case for the Court to consider. The police interrogated the suspect in secret and commenced the interrogation without informing him of any rights. Together with the other three cases the Court was considering, *Miranda* seemed to provide an excellent opportunity for clarifying the scope of a suspect's right to the assistance of counsel during pretrial interrogation.

Before hearing oral argument in *Miranda* and the other three cases before it, the Court received briefs from three amici curiae[21] as well as the parties to the cases. One of these amicus briefs, the American Civil Liberties Union brief primarily authored by Professor Anthony G. Amsterdam,[22] developed the constitutional argument sketched in Kamisar's article.

Unlike the other briefs, Amsterdam's brief based its argument primarily on the Fifth Amendment privilege. Although the Court had held in 1964 that the Fifth Amendment privilege applied to the states,[23] it had never suggested that police questioning of a suspect prior to trial could result in a violation of the privilege. Nevertheless, Amsterdam's brief stated that the Supreme Court cases contemplated a "marriage of the Fifth Amendment and the Sixth Amendment right to counsel."[24] In an effort to establish the coercive atmosphere of the interrogation, moreover, his brief quoted extensively from police interrogation manuals, concluding that police interrogators' "basic attitude is one of getting the subject to confess despite himself—by trapping him into it, deceiving him, or by more direct means of overbearing his will."[25]

In *Miranda v. Arizona*,[26] the Court essentially adopted the Amsterdam brief's view of the constitutional issue presented. It stated that it had granted certiorari to determine whether the admission of confessions against the four defendants resulted in violations of the defendants' Fifth Amendment privilege and "to give concrete constitutional guidelines for law enforcement agencies and courts to follow."[27] By shifting its constitutional focus, the Court essentially "displaced" *Escobedo*.[28] From that point on, *Miranda*'s detailed warning and waiver requirements, which have been interpreted and revised by post-*Miranda* cases, provided the most important constitutional guidelines for police seeking to interrogate suspects.

Although *Miranda* has often been viewed as a single constitutional ruling, the Court's decision was in fact predicated on three holdings:[29] first, the Court held that the Fifth Amendment privilege[30] applies not only at trial or in proceedings before a legislative committee, but also to the "informal compulsion exerted by law-enforcement officers during in-custody questioning."[31] Second, it concluded that, unless adequate protective devices are established to protect a suspect from the pressures of custodial interrogation, such interrogation will automatically result in compulsion.[32] Finally, it held that, in the absence of other safeguards, statements obtained from a suspect as a result of custodial interrogation will not be admissible unless the officer conducting the interrogation first warned the suspect of four rights, including the right to remain silent and the right to have an attorney present during interrogation,[33] and the suspect voluntarily and intelligently waived those rights.[34]

The second holding seemed especially problematic. On what basis could the Court conclude that custodial interrogation would automatically result in compulsion? Did the Court mean to equate compulsion within the meaning of the Fifth Amendment privilege with coercion under the due process voluntariness test? If so, how could it conclude that a single question posed by an officer to a suspect in custody would result in compulsion? And, if not, what did compulsion mean?

The majority made some effort to address these questions. After acknowledging that we lack "knowledge as to what in fact goes on in the interrogation rooms,"[35] the majority referred to the interrogation manuals cited in Amsterdam's brief, observing that they provided "[a] valuable source of information about present police practices."[36] Over its next six pages, the majority discussed interrogation techniques described in the interrogation manuals, devoting most of this space to tactics described in the *Inbau Manual,* including that manual's advice as to how an interrogator should deal with the situation in which a suspect either refuses to speak to the police or asks to have an attorney present.[37] Drawing upon these descriptions, the Court intimated that questioning suspects at the police station often involves interrogation practices in which the police not only undermine the suspect's "will to resist" but when necessary "resort to deceptive stratagems such as giving [him] false legal advice" and "then persuade, trick, or cajole him out of exercising his constitutional rights."[38]

In equating custodial interrogation with compulsion, however, the Court did not assume that police interrogators always employed the techniques described in the manuals. Rather, the Court stated that, even if the police employ neither brutality, the third degree, nor the stratagems described in the manuals, "the very fact of custodial interrogation exacts a heavy toll on individual liberty and trades on the weakness of individuals."[39] Adverting to the four cases before it, the Court observed that it "might not find the defendants' statements to have been involuntary in traditional terms,"[40] but concluded that safeguards to protect the defendants' Fifth Amendment rights were nevertheless necessary: "Unless adequate protective devices are employed to dispel the compulsion inherent in custodial surroundings, no statement obtained from the defendant can truly be the product of his free choice."[41]

With respect to at least two questions that were potentially significant, the Court's opinion was ambiguous. Did it mean that the *Miranda* safeguards were necessary to prevent the police from obtaining confessions that would be "involuntary in traditional terms" (i.e., under the due process test)? Or did it mean that the safeguards were necessary to prevent the police from obtaining confessions that would be "compelled" under a new (stricter) Fifth Amendment test? And regardless of the meaning of compulsion, did the Court mean that confessions obtained in the absence of the safeguards would actually be compelled? Or did it mean that the safeguards were necessary to provide sufficient assurance that statements obtained in violation of the privilege would not be introduced into evidence?

In reacting to *Miranda,* commentators did not discuss these theoretical questions; instead, they focused on the basic constitutional and policy issues, addressing especially whether the Court's decision provided sufficient protection of suspects' rights and whether it placed undue burdens on law enforcement. Liberal critics expressed the view that *Miranda* did not provide suspects with adequate Fifth Amendment protection because it "did not take the final step of stating the privilege cannot be fully assured unless a suspect's lawyer is present during the police interrogation."[42] The basis for this criticism was that the police could not be expected to fulfill two conflicting roles at the same time.[43] As law enforcement officers seeking to solve crimes, police interrogators' primary role is to obtain reliable incriminating statements from suspects. *Miranda* also gives them the role, however, of protecting the constitutional rights of those same suspects. When burdened with these conflicting responsibilities, police could not be expected to provide the *Miranda* warnings in a way that would effectively protect suspects' rights.

Critics who believed the Court had placed undue burdens on law enforcement were more numerous and less measured in their attacks on *Miranda*. One police chief complained that the Court had mistakenly interpreted the Constitution so as to provide "a shield for criminals."[44] Criticism of this type spread beyond those ostensibly associated with law enforcement. Professor Otis Stephens pointed out that "an array of Supreme Court critics" accused the Warren Court of " 'coddling criminals,' 'handcuffing police,' and otherwise undermining 'law and order' at the very time when police faced their most perilous and overwhelming challenge."[45]

Indeed, for at least two years after the *Miranda* decision, conservative criticism of the Supreme Court was not only intense and passionate but often near the center of the political debate. During his 1968 presidential campaign, Richard Nixon issued a position paper on crime. In that paper, he chastised the Supreme Court for contributing to the low conviction rate of serious criminals: "The *Miranda* and *Escobedo* decisions . . . have had the effect of seriously ham stringing [*sic*] the peace forces in our society and strengthening the criminal forces."[46] He added that "the cumulative effect [of] these decisions has been to very nearly rule out the 'confession' as an effective and major tool in prosecution and law enforcement"[47] and urged Congress to enact "proposed legislation that—dealing with both *Miranda* and *Escobedo*—would leave it to the judge and the jury to determine both the voluntariness and the validity of any confession."[48]

The legislation Nixon referred to became 18 U.S.C. § 3501, the statute considered by the Court in *Dickerson*. As Kamisar's examination of § 3501 shows,[49] Congress's purpose in enacting § 3501 was to make "the pre-*Escobedo*, pre-*Miranda* 'due process' . . . 'voluntariness' rule the sole test for the admissibility of confessions in federal prosecutions, thereby purporting to 'overrule' by legislation the Warren Court's two most famous confession cases."[50] Since even those most opposed to *Miranda* believed that Congress could not overrule that decision in the absence of a constitutional amendment, however, § 3501 was rarely used by federal prosecutors.[51] Until the new assault on *Miranda*, which precipitated the Court's decision in *Dickerson*, the statute had fallen into desuetude, a relic of the 1968 Congress's antipathy toward *Miranda*.

NOTES

1. U.S. CONST. amend. VI.
2. *See, e.g.,* Spano v. New York, 360 U.S. 315, 327 (1959) (concurring opinion of Stewart, J.) (right attaches at point of indictment); Crooker v. California, 357 U.S. 433, 443 (1958) (dissenting opinion of Douglas, J.) (right attaches at point of arrest).
3. 377 U.S. 201 (1964).
4. 378 U.S. 478 (1964).
5. *Massiah,* 377 U.S. at 206.
6. *Escobedo,* 378 U.S. at 491.
7. 378 U.S. at 491–92. *See generally* Geoffrey R. Stone, *The Miranda Doctrine in the Burger Court,* 1977 SUP. CT. REV. 99, 103.
8. *See, e.g.,* Arnold N. Enker & Sheldon H. Elsen, *Counsel for the Suspect:* Massiah v. United States, *and* Escobedo v. Illinois, 49 MINN. L. REV. 47 (1964). *See generally* Stone, *supra* note 7, at 103.
9. Yale Kamisar, *Equal Justice in the Gatehouses and Mansions of American Criminal Procedure, in* CRIMINAL JUSTICE IN OUR TIME 11–38 (A. Howard ed., 1965), *reprinted in* KAMISAR, ESSAYS, *supra* chapter 1, note 24, at 27–40.
10. KAMISAR, ESSAYS, *supra* chapter 1, note 24, at 31–32.
11. See *supra* chapter 2.
12. *See, e.g.,* Ernest Hopkins, *The Lawless Arm of the Law,* ATLANTIC MONTHLY, Sept. 1931, at 279, 280–81, quoted in KAMISAR, ESSAYS, *supra* chapter 1, note 24, at 31. During the nineteenth century, *Bram v. United States,* 168 U.S. 532 (1897), held that the Fifth Amendment privilege applied to police questioning of a suspect in custody. Until 1964, however, when *Malloy v. Hogan,* 378 U.S. 1 (1964) held that the Fifth Amendment privilege applied to the states, *Bram's* holding only applied in federal cases. From the 1930s until *Miranda* was decided, moreover, *Bram's* Fifth Amendment holding had little impact even in the federal courts. *See generally* Lawrence Benner, *Requiem for Miranda: The Rehnquist Court's Voluntariness Doctrine in Historical Perspective,* 67 WASH. U. L.Q. 59, 110–12 (1989).
13. KAMISAR, ESSAYS, *supra* chapter 1, note 24, at 37.
14. 304 U.S. 458 (1938).
15. See KAMISAR, ESSAYS, *supra* chapter 1, note 24, at 38.
16. See *supra* chapter 4.
17. LIVA BAKER, MIRANDA: CRIME, LAW, AND POLITICS 12 (1983) (hereinafter BAKER, MIRANDA).
18. *Id.*
19. For example, Miranda said in his statement that he asked the woman he had raped to "say a prayer" for him, a statement that corroborated the woman's account of his last words to her. Compare *id.* at 5 with *id.* at 14.
20. *Id.* at 14.
21. The three parties who filed amicus briefs in *Miranda* were the American Civil Liberties Union (supporting the defendants), the

National District Attorney's Association (supporting the government), and the New York attorney general joined by the attorneys general of more than half the states (supporting the government).

22. BAKER, *MIRANDA*, *supra* note 17, at 108.

23. Malloy v. Hogan, 378 U.S. 1, 6 (1964).

24. BAKER, *MIRANDA*, *supra* note 17, at 108.

25. *Id.*

26. 384 U.S. 436 (1966).

27. 384 U.S. at 441–42.

28. KAMISAR, ESSAYS, *supra* chapter 1, note 24, at 163.

29. *See generally* Steven J. Schulhofer, *Reconsidering Miranda*, 54 U. CHI. L. REV. 435, 436 (1987) (observing that *Miranda*'s "complex series of holdings" may be "subdivided in various ways, but three conceptually distinct steps were involved in the Court's decision").

30. *Miranda*, 384 U.S. at 461.

31. *Id.* at 461.

32. *Id.* at 458.

33. *Id.* at 468–70. In addition, the police were required to warn the suspect that anything he said could and would be used against him, *id.* at 469, and that, if he wanted to consult with a lawyer but could not afford one because of indigence, a lawyer would be appointed to represent him. *Id.* at 473.

34. *Id.* at 475.

35. *Id.* at 448.

36. *Id.*

37. *Id.* at 454. For the *Inbau Manual*'s advice on these issues, see *supra* chapter 3.

38. *Id.* at 455.

39. *Id.* at 455.

40. *Id.* at 457.

41. *Id.* at 458.

42. N.Y. TIMES, June 14, 1966, at 25 (quoting statement of John de J. Pemberton Jr., then director of the ACLU, quoted in KAMISAR, ESSAYS, *supra* chapter 1, note 24, at 47–49 n.11).

43. See Richard H. Kuh, *Some Views on Miranda*, 35 FORDHAM L. REV. 233, 235 (1966); Brief of Edward L. Barret Jr., as amicus curiae, at 9; People v. Dorado, 42 Cal. Rptr. 169, 398 P.2d 361 (1965) (on rehearing). *See generally* KAMISAR, ESSAYS, *supra* chapter 1, note 24, at 47–49 n.11.

44. BAKER, *MIRANDA*, *supra* note 17, at 176 (quoting Philadelphia Police Commissioner Edward J. Bell).

45. OTIS H. STEPHENS JR., THE SUPREME COURT AND CONFESSIONS OF GUILT 165 (1973).

46. See Yale Kamisar, *Can (Did) Congress "Overrule" Miranda?* 85 CORNELL L. REV. 883, 900 (2000) (hereinafter Kamisar, *Congress*) (quoting from 114 CONG. REC. 12, 936–38 which sets forth the text of presidential candidate Nixon's May 8, 1968, position paper on crime).

47. *Id.*

48. *Id.*

49. See Kamisar, *Congress*, *supra* note 46, at 887–909.

50. *Id.* at 885.

51. See Paul G. Cassell, *The Statute That Time Forgot: 18 U.S.C. § 3501 and the Overhauling of Miranda*, 85 IOWA L. REV. 175, 197–219 (1999) (providing a detailed account of the Department of Justice's sporadic efforts to use the statute).

CHAPTER 6

Miranda's **Subsequent History**

Within a few years after the *Miranda* decision, it became obvious that those who had predicted the decision would have a crippling effect on law enforcement had miscalculated. The police were able to comply with *Miranda* and still obtain confessions. In fact, studies conducted during the 1960s and early 1970s suggested that *Miranda* had had little adverse effect on the police's ability to solve crimes.[1] In an article published in 1977, moreover, Professor Jerald Israel reported that the police with whom he had spoken generally acknowledged that "the *Miranda* warnings cause[d] little difficulty" so long as the requirement that they be given was "limited to arrested persons at the police station or in similar settings."[2] *Miranda*'s impact on law enforcement thus appeared to be negligible.

Miranda might have had more effect, of course, if the Court had interpreted the decision expansively—giving substance, for example, to the rule that the government must meet "a heavy burden" to establish that the defendant "waived his [Fifth Amendment] privilege"[3] or making it clear that a confession that would not be involuntary under the due process test could nevertheless be compelled within the meaning of the Fifth Amendment privilege.[4] Following Nixon's election as president in 1968, however, the changing composition of the Court made it unlikely that the Court would interpret *Miranda* expansively. During his first term, Nixon appointed four justices who appeared to share his conservative constitutional principles: Warren Burger, who replaced Earl Warren as chief justice, William Rehnquist, the present chief justice, Harry Blackmun, and Lewis Powell. In view of the Burger Court's conservative pro–law enforcement orientation, the question was not whether *Miranda* would be liberally interpreted but rather whether the newly comprised Court would allow the Warren Court's landmark decision to survive.

During the late 1960s and 1970s, the Burger Court in fact manifested considerable hostility toward *Miranda*. When defendants challenged the admission of evidence on the basis of *Miranda,* the Court consistently "interpreted *Miranda* so as not to exclude the challenged evidence."[5] As

Professor Geoffrey Stone documented, moreover, the Court's first ten decisions "concerning the scope and application of *Miranda*" indicated that the Court was predisposed toward limiting the decision as narrowly as possible. In holding that statements obtained in violation of *Miranda* may be used for the purpose of impeaching a defendant's credibility,[6] for example, the Court rejected *Miranda's* unambiguous language to the contrary,[7] stating that *Miranda's* discussion of impeachment evidence's admissibility "was not at all necessary to the Court's holding and cannot be regarded as controlling."[8] And in deciding whether a parolee should be given *Miranda* warnings before being interrogated at police headquarters,[9] the Court—after determining that the defendant was not in custody within the meaning of *Miranda*[10]—refused to consider the possibility of applying *Miranda* to a situation where the atmosphere in which the suspect was interrogated was arguably as coercive as the atmosphere in *Miranda*. Instead, after stating that *Miranda* was concerned with custodial interrogation, the Court declared, "It was *that* sort of coercive environment to which *Miranda* by its terms was applicable, and to which it is limited."[11] Based on these decisions, it appeared that the Court was moving toward dismantling *Miranda*[12] or at least diluting it to the point where it would impose only minimal restrictions on the police.

During the 1980s, however, the Court's attitude toward *Miranda* seemed to change. In 1981, it decided two cases in which its record of refusing to exclude evidence on the basis of *Miranda* was broken.[13] In one of these cases, *Edwards v. Arizona*,[14] the Court held that when a suspect responds to the *Miranda* warnings by invoking his right to have an attorney present at questioning, the police are precluded from interrogating the suspect without counsel "unless the accused himself initiates further communications, exchanges or conversations with the police."[15] *Edwards's* holding, which was refined in later cases,[16] provided considerable protection for suspects who invoked their right to have an attorney present during an interrogation. In *Rhode Island v. Innis*,[17] decided one year earlier, moreover, the Court adopted a relatively expansive definition of interrogation within the meaning of *Miranda*,[18] even while declining to find that the defendant before it was subject to interrogation.[19] These cases indicated that, while the Court might still be disinclined to expand *Miranda*, it was not willing to dismantle it; rather it seemed resolved to insure that the decision's core safeguards provided real protection to suspects subjected to interrogation.

The Court's more receptive attitude toward *Miranda* was also reflected in the tone of its references to the decision. In the *Innis* case, Chief Justice Burger, who had been an impassioned critic of *Miranda*,[20] stated that "law enforcement practices ha[d] adjusted to its strictures" and that he would "neither overrule *Miranda*" nor "disparage it."[21] In later decisions, the Court referred to *Miranda's* "virtues,"[22] especially the "clarity of its bright line rules."[23] And in *Withrow v. Williams*,[24] a case that held that federal courts are required to consider federal habeas cases in which state prisoners attack their convictions on the basis of *Miranda* violations, the Court stated that "in protecting a defendant's Fifth Amendment privilege against self-incrimination, *Miranda* safeguards a 'fundamental trial right.'"[25] By the latter part of the twentieth century, it thus appeared that the Court had come to accept *Miranda*, acknowledging that the decision "as written strikes a proper balance between society's legitimate law enforcement interests and the protection of the defendant's Fifth Amendment rights."[26]

During the past two decades, however, conservative commentators, especially Joseph D. Grano and Paul G. Cassell, have mounted a new assault on *Miranda*. In a forceful article,[27] Grano laid the groundwork for the current constitutional attack on *Miranda* by arguing that the Court's analysis in support of imposing the waiver and warning requirements showed that it was improperly promulgating prophylactic rules. This argument provided the basis for Cassell's constitutional attack on *Miranda* in *Dickerson*.

Grano also criticized *Miranda* on policy grounds. In writings that have resonated with other conservatives, he attacked the Court's decision on the basis that it is truth-defeating,[28] unprincipled,[29] and elevates form over substance.[30] While these arguments do not relate to the constitutional issue considered in *Dickerson*, they address basic questions relating to the values that the Supreme Court should seek to promote in regulating police interrogation practices.

Grano's writing undoubtedly influenced thinking about these basic questions and thereby contributed to an intellectual climate more receptive to assaults on *Miranda*. In an important sense, therefore, Grano has blazed the path for the "indefatigable"[31] Paul G. Cassell, the man who has sometimes been given sole responsibility for reviving the *Miranda* debate.[32] Grano's criticisms of *Miranda* also provide a lens through which one may view some of the Supreme Court's judgments relating to how the balance should be struck between promoting law enforcement interests and protecting individual rights. In order to illuminate some of these critical value judgments, I will consider Grano's policy attacks on *Miranda*, focusing especially on the difference between Grano's underlying value choices and those implicitly adopted by *Miranda*.

Miranda as Truth-Defeating

One of Grano's central premises is that "the discovery of truth will be a dominant concern of any rational criminal justice system."[33] Accordingly, he takes the position that "draconian measures that would eliminate or sharply reduce the number of reliable confessions produced by police interrogation cannot be defended."[34] Since *Miranda* results in the exclusion of reliable confessions, *Miranda*'s warning and waiver requirements at least create a serious problem for our criminal justice system. In essence, *Miranda*'s requirements are dubious because they are "truth-defeating."[35]

In fairness to Grano, he never states that *Miranda* should be overruled simply because its requirements result in the exclusion of reliable evidence. Rather, he carefully examines whether, even though *Miranda* leads to the loss of such evidence, the decision may be justifiable on some other basis. Drawing from Grano's work, however, other commentators have suggested that *Miranda* should be overruled primarily because it is "truth-defeating." Former attorney general Ed Meese, for example, stated that "it is clearly wrong to see [*Miranda*'s] truth-defeating changes as constituting a deeply rooted part of our legal heritage."[36] And Judge Harold Rothwax criticized *Miranda* on the ground that it "accentuate[s] just those features in our system that manifest the least regard for truth-seeking."[37]

The criticism of *Miranda* as "truth-defeating" is curious. *Miranda*'s requirements do, of course, result in the exclusion of some trustworthy confessions. But for at least a decade prior to *Miranda,* application of the due process voluntariness test also resulted in the exclusion of trustworthy confessions. In *Rogers v. Richmond,* in fact, the Court expressly stated that a confession that is shown to be reliable may nevertheless be excluded as involuntary.[38]

Thus the charge that the Court's constitutional doctrine was "truth-defeating" should have been directed at the Court's due process voluntariness decisions rather than at *Miranda*. By the time *Miranda* was decided, it had been well established that the Court's constitutional restraints on interrogation practices would sometimes result in the exclusion of reliable statements.[39] Conservative commentators' suggestions that *Miranda* represented a break from our criminal system's tradition of excluding only untrustworthy statements are, therefore, incorrect. In holding that constitutional constraints sometimes mandated the exclusion of reliable statements, *Miranda* was consistent with a long line of previous Supreme Court decisions.

Miranda as Unprincipled

Grano's argument that *Miranda* is unprincipled stems from his analysis of the appropriate relationship between the police and suspects. While Grano's explanation of the Court's shifting perception of this relationship highlights the ways in which the Court's view of *Miranda* has changed over thé past three decades, the present Court's altered view of *Miranda* does not establish either that *Miranda* was wrong when it was decided or that the present Court's failure to overrule it is unprincipled.

In both *Escobedo* and *Miranda,* Grano observes, the Court obliquely referred to the need to redress the inequality between interrogating officers and suspects subjected to custodial interrogation.[40] While admitting that "most suspects are not an equal match for their interrogators at the police station,"[41] Grano maintains that, in view of our goal of obtaining reliable evidence, redressing the balance of equality is not desirable. As he puts it, "[I]f we want guilty defendants to confess, equality between defendants and interrogators is antithetical to our goal."[42]

Grano does not deny that redressing the balance of advantage at the police station will be desirable if alleviating the inequality between interrogators and suspects serves other legitimate ends, such as "the achievement of truth or the prevention of inappropriate police tactics."[43] He maintains, however, that the balance struck by the Court in *Miranda* was inappropriate because the Court's alteration of the relationship between interrogators and suspects was based on the mistaken view that redressing the inequality between the two was a valid end in itself.

In arguing that *Miranda* should be overruled, moreover, Grano returns to this theme. He argues that post-*Miranda* cases, such as *Moran v. Burbine,*[44] have repudiated *Miranda*'s view of the proper relationship between interrogator and suspect. In holding that interrogators did not have to advise the suspect that a lawyer had telephoned the police station on his behalf, the *Burbine* majority said:[45]

> No doubt the additional information would have been useful to [the suspect]; perhaps even it might have affected his decision to confess. But we have never read the Constitution to require that the police supply a suspect with a flow of information to help him calibrate his self-interest in deciding whether to speak or stand by his rights.

As Grano points out, *Burbine*'s approach exemplifies the post-*Miranda* Court's altered view as to the proper relationship between interrogators and suspects. The language quoted from *Burbine* shows that the Court no longer views redressing the inequality between interrogators and suspects as desirable for its own sake. Moreover, whereas *Miranda* said that the need for police interrogation had been overstated,[46] *Burbine* said that the need for such interrogation "cannot be doubted."[47] As I have already indicated,[48] the Court's shifting view of the proper relationship between interrogator and suspect is reflected in many of its post-*Miranda* decisions.

After pointing out that post-*Miranda* cases reflect an altered view of the relationship between interrogators and suspects, Grano asserts that the Court should alleviate the tension between *Miranda*'s and post-*Miranda* cases' view of the relationship by overruling *Miranda*. Although Grano accepts that *Miranda* represented a compromise "between adhering to the voluntariness approach and taking an even more radical position,"[49] he asserts that the "compromise" can no longer be defended on any principled basis. There is thus an irreconcilable conflict between *Miranda*'s underlying premises, which essentially "challenge the legitimacy of police interrogation,"[50] and the present Court's recognition that redressing the inequality between interrogators and suspects is neither desirable nor constitutionally required.

Much of what Grano says is indisputable. Post-*Miranda* cases undoubtedly differ from *Escobedo* and *Miranda* with respect to their view of the proper relationship between interrogators and suspects. Unlike *Miranda*, moreover, the post-*Miranda* cases clearly accept the premise that police interrogation is necessary for effective law enforcement. As a result, there is certainly some tension between *Miranda*'s requirement that suspects be protected from interrogation unless they voluntarily and intelligently waive their constitutional rights and later cases' recognition that the police should generally be allowed the opportunity to engage in noncoercive interrogation.

Does it follow that *Miranda* should be overruled? In *Burbine*, one of the cases that Grano identifies as reflecting the Court's altered view of the proper relationship between interrogators and suspects, the post-*Miranda* Court stated that *Miranda* "*as written* strikes the proper balance between society's legitimate law enforcement interests and the protection of the defendant's Fifth Amendment rights."[51] In emphasizing that the decision *as written*[52] struck the appropriate balance, the Court, of course, implied that *Miranda* should not be interpreted so as to provide additional protections beyond those encompassed in its holding. The Court has expressed similar views in other post-*Miranda* cases that have refused to expand the circumstances under which giving a suspect the *Miranda* warnings is required to dissipate a coercive atmosphere.[53]

In a later post-*Miranda* case, moreover, the Court emphasized that the "primary protection afforded suspects subjected to custodial interrogation is the *Miranda* warnings themselves,"[54] adding that "full comprehension of the right to remain silent and request an attorney [is] sufficient to dispel whatever coercion is inherent in the interrogation process."[55] In contrast to *Miranda*, the post-*Miranda* cases thus reflect the view that warning suspects of their constitutional rights in a way that informs them of those rights is sufficient to dispel the coercion inherent in custodial interrogation. Providing protections that go beyond warning suspects of their rights is thus generally unnecessary.*

Does it follow, as Grano asserts, that the Rehnquist Court's failure to overrule *Miranda* is unprincipled? The Rehnquist Court certainly shares Grano's view that redressing the inequality between interrogators and suspects is not desirable for its own sake. The present Court, moreover, does not want to eliminate police interrogation of suspects. The Court has concluded, however, that providing suspects with *Miranda* warnings will not have these effects. Rather, the warnings will reduce the likelihood of coercive interrogation without significantly affecting the extent to which interrogators are able to obtain confessions. If *Miranda* represented one compromise through which the Court sought to strike an appropriate balance between allowing interrogating officers to obtain incriminating statements and protecting suspect's constitutional rights, the Court's post-*Miranda* cases have crafted a different compromise. Although the Burger and Rehnquist Courts' modifications of *Miranda* have undoubtedly produced some tension and ambiguity,[56] the Court's new compromise should not be viewed as unprincipled simply because it is based on different premises from the compromise adopted by *Miranda*.

Elevating Form over Substance

Grano asserts that "*Miranda*'s rigidity" has produced a "judicial formalism that cannot be a source of pride to American jurisprudence."[57] After

---

* The *Edwards* line of cases, however, constitutes an important exception to this principle. In *Edwards v. Arizona*, 451 U.S. 477 (1981), the Court held that once a suspect invokes his right to have counsel present during custodial interrogation, the police are not permitted to interrogate him unless counsel is present or the accused himself initiates further exchanges with the police. For later cases applying and, in some respects, expanding *Edwards*, see *Minnick v. Mississippi*, 498 U.S. 146 (1990); *Arizona v. Roberson*, 486 U.S. 475 (1988). *See generally* Kamisar, *Confessions, Search and Seizure, and the Rehnquist Court*, 34 TULSA L.J. 465, 474–75 (1999).

pointing out that *Miranda* has "added a rigid set of procedural requirements that must be satisfied before the voluntariness test takes over,"[58]
he complains that courts have become unduly focused on whether these
requirements have been met. To illustrate, he discusses several cases in
which courts addressed issues that need to be decided under *Miranda*,
such as whether a suspect was in custody or whether police conduct constituted interrogation.[59] In these cases, the judges considering these
issues disagreed, and the courts deciding them did not focus on whether
the suspect's incriminating statements were compelled. Grano therefore
concludes, "Instead of either bringing clarity to the law or helping courts
to identify situations where the potential for compulsion is great,
Miranda has induced judges at all levels to split hairs over the meaning of
black-letter rubrics."[60]

Grano's complaints about *Miranda*'s formalism obviously struck a
chord with Judge Rothwax. In a popular book that criticizes various
aspects of our system of justice,[61] Rothwax characterizes *Miranda* as "the
triumph of formalism."[62] Echoing Grano, he observes that "courts are
forced to decipher and apply rigid principles—often with no consideration of the Fifth Amendment's underlying concern with compulsion."[63]
After discussing some of the same cases discussed by Grano, he points
out that "there is no agreement among legal experts on the boundary of
the law,"[64] and states, "That in itself should be cause for alarm."[65]

Like Grano, Rothwax is also concerned that courts addressing
Miranda issues are not focusing on whether suspects were in fact compelled to incriminate themselves. Indeed, he directs his harshest criticism
at the result in *People v. Ferro*,[66] a case in which the New York Court of
Appeals held that introducing the defendant's incriminating statements
violated *Miranda* because a detective induced the statements by placing
stolen furs in front of him, conduct that the Court of Appeals concluded
constituted interrogation within the meaning of *Miranda*.[67] Rothwax
characterizes this as "a horrifying example of the formalism that has
evolved around *Miranda*."[68] He adds, "To say that the detective's action
was compulsion is, frankly, insane. We let a convicted murderer go free
for this? Liberal or conservative, any thinking person should be deeply
offended by the result."[69]

Stripped of its rhetoric, these attacks on *Miranda*'s formalism can be
reduced to three points: (1) with respect to certain issues that must be
decided under *Miranda*, the lines are unclear; (2) in deciding whether a
suspect's statements were obtained in violation of *Miranda*, courts do not
consider whether the suspect's statements were compelled; (3) the issues
courts are forced to consider under *Miranda* do not "identify situations

where the potential for compulsion is great."[70] Although the first two points are true, they do not show that *Miranda* has introduced a pernicious formalism into American jurisprudence. Rather, they are simply inevitable by-products of the Court's efforts to restrict compulsion at the police station by imposing prophylactic rules. If it were correct, the third point would pose a serious objection to *Miranda,* suggesting that its rules are not properly directed toward alleviating the potential for compulsion at the police station. As I will show, however, the third point is incorrect.

It is hardly surprising that the boundaries for determining whether there has been a *Miranda* violation are not always clear. *Miranda*'s requirements only apply when a suspect is subjected to custodial interrogation.[71] Although *Miranda* and its progeny have provided definitions of custody[72] and interrogation,[73] these definitions do not provide litmus tests that judges can apply to produce predictable results in every case. Custody, for example, has been defined as coming into effect when a reasonable person in the suspect's situation would perceive that his "freedom of action is curtailed to a 'degree associated with formal arrest.'"[74] In most cases, this definition will enable courts to determine whether or not a suspect is in custody. At the margins, however, there will inevitably be close cases. Just as reasonable judges may disagree as to whether a suspect was arrested, they will sometimes disagree with respect to whether a suspect's freedom was restrained to a "degree associated with a formal arrest." Disagreements as to whether close cases fall inside or outside the boundaries marked by *Miranda* and its progeny do not reflect a problem with those boundaries, but rather should be viewed as an inevitable by-product of our adjudicatory system.

Moreover, if the unclear boundaries provided by *Miranda* and its progeny are cause for "alarm," what should be said of the boundaries provided by the pre-*Miranda* voluntariness test? That test required courts to determine such questions as whether the government conduct "was such as to overbear [the suspect's] will to resist and bring about confessions not freely self-determined,"[75] or whether the suspect's "will [was] overborne and his capacity for self-determination critically impaired."[76] Are these tests more illuminating than the ones provided by *Miranda*? Grano finds "substantial merit"[77] in Kamisar's observation that those tests appeared to be little more than labels that were designed to "beautify" interrogation methods that the Court approved while "vilify[ing]" others that the Court disapproved.[78] In terms of providing guidelines for decision, therefore, *Miranda* is clearly superior to the pre-*Miranda* voluntariness test. Whereas the voluntariness test provided very little guidance for the police or lower courts,[79] *Miranda* and its progeny provide them with objective criteria that will lead to predictable results in most cases.

Nor is it surprising that a court addressing whether a suspect's statement was obtained in violation of *Miranda* does not consider whether the suspect's statement was compelled. Grano, of course, believes that the Court should not have provided prophylactic safeguards designed to protect suspects against the potential for compulsion. Since the Court did provide such safeguards, however, the question whether there has been a *Miranda* violation is inevitably separate from the question whether there has been compulsion. In deciding whether a suspect's statement was obtained in violation of *Miranda*, there is no reason for a court to consider whether the statement was compelled or to be influenced by a conclusion that the statement does not appear to have been compelled. *Miranda*'s requirements are designed to provide safeguards against compulsion, not to exclude compelled statements.

If the issues *Miranda* requires courts to deal with do not even "identify situations where the potential for compulsion is great," however, *Miranda*'s prophylactic rules are seriously deficient. The rules were designed to protect suspects from potential compulsion. If courts are forced to find violations of *Miranda*'s rules when there is no significant potential for compulsion, then the rules are not doing the job they were intended to perform.

Miranda's premise was that, in the absence of safeguards, custodial interrogation creates a potential for compulsion. Grano and Rothwax both apparently believe that the *Ferro* case, among others, demonstrates that this premise is incorrect. They would apparently maintain that the police conduct in *Ferro* creates absolutely no potential for compulsion. A fuller consideration of the *Ferro* case, however, shows that this conclusion is incorrect.

In *Ferro*, a woman was murdered in her home during the course of a robbery in which furs were stolen. A week later, the defendant was arrested for the murder and taken to the precinct station where the *Miranda* warnings were read to him. In response, the defendant declined to answer questions, asserting his right to remain silent. The defendant was then moved to a detention cell. Shortly after that, Detective Hudson placed the furs that had been stolen from the murdered woman's apartment "right in front of the cell a foot away from [the defendant]."[80] The furs prompted an immediate response. According to a detective, "there was one continuous conversation which began as soon as the furs were placed on the floor in front of the cell."[81] The conversation culminated in the defendant requesting to speak to an Italian detective. When Detective Cassi introduced himself to the defendant, the defendant soon made incriminating statements to that detective.

In *Miranda,* the Court stated that if an individual in custody indicates that "he wishes to remain silent, the interrogation must cease."[82] Based on that rule, the New York Court of Appeals properly concluded that the critical question was whether the placing of the stolen furs in front of the defendant constituted interrogation. In *Rhode Island v. Innis,*[83] the Court defined interrogation under *Miranda* to include not only express questioning but also "any words or actions on the part of the police that the police should know are reasonably likely to elicit an incriminating response."[84] Applying that test, the New York Court of Appeals concluded that Hudson's act of placing the furs in front of the defendant constituted interrogation.

Does *Ferro* exemplify a case in which there is no potential for compulsion within the station house? In response to the *Miranda* warnings, the suspect indicated that he did not wish to answer questions. Suppose that the police had simply continued to question him. Would that create a potential for compulsion? At a minimum, the interrogator's continued questioning would suggest to the suspect that the police had no intention of honoring his assertion of his right to remain silent, leading him to believe that the questioning might continue until he gave the police the answers they were looking for. The interrogator's questions would thus create exactly the kind of police-dominated atmosphere that the Court was concerned about in *Miranda.* Although Grano may not agree, the Court's conclusion that this atmosphere creates a potential for compulsion seems reasonable.

Would it make a difference if the interrogator asked the suspect only one question? The suspect would still be led to believe that the police were not prepared to honor his invocation of his right to remain silent. Nevertheless, the potential for compulsion would depend on the circumstances. If the question seemed relatively innocuous or was asked in a mild tone of voice, it might exert relatively little pressure on the suspect. On the other hand, if a detective insistently asked a critical question—"Who stabbed that woman?" for example—it might exert significant pressure on the suspect. As *Miranda* recognized, however, deciding the extent to which specific questions exert pressure on a suspect is extremely difficult. Because the potential for compulsion is present, police are forbidden from asking any questions unless the suspect first waives his *Miranda* rights.

Will the potential for compulsion be less when, instead of asking a question, the interrogator engages in conduct that has the force of a question? Again, it depends on the circumstances. In some cases, conduct would be likely to exert more pressure than a question. Handing the suspect an accomplice's confession in which the accomplice named the suspect as the killer would be likely to exert very significant pressure on the suspect. Showing the suspect a picture of the victim's murdered body would also exert significant pressure. Depending on the circumstances, placing stolen furs in front of the suspect, as the police did in *Ferro*, might exert significant pressure by communicating to the suspect the strength of the government's evidence against him.[85] If *Miranda*'s presumption of compulsion applies when the police ask a single question, it should also apply when the police engage in conduct that will have the same effect as a question.

Grano and Rothwax might insist, however, that a single act, such as placing stolen furs in front of the suspect, is unlikely to have much coercive effect. Even though the suspect may be aware that the police have the goods on him, he would not feel compelled to speak. Assuming this is true, where should we draw the line? Suppose that placing the furs in front of the defendant had not been effective in *Ferro:* Would the detective also be allowed to place the murder weapon in front of the defendant? And then to hand him a ballistics report? And then to show him additional reports indicating that his fingerprints were found on the gun? How long should the game of charades be allowed to continue? Would the interrogators be allowed to pursue it long enough to "convince the suspect not only [that] guilt [has] been detected, but also that it can be established by the evidence currently available or that will be developed before the investigation is completed," as recommended in the *Inbau Manual*?[86] Since there is a potential for compulsion as soon as the interrogator begins interrogating a suspect who has invoked his right to remain silent, *Miranda* cuts off interrogation at that point, thereby avoiding the difficulties of determining on a case-by-case basis whether an interrogator's particular questions or conduct actually resulted in compulsion.

The argument that *Miranda* has produced a pernicious form of "judicial formalism" sounds intriguing. When analyzed, however, this argument adds little or nothing to Grano's case against *Miranda*. *Miranda* provided safeguards designed to protect suspects subjected to custodial interrogation from potential compulsion. Grano believes that the Court's adoption of these prophylactic safeguards was improper. If Grano's view is correct, then courts should consider only whether particular suspects' statements were compelled in violation of the Fifth Amendment. If Grano is not correct, then *Miranda* properly directed courts to consider issues that do not directly relate to whether a suspect's statements were compelled. In determining whether *Miranda*'s prophylactic safeguards were met, courts will inevitably focus on questions that have nothing to do with whether the particular suspect was compelled to incriminate himself or, even, whether there was a strong likelihood that the suspect was so compelled. Through addressing these questions properly, however, courts will insure that *Miranda*'s prophylactic safeguards will provide additional protection against coercive custodial interrogation. Whether or not one agrees with the prophylactic safeguards, courts attempting to enforce the safeguards are not elevating form over substance. Rather, by complying with the Court's mandate, they are applying safeguards designed to reduce the potential for compulsion.

Although Grano may have blazed the path for Cassell, by the mid-1990s Cassell was undoubtedly "the nation's leading critic of *Miranda*."[87] Moreover, if Grano formulated the theoretical basis for the new assault on *Miranda*, Cassell also played a significant role in precipitating a climate in which the public and the Court might be more receptive to an attack on the Warren Court's most famous decision. Before seeking to overturn *Miranda* in the *Dickerson* case, Cassell wrote a series of articles that were designed to show that *Miranda*'s warnings and waiver requirements had reduced interrogators' ability to obtain confessions from suspects, thereby resulting in substantial costs—in terms of lost convictions—to law enforcement.[88] In both his scholarly work[89] and in an appearance on television[90] he even referred to *Miranda* as the most harmful decision to law enforcement in the last fifty years. In addition, as the attorney representing the Washington Legal Foundation and the Safe Streets Coalition, Cassell precipitated the legal challenge to *Miranda* considered by the Court in *Dickerson*.

The next two chapters address Cassell's empirical and legal assault on *Miranda*. Chapter 7, which considers the ways in which the police have adapted to *Miranda*, provides a substantial basis for doubting Cassell's assertions relating to *Miranda*'s harmful effect on law enforcement. Chapter 8 directly deals with Cassell's constitutional attack on *Miranda*, assessing his constitutional argument in light of *Dickerson*'s response to that argument.

NOTES

1. *See, e.g.*, Richard Seeburger & R. Stanton Wettick Jr., *Miranda in Pittsburgh—a Statistical Study*, 29 U. Pitt. L. Rev. 1, 11–16 (1967) (finding that in one detective division within Allegheny

County, after *Miranda*, suspects' confessions significantly declined, but the conviction rate remained about the same); Michael Wald et al., *Interrogation in New Haven: The Impact of Miranda*, 76 YALE L.J. 1519, 1523 (1967) (concluding that *Miranda* handicapped police in New Haven, Connecticut, from obtaining a confession necessary for conviction in only 6 of 127 cases); James W. Witt, *Non-coercive Interrogation and the Administration of Criminal Justice: The Impact of Miranda on Police Effectuality*, 64 J. CRIM. L. & CRIMINOLOGY 320, 325 (1973) (concluding that the post-*Miranda* "success" rate for police interrogations in a California city declined only 2 percent).

2. Jerold Israel, *Criminal Procedure, the Burger Court, and the Legacy of the Warren Court*, 75 MICH. L. REV. 1320, 1383 (1977).

3. *Miranda*, 384 U.S. at 475. One commentator, for example, suggested that "the burden of proving waiver might . . . require the prosecution to provide detailed evidence of the interrogation in order to show that as a whole it was not coercive." *The Supreme Court, 1965 Term*, 80 HARV. L. REV. 201, 206 (1966).

4. See *supra* chapter 5.

5. Geoffrey R. Stone, *The Miranda Doctrine in the Burger Court*, 1977 SUP. CT. REV. 99, 100.

6. Harris v. New York, 401 U.S. 222 (1971).

7. See *Miranda*, 384 U.S. at 477.

8. *Harris*, 401 U.S. at 224.

9. Oregon v. Mathiason, 429 U.S. 492 (1977).

10. 429 U.S. at 495 (defendant not in custody because he voluntarily came to the police station, where he was immediately informed he was not under arrest; throughout the interview there was no indication that his freedom to depart was restricted; and, at the end of the interview, he left the police station without hindrance). *See generally* Stone, *supra* note 5, at 151–54.

11. 429 U.S. at 495 (emphasis in original).

12. Stone, *supra* note 5, at 169.

13. See Edwards v. Arizona, 451 U.S. 477 (1981); Estelle v. Smith, 451 U.S. 454 (1981).

14. 451 U.S. 477 (1981).

15. 451 U.S. at 485.

16. *See, e.g.*, Minnick v. Mississippi, 498 U.S. 146 (1990) (holding that, under *Edwards*, defendant's invocation of his right to have counsel present at interrogation bars the police from conducting police-initiated interrogation even after the defendant has consulted with an attorney); Arizona v. Roberson, 486 U.S. 675 (1988) (holding that, under *Edwards*, defendant's invocation of his right to have counsel present at interrogation bars the police from conducting police-initiated interrogation as to any crime, not just the crime as to which defendant invokes the right to have counsel present).

17. 446 U.S. 291 (1980)

18. 446 U.S. at 301: "The term interrogation under *Miranda* refers not only to express questioning, but also to any words or actions on the part of the police (other than those normally attendant to arrest and custody) that the police should know are reason-

ably likely to elicit an incriminating response from the suspect."

19. *See id.* at 302–03.

20. BAKER, *MIRANDA, supra* chapter 5, note 17, at 323.

21. *Innis,* 446 U.S. at 304 (concurring opinion of Burger, C.J.)

22. *See, e.g.,* Fare v. Michael C., 442 U.S. 707, 718 (1979).

23. *See, e.g.,* Berkemer v. McCarty, 468 U.S. 420, 430 (1984); *Fare,* 442 U.S. at 718.

24. 507 U.S. 680 (1993).

25. 507 U.S. at 691, quoting from United States v. Verdugo-Urquidez, 494 U.S. 259, 264 (1990).

26. Moran v. Burbine, 475 U.S. 412, 424 (1986); *id.* at 433 n.4.

27. GRANO, CONFESSIONS, *supra* chapter 4, note 7, at 16.

28. *See generally* W. LaFAVE & J. ISRAEL, CRIMINAL PROCEDURE 285–86 (1985); *see also supra* note 2, at 1383.

29. *Miranda,* 384 U.S. at 474.

30. 446 U.S. 291 (1980).

31. Yale Kamisar, *Confessions, Search and Seizure, and the Rehnquist Court,* 34 TULSA L.J. 465, 470 (1999) (hereinafter Kamisar, *Rehnquist Court*).

32. See Roger Parloff, *Miranda on the Hot Seat,* NEW YORK TIMES, Sept. 26, 1999, at 84, 87. *See also CBS News: 60 Minutes* (CBS television broadcast, May 28, 2000).

33. GRANO, CONFESSIONS, *supra* chapter 4, note 7, at 16.

34. *Id.* at 55.

35. Joseph D. Grano, *Ascertaining the Truth,* 77 CORNELL L. REV. 1061, 1063 (1992).

36. Edwin Meese III, *Promoting Truth in the Courtroom,* 40 VAND. L. REV. 271, 273 (1987).

37. HAROLD J. ROTHWAX, GUILTY: THE COLLAPSE OF CRIMINAL JUSTICE 86 (1996) (hereinafter ROTHWAX, GUILTY).

38. *Rogers,* 365 U.S. 534, 540–41 (1961).

39. *See* Yale Kamisar, *Remembering the "Old World" of Criminal Procedure: A Reply to Professor Grano,* 23 U. MICH. J.L. REFORM 537, 585 (1990).

40. GRANO, CONFESSIONS, *supra* chapter 4, note 7, at 33.

41. *Id.*

42. *Id.* at 34.

43. *Id.* at 34.

44. 457 U.S. 412 (1986).

45. *Burbine,* 475 U.S. at 422.

46. *Miranda,* 384 U.S. at 481.

47. *Burbine,* 475 U.S. at 426.

48. See *supra* text accompanying notes 5–12.

49. GRANO, CONFESSIONS, *supra* chapter 4, note 7, at 217.

50. *Id.* at 218.

51. *Burbine,* 475 U.S. at 424 (emphasis added); *id.* at 433 n.4.

52. See *id.* at 433 n.4.

53. *See, e.g.,* Oregon v. Mathiason, 429 U.S. 492, 495 (1977) (per curiam).

54. Davis v. United States, 512 U.S. 452, 460 (1994).

55. *Id.,* quoting from *Burbine,* 475 U.S. at 412.

56. See Stone, *supra* note 5, at 99.

57. GRANO, CONFESSIONS, *supra* chapter 4, note 7, at 207.

58. *Id.*

59. *Id.* at 207–13.

60. *Id.* at 215.

61. ROTHWAX, GUILTY, *supra* note 37.

62. *Id.* at 82.

63. *Id.*

64. *Id.* at 84.

65. *Id.*
66. 472 N.E.2d 13 (N.Y. 1984).
67. 472 N.E.2d at 17.
68. *Id.* at 85.
69. *Id.*
70. GRANO, CONFESSIONS, *supra* chapter 4, note 7, at 215.
71. *Miranda,* 384 U.S. at 358.
72. See Berkemer v. McCarty, 468 U.S. 420, 440 (1984).
73. See Rhode Island v. Innis, 446 U.S. 291, 300–302 (1980).
74. *Berkemer,* 468 U.S. at 440, quoting from California v. Beheler, 463 U.S. 1121, 1125 (1983) (per curiam).
75. Rogers v. Richmond, 365 U.S. 534, 544 (1961).
76. Culombe v. Connecticut, 367 U.S. at 602 (Frankfurter, J., concurring).
77. GRANO, CONFESSIONS, *supra* chapter 4, note 7, at 65.
78. *Id.*
79. See *supra* chapter 4.
80. 472 N.E.2d at 15.
81. *Id.*
82. *Miranda,* 384 U.S. at 474.
83. 446 U.S. 291 (1980).
84. *Innis,* 446 U.S. at 301.
85. Through this act, the police could begin the process of communicating to the suspect that they had an irrefutable case against him, one of the techniques recommended in the *Inbau Manual.* See INBAU ET AL., *supra* chapter 1, note 23, at 131.
86. *Id.*
87. Kamisar, *Rehnquist Court, supra* note 31, at 470.
88. *See* Paul G. Cassell & Richard Fowles, *Handcuffing the Cops? A Thirty Year Perspective on Miranda's Harmful Effects on Law Enforcement,* 50 STAN. L. REV. 1055 (1998); Paul G. Cassell, *All Benefits, No Costs: The Grand Illusion of Miranda's Defenders,* 90 Nw. U. L. REV. 1084 (1996); Cassell, *Miranda's Social Costs, supra* chapter 1, note 26.
89. Cassell & Fowles, *supra* note 88, at 1132.
90. *CBS News: 60 Minutes, supra* note 32.

CHAPTER 7

How Modern Interrogators Have Adapted to *Miranda*

In order to assess *Miranda*'s current impact on law enforcement, it is necessary to focus on how *Miranda*'s requirements operate today. Over the past three and a half decades, *Miranda* has changed. As a result of the Burger and Rehnquist Courts' post-*Miranda* decisions, *Miranda* is no longer one case but rather a body of rules that provide less strict safeguards than the original decision. Moreover, as the obstacles posed to interrogators have become less formidable, interrogators' strategies for surmounting the remaining obstacles have become more sophisticated. As a result, *Miranda*'s adverse impact on law enforcement might be expected to be less today than it was in the past.

Even so, the data relating to *Miranda*'s actual effect on interactions between police and suspects is surprising. Based on empirical studies conducted during the past decade, it appears that in serious cases, more than 80 percent of suspects waive their *Miranda* rights and make some kind of statement to the police.[1] Why do so many suspects choose to relinquish their important Fifth Amendment protections? In what way should this striking statistic affect our response to *Miranda*?

In this chapter, I will address the first of these questions. After sketching some of the changes effected by post-*Miranda* decisions, I will explain some of the strategies interrogators employ to induce *Miranda* waivers. Drawing primarily from transcripts of interrogations conducted over the past decade, I will show that interrogators employ a variety of strategies, some of which are specifically designed to circumvent *Miranda*'s requirements. After showing examples of each strategy, I will discuss whether the incriminating statements obtained as a result of the strategy employed would be likely to be found admissible under prevailing post-*Miranda* doctrine. At the end of this chapter, I will draw some conclusions as to how interrogators' adaptions to *Miranda* have altered *Miranda*'s effect on law enforcement. In later chapters, I will consider how these conclusions should affect our response to *Miranda*.

Post-*Miranda* Decisions Weakening
Miranda's Requirements

During the past thirty-five years, the Court has decided more than thirty cases in which some aspect of *Miranda* was at issue.[2] In many of these cases, the Court has reinterpreted *Miranda*'s language so as to provide less protection to suspects than *Miranda* appeared to provide.[3] In assessing the constitutional obstacles that *Miranda* now presents to interrogators seeking to obtain statements from suspects, two lines of post-*Miranda* decisions are particularly significant. First, post-*Miranda* decisions addressing the prerequisites of a valid waiver provide at least the broad outlines of the legal framework within which interrogators must operate when trying to induce a suspect to waive his *Miranda* warnings. Second, post-*Miranda* decisions holding that statements obtained in violation of *Miranda* may be used for impeachment or to obtain other evidence that will be admissible against the suspect provide insight into the nature of the options that will be available to the police when a suspect invokes his *Miranda* rights.

In *Miranda* itself, the Court indicated it was adopting stringent waiver requirements, which included imposing a heavy burden of proof on the government[4] and prohibiting interrogators from inducing a waiver through "trickery" or "cajolery."[5] Post-*Miranda* decisions have been less strict, however, in mandating specific requirements designed to insure that suspects freely waive their *Miranda* rights. The tests employed vary depending on the context in which the waiver issues arise; when interpreted by lower courts, however, these tests generally provide interrogators with considerable freedom to induce waivers.

Miranda also seemed to indicate that statements obtained in violation of *Miranda* would not be admissible for any purpose.[6] Post-*Miranda* cases have held, however, that such statements may be admitted to impeach a suspect's credibility if he testifies in his own behalf,[7] and that evidence derived from such statements may be admissible in the government's case in chief.[8] Based on these cases, interrogators dealing with suspects who have asserted their *Miranda* rights still have a limited opportunity to circumvent *Miranda*. When seeking statements that will be admissible for the purpose of impeachment or that they hope will lead to other incriminating evidence, interrogators may employ any interrogation tactics not prohibited by the due process voluntariness test.[9]

The significance of the Court's post-*Miranda* cases should not be overestimated. As interpreted by the lower courts, these cases provide the legal framework within which interrogators must operate; nevertheless, the rules stated in reported cases are not likely to provide an accurate picture of the strategies employed by interrogators. First, the police interpret and apply those rules in light of their particular concerns. In some instances, this may lead them to interpret *Miranda* strictly. In order to ensure that incriminating statements obtained by interrogators will be admissible, interrogators may be advised to adhere to the letter of *Miranda*'s requirements. In other instances, however, the police may interpret the post-*Miranda* cases so as to maximize the extent to which interrogators will be able to obtain incriminating statements likely to be admissible. In determining whether incriminating statements are likely to be admissible, moreover, the police may take into account two factors favoring admissibility: first, lower courts (especially trial courts) are inclined to interpret post-*Miranda* doctrine in a way that is favorable to the police;[10] and, second, at least in cases where the interrogation is not recorded or otherwise transcribed, police testimony can be shaped so as to reduce the likelihood of a finding of nonwaiver.[11]

Interrogators' Strategies for Inducing *Miranda* Waivers

From an interrogator's perspective, *Miranda*'s requirements present various obstacles to a successful interrogation. In most cases, the primary obstacle arises when the interrogator first gives *Miranda* warnings to the suspect. Although the interrogator hopes that the suspect will waive his *Miranda* rights and respond to questions, the suspect may invoke his rights and refuse to speak to the interrogator. Even if the suspect elects to waive his rights, *Miranda* still presents a theoretical obstacle in that the suspect could choose to invoke one of his *Miranda* rights during the interrogation, declining to make further statements. In practice, however, once the suspect waives his rights, the interrogator will generally be able to conduct an interrogation that will be successful in that at least some valuable statements will be obtained.*

If the suspect responds to the *Miranda* warnings by invoking either his right to remain silent or his right to have an attorney present at questioning, *Miranda*'s requirements present further obstacles to interroga-

---

* From an interrogator's perspective, statements that the suspect believes to be exculpatory can be just as useful as an admission of guilt. As David Simon observes, "[M]any of those who cannot be lured over the precipice of self-incrimination can still be manipulated into providing alibis, denials and explanations—statements that can be checked and rechecked until a suspect's lies are the greatest evidentiary threat to his freedom." SIMON, HOMICIDE: A YEAR ON THE KILLING STREETS 210 (1991).

tors. The strategies employed to surmount these obstacles will be considered in the next section. In this section, I will consider four strategies interrogators employ to obtain *Miranda* waivers when initially confronting suspects. After presenting examples of each strategy, I will briefly consider whether the strategies illustrated by these examples are legally permissible.

1. Delivering *Miranda* Warnings in a Neutral Manner

Some interrogators deliver the *Miranda* warnings in as simple a manner as possible. Before engaging in any conversation with the suspect, they simply read the warnings from a standard preprinted *Miranda* form card. After reading the warnings, such interrogators typically ask the suspect two questions: Do you understand your rights? Do you wish to waive them? If the suspect answers yes to both questions, interrogators typically ask for and receive the suspect's signed statement that he understands his *Miranda* rights and is waiving them.

Is the strategy legally permissible? One purpose of delivering *Miranda* warnings in this way is to ensure that the suspect's waiver will be valid. Under *North Carolina v. Butler*,[12] even if the suspect never explicitly waives his rights, reading the *Miranda* warnings to him will be sufficient to establish a waiver so long as the judge hearing the case determines that the suspect understood the *Miranda* warnings and voluntarily waived them.[13] Since judges are generally not predisposed toward finding *Miranda* violations, simply reading the *Miranda* warnings to suspects will generally be sufficient to establish a valid waiver; and, in the absence of unusual circumstances,[14] reading the warnings and obtaining a signed statement from the suspect that he understands the warnings and is waiving his rights will always be sufficient.

2. De-emphasizing the Significance of the *Miranda* Warnings

Perhaps the most common strategy employed by interrogators seeking *Miranda* waivers is to de-emphasize the significance of the required warnings. Interrogators employing this strategy typically engage in rapport-building small talk with their suspects before mentioning the *Miranda* warnings. In order to de-emphasize the significance of the warnings, the interrogator then portrays the reading of them as an unimportant bureaucratic ritual and communicates, implicitly or explicitly, that he anticipates that the suspect will waive his rights and make a statement.

Interrogators may attempt to de-emphasize *Miranda* warnings in several ways. One strategy relies on simply becoming less animated while reading the warnings. Some detectives read the warnings in a perfunctory tone of voice, suggesting that the warnings are a bureaucratic form that do not merit the suspect's concern. Others read the warnings quickly, without pausing or looking at the suspect until they request his signature on the waiver form, implying through their conduct that the warnings are merely a matter of routine that necessarily precedes the anticipated questioning.

Another way to de-emphasize the warnings is to call attention to them in a way that suggests that they are simply part of a routine procedure. Interrogators employing this strategy typically tell the suspect that the warnings are a mere formality that they need to dispense with prior to questioning:

> INTERROGATOR: Okay, let, let me go ahead and do this here real quick, like I said so don't let this ruffle your feathers or anything like that—it's just a formality that we have to go through, okay. As I said this is a *Miranda* warning and what it says is that you have the right to remain silent, anything you say can be used against you in a court of law, you have the right to the presence of an attorney to assist you prior to questioning and to be with you during questioning if you so desire, and if you cannot afford an attorney you have the right to have an attorney appointed for you prior to questioning. Do you understand these?
>
> SUSPECT: Yeah.
>
> INTERROGATOR: Okay. Any questions about those at all?
>
> SUSPECT: [*Shakes head side to side*][15]

Interrogators may also try to de-emphasize the *Miranda* warnings by referring to their dissemination in popular movies and TV shows. By placing the warnings in this context, an interrogator may be able to reinforce the idea that the warnings are a formality. For example:

> INTERROGATOR: Before we talk to anybody about anything, there's a thing called *Miranda* and I don't know if you've heard about it, if you've seen it on TV, um, the, just to cover ourselves and to cover you, to protect you, we need to, to advise you of your *Miranda*

rights and we need to know that you understand 'em and that you can hear them, so if you'll speak up for us, okay? Jeff.

SUSPECT: Yeah.[16]

Is the strategy legally permissible?   When interrogators employ this strategy, suspects may attack the validity of their *Miranda* waivers, arguing that they did not make an intelligent waiver as required by *Miranda*. De-emphasizing the warnings arguably trivializes the warnings' legal significance. Instead of understanding that the waiver decision provides him with a critical opportunity to invoke important constitutional protections, the suspect is led to believe that waiving his rights is a bureaucratic formality, an action to be performed without consideration as a matter of routine.

Based on the original *Miranda* opinion, this argument would appear to have force. *Miranda* stated that the government would have to surmount the "heavy burden" of demonstrating that the suspect "knowingly and intelligently waived his privilege against self-incrimination and his right to retained or appointed counsel."[17] Under this standard, interrogation strategies designed to de-emphasize the warnings' significance would be suspect. An intelligent waiver would presumably require a full understanding of the consequences of relinquishing one's rights to remain silent and to have counsel present at questioning.

Post-*Miranda* cases, however, have significantly modified the definition of an intelligent *Miranda* waiver. *Colorado v. Spring*[18] held that a suspect may validly waive his *Miranda* rights even though he is not aware of the magnitude of the charges against him.[19] And *Moran v. Burbine*[20] held that a suspect may waive his *Miranda* rights (including the right to have an attorney present at questioning) even though he is unaware of the fact that a lawyer has been retained to represent him.[21] Based on these cases, the government can establish a valid *Miranda* waiver by simply demonstrating that the suspect understood the meaning of the *Miranda* warnings; it need not show that he understood the consequences of waiving his rights. Thus strategies designed to de-emphasize the significance of the *Miranda* rights will be legally permissible.

3.   Providing the Suspect with an Opportunity to Tell His Side of the Story

One of the most effective strategies for inducing a *Miranda* waiver is to tell the suspect that waiving his rights will provide him with an opportunity to tell his side of the story. Often, an interrogator will utilize this strategy to convince the suspect that the warnings are merely a formality. A standard example is as follows:

> Listen, Joe, I talked to the witnesses and they all say you're involved in this thing. But before I file any charges, I'd like to get your side of the story. I want to hear you tell me what you did—and what you didn't do. But first, I gotta read you your rights. You watch TV, you know the drill . . .[22]

By emphasizing that the suspect will have an opportunity to tell his story to the police, the interrogator makes it clear why the warnings are simply a formality. If the suspect wants to tell the interrogator his side of the story, he will first need to waive his rights. Since the suspect will generally want to tell his side of the story to the interrogator, waiving his rights becomes a matter of routine.

In order to make the option of telling his story even more attractive, the interrogator will sometimes try to convince the suspect that the content of his story will have important consequences. One approach is to suggest that the witness or witnesses against the suspect are being viewed with skepticism:

> INTERROGATOR: I don't think this woman was telling us the whole truth. Okay. I think that it's not, probably not as significant as she's letting on at this point. Okay. So this is why you're here. Now I'd like to talk to you about what this woman is saying, we've more or less ah, you know, if we just talk to her and she alleges this felony crime occurred, then we're more or less obligated to make an arrest.

> SUSPECT: Uh-huh.

> INTERROGATOR: And I know there's more to it and I know, I know you were there. That's not a problem because, because we have, that, that ain't no big deal. But I also need to know the real truth because I'm not sure she's telling us the whole story.

> SUSPECT: What, what is she trying to say?

> INTERROGATOR: Well, she's alleging that you pointed the gun at her.

SUSPECT: Uh-uh [*negative*]. Nah-uh.

INTERROGATOR: [*Unintelligible.*] Alright before we, before we do that, I, like I said I know there's more to this story than she's telling us. But—

SUSPECT: I don't even know her, you know what I'm saying (unintelligible)—

INTERROGATOR: Whoa, whoa, whoa. I can't take your statement until we get through that *Miranda* issue.

SUSPECT: Oh.

INTERROGATOR: You can't tell me anything until we get through that.[23]

By stating to the suspect that he did not think the victim was "telling . . . the whole truth" about the suspect's conduct, the interrogator clearly suggested to the suspect that if he presented a different version of the critical events, the interrogator would be inclined to believe him and to take appropriate action on the basis of that belief. In this example, the interrogator's strategy was so effective that the suspect viewed the *Miranda* warnings as a needless impediment to his goal of telling his side of the story.

Sometimes interrogators will be even more explicit, explaining to the suspect why telling his side of the story will have vitally important consequences for his future. The interrogation of McConnell Adams depicts a particularly masterful employment of this strategy:

INTERROGATOR: McConnell, what we're going to ask you basically is going to change your life, Okay. Your life has changed right now. Okay?

SUSPECT: Okay.

INTERROGATOR: Uhm, it ain't going to be like it was before you were arrested. Your actions from this point on dictate how your life is going to be. Okay? There were some—there are some very, very important questions Sgt. Sutton and I would like to ask you. . . .

> What we're going to get at is the truth. And I already have all of it, as to how things occurred, where they occurred, everything else. What I really need from you is the whys and an explanation so that the world knows that McConnell isn't a cold hearted, stone killer. You're not an assassin, you're not a serial killer, something happened that went wrong that day, cause I know murder wasn't your intention. . . . The reason why can only come from you. Okay? And that's what we're going to delve into.[24]

By telling Adams that his answers to their questions are going to "change his life," the interrogators communicate a twofold message: first, Adams is going to answer their questions; second, the answers he gives will have an important positive or negative effect on his situation. At this point, Adams is likely to wonder what answers will improve his situation. The interrogator then makes it clear. He tells Adams that they know what he did; but they need to determine "the whys . . . so that the world knows that McConnell isn't a cold hearted, stone killer." Upon hearing this, Adams understands that he can help himself by convincing the interrogators that he is not a "cold hearted" killer, but, rather, as they surmised, someone who did not intend to kill. Adams also understands, however, that before he can make any statement to the interrogators, he must waive his *Miranda* rights. Predictably, Adams elected to waive his *Miranda* rights and to make a statement admitting the killing.[25]

Is the strategy legally permissible?　A suspect might argue that this strategy employed in these examples is impermissible for either of two reasons: first, in all cases, the strategy vitiates the suspect's waiver; second, at least in cases where, prior to giving the *Miranda* warnings, the interrogator makes statements that seem to call for a response, the interrogator has violated *Miranda* by improperly interrogating the suspect before the suspect validly waived his rights. Though both these arguments are plausible, they need to be evaluated in light of the post-*Miranda* doctrinal developments.

　　The argument that the strategy vitiates the suspect's *Miranda* waiver could be based on *Miranda*'s language. *Miranda* stated that "any evidence that the accused was threatened, tricked, or cajoled into a waiver" would vitiate the waiver.[26] Under the most common definition of cajolery,[27] this language would seem to prohibit the police from persuading suspects to waive their rights through the offer of inducements. When interrogators use the strategy described in these examples, suspects are being offered an inducement to waive their rights. In every example, the interrogator makes it clear to the suspect that he will be able to tell his "side of the story" only if he waives his rights. This in itself constitutes an inducement to the suspect.

Post-*Miranda* cases have not expressly repudiated *Miranda*'s "trickery" or "cajolery" language. They have emphasized, however, that the validity of a *Miranda* waiver turns on whether the waiver is voluntary and intelligent.[28] By articulating this standard, the post-*Miranda* cases clearly suggest that interrogators' use of inducements or persuasion will not necessarily render a suspect's resulting waiver invalid. Rather, the question of a waiver's validity will be determined by a totality of circumstances test that depends on an evaluation of all factors relating to the waiver's voluntariness.[29]

This "totality of circumstances" test is analogous to the due process voluntariness test under which courts evaluated myriad factors to determine the voluntariness of a suspect's confession.[30] In practice, lower courts have applied both tests so that interrogators are allowed considerable leeway. In determining whether a suspect's *Miranda* waiver is valid, lower courts invariably conclude that police inducements alone are not sufficient to vitiate the waiver.[31] On the other hand, courts are likely to hold that *Miranda* waivers induced through affirmative misrepresentations or misleading statements are invalid.[32] In one case,[33] for example, a court held that an officer rendered the suspect's waiver invalid by telling him that if he asked for an attorney he would forfeit any opportunity to talk to the police or cooperate with the government. The court held that the interrogator's ultimatum (stating that this was the suspect's only opportunity to cooperate) made his statements false or misleading and this was sufficient to render the suspect's waiver involuntary.[34] In the absence of unusual circumstances of this type, however, lower courts have been unlikely to hold that a suspect's *Miranda* waiver is involuntary because it was induced through the strategy of telling him that waiving his rights will provide him an opportunity to tell his side of the story.

In at least some of the situations described above, the suspect would have a strong argument that the officer interrogated him before he received his *Miranda* warnings. In McConnell Adams's case, for example, the officer told the suspect, "What I really need to know from you is the whys and an explanation so that the world knows that McConnell isn't a cold hearted, stone killer." A reasonable person in Adams's position would certainly view that statement as the functional equivalent of a question. The officer is telling Adams that he wants him to explain the reasons for his conduct. Under *Rhode Island v. Innis*,[35] a post-*Miranda* decision, statements that are the functional equivalent of questions will generally constitute interrogation.[36] Thus, Adams seems to have a plausible claim that the police violated *Miranda* by interrogating him before informing him of his rights. Since his statements were obtained in violation of *Miranda,* they should not be admissible.[37]

Even if the government were to concede that Adams was interrogated in violation of *Miranda,*[38] however, it would still have a strong argument that Adams's statements should not be excluded. In *Oregon v. Elstad,*[39] the Court dealt with a situation in which the police interrogated a suspect in custody without giving him the *Miranda* warnings, obtained an incriminating statement, and then, after taking the suspect to the police station, giving him *Miranda* warnings and receiving a signed waiver, obtained additional incriminating statements. After observing that the suspect's first incriminating statement would be inadmissible because it was obtained in violation of *Miranda,*[40] the Court held that the suspect's later statements—which were made after *Miranda's* warnings and waiver requirements were ostensibly met—would be admissible so long as the second statement was "voluntarily made"[41] and, prior to giving that statement, the suspect knowingly and voluntarily waived his *Miranda* rights.[42]

Elstad arguably applies to Adams's case. If Adams had interrupted the officer's initial remarks and said, "I'm not a stone killer. I didn't mean to kill him," that statement would be inadmissible; but Adams's later statements—given after the *Miranda* warnings and waiver requirements were met—would be admissible so long as Adams's *Miranda* waiver was voluntary and intelligent and his second statement was voluntarily made, requirements that in practice would be easily satisfied.[43] Adams's actual case differs from the hypothetical only in that the suspect made no initial incriminating statement. This difference only strengthens the government's argument for admissibility. If subsequent *Miranda* warnings can eliminate the taint of a prior *Miranda* violation even when the violation produced an incriminating statement that might lead the suspect to believe that he had already relinquished his right to remain silent,[44] then, surely, subsequent *Miranda* warnings will be sufficient to eliminate the taint of an initial *Miranda* violation that did not immediately produce an incriminating statement.

Adams might argue that in his case the connection between the *Miranda* violation and the subsequent incriminating statement is much more direct than it was in *Elstad.* In contrast to *Elstad,* where the violation of *Miranda* was apparently inadvertent,[45] the detective in *Adams* improperly interrogated the suspect for the specific purpose of trying to persuade him to waive his *Miranda* rights. Moreover, in Adams's case, unlike in *Elstad,* the improper interrogation, the *Miranda* warnings and waiver, and the subsequent interrogation that elicited incriminating statements all occurred in rapid succession.

From a policy perspective, these differences appear significant. If the police are permitted to exploit *Miranda* violations so as to obtain evidence directly emanating from such violations, then the protection provided by *Miranda*'s safeguards is tenuous indeed. *Elstad,* however, seemed adamant in insisting that statements stemming from a *Miranda* violation would not be excluded so long as the statements were shown to be voluntary and the police complied with *Miranda*'s requirements before obtaining them. Because of *Elstad,* lower courts predisposed toward admitting suspects' incriminating statements can readily reject the argument that statements should be excluded because police interrogated suspects prior to giving them the *Miranda* warnings.

4. Convincing the Suspect That the Interrogator Is Acting in His Best Interests

Another strategy for obtaining *Miranda* waivers is to convince the suspect that the interrogator is acting in his best interests. Interrogators employing this strategy seek to create the appearance of a nonadversarial relationship between the interrogator and the suspect. Before reading the *Miranda* warnings, the interrogator portrays himself as someone who is trying to help the suspect. If the strategy is successful, the suspect will inevitably view the *Miranda* safeguards as insignificant. He will naturally want to waive his right so that he can receive assistance from the interrogator.

Interrogators employing this strategy will sometimes simply present themselves as a friend of the suspect, perhaps drawing on a past relationship:

INTERROGATOR: I consider myself to be a friend of yours.

SUSPECT: Yeah, you're a friend of mine, Bill, all right.

INTERROGATOR: We've had hot fudge sundaes together, and we've exchanged Christmas letters and—we've done various things like that.

SUSPECT: Yeah.[46]

Although the interrogator did not further elaborate as to their friendship, his reference to it might be sufficient to convince the suspect that he should waive his rights so that he could explain to his "friend" what happened.

When the interrogator has no preexisting relationship with the suspect, he may employ this strategy by explaining that he wants to "help people"[47] or that he and other interrogators want to help the suspect deal with his specific problem. In dealing with Prudencio Sanchez, a suspect who was accused of sexually molesting his daughter, the interrogator employed the latter approach. Before reading the *Miranda* warnings to Sanchez, the interrogator told Sanchez the evidence indicated he had had sex with his daughter but added that this did not mean that he was a terrible person. Rather, it showed that he needed help. The interrogator then elaborated this theme as follows:

> We think you have a problem and you need help before that problem gets bigger, you have to get help from a professional who can give you some advice so that you can continue with your life and go forward, because if you don't do anything about this, what you have done with your daughter, it will go to something worse, it's going to get worse and that will cause you more damage, to you and your family or the other person who you do this to. Because it's not normal; but neither are you a very dangerous person, you are not a criminal who's going to frighten people. But that there are people who need help for your problem, we believe that you are a person who needs professional help to give you advice, so that this does not happen again and you can go on with your life. Right now you have several problems with your family with this, and you have to take care of one by one because if you don't take care of any, you are not going to be well, mentally, you are not going to be well. And that's one of the reasons why we are here. Not just to tell you "you're lying" and it's now over, no, what we want is to [know] how did this problem come about, how did it start and why, and to find someone who can give you advice and who can give you some good guidance so that you can go on instead of being stuck here, and that just because, because this happened my life is over. No, you have to think about your future. You're what, 33 years old? 33 years, you're relatively young, you have to think about your children.[48]

Shortly after this statement, the detective read Sanchez the *Miranda* warnings and Sanchez waived his rights. By the time the warnings were read, Sanchez was very likely convinced that the interrogators were acting in his interest in the sense that they were seeking to obtain the right kind of help or treatment for him. Sanchez would naturally believe that in order to obtain the interrogators' assistance, he would need to waive his rights and explain exactly what happened.

In other situations, interrogators employ a less direct variation of this strategy. Without stating that they are acting in the suspect's interest, the interrogator suggests to the suspect, either directly or implicitly, that he will be able to help the suspect only if the latter waives his rights and makes a statement. In McConnell Adams's case, for example, the message to the suspect was that he could help himself only if he made a statement in which he showed that he was not a cold-hearted killer. In Vincent Yarborough's case, the suspect's options, though less clearly stated, were equally obvious. After telling the suspect he was arrested for two murders and assault, the interrogator read him his rights and asked him if he understood. The interrogation then proceeded as follows:

SUSPECT: Uh huh. Wait a minute, but what you're saying, I'm being arrested for, for what'd you say, two—

INTERROGATOR 1: Actually for two homicides, or one, one homicide and one beat, and one felony assault.

SUSPECT: Oh no.

INTERROGATOR 2: Yeah, unless we can find a reason or explanation for, for what happened, that's, we have no choice based on what we have.

INTERROGATOR 1: So do you understand your rights?

SUSPECT: Yeah, I understand what you're sayin.

INTERROGATOR 1: Okay, do you want to talk to us about it?

SUSPECT: Yeah, I'll talk [*inaudible*].[49]

The interrogator's statement to the effect that they had "no choice" with respect to the charges unless they could "find a reason or explanation for . . . what happened" clearly suggested that if the suspect could provide an explanation for what happened, there was a possibility the interrogators would reduce the charges. Although the interrogators did not state that they were acting on the suspect's behalf, their statements would lead the suspect to believe that the interrogators might help him if he waived his rights and made a statement.

Is the strategy legally permissible? When this strategy is employed, suspects may attack the validity of their *Miranda* waivers on the ground that waivers induced through express or implied promises of leniency are involuntary. In all of the examples presented, the interrogator's statements would lead the suspect to believe that waiving his *Miranda* rights might lead to more lenient treatment from the police. In Yarborough's case, for example, the suspect would believe that waiving his rights could precipitate reduced government charges. And in Sanchez's case, the suspect would believe that waiving his rights provided the best possibility for obtaining the treatment he needed. Just as confessions induced by express or implied promises of leniency were originally inadmissible,[50] suspects could argue that *Miranda* waivers induced by such promises should also be invalid.

As with *Miranda* waivers obtained through other kinds of inducements, *Miranda's* language provides some support for this argument. Even if "cajolery" cannot be interpreted to include all inducements, the "threatened, tricked, or cajoled" language is arguably broad enough to cover express or implied promises of leniency. Such promises constitute unusually strong types of persuasion.

Moreover, even under the "totality of circumstances" test applied by post-*Miranda* cases, inducing a *Miranda* waiver through an express or implied promise of leniency would arguably be sufficient to render the waiver invalid. In finding suspects' confessions involuntary under the due process voluntariness test, the Court sometimes viewed such promises as significant factors in support of its conclusion.[51] If *Miranda's* language relating to a strict standard of waiver is to have any force, more stringent restrictions should be imposed on interrogators seeking to obtain a *Miranda* waiver than on those seeking to obtain a confession. Arguably, therefore, waivers induced by express or implied promises of leniency should be invalid.

At least one lower court has endorsed this principle. In *Commonwealth v. Gibbs*,[52] the Pennsylvania Supreme Court held that a *Miranda* waiver induced by an interrogator's promise to inform the prosecutor of the suspect's cooperation was invalid because "[p]romises of benefits or special considerations . . . comprise the sort of persuasion or trickery which easily can mislead suspects into giving confessions."[53] Other lower courts have held that specific promises of leniency[54] or admonitions relating to the danger of noncooperation[55] will render the suspect's *Miranda* waiver invalid. Most courts, however, have held that "[p]romises of leniency, without more, do not invalidate a *Miranda* waiver."[56] As with other types of inducements, express or implied promises of leniency are viewed as simply a factor to be considered in determining the voluntariness of the waiver.

Under this test, the strategy employed in all of the examples described could properly be found to be permissible. When evaluating the pressures generated by suggesting to a suspect that waiving his rights could lead to reduced charges or to providing appropriate treatment for the suspect's problem, lower courts would be able to take into account the suspect's background, the environment in which the strategy was employed, and other circumstances that might ameliorate the strategy's coercive effect. Thus in applying the "totality of the circumstances" test, lower courts might easily find that *Miranda* waivers produced by the strategies in the examples cited above would be valid.

Interrogators' Strategies When Suspects Invoke Their *Miranda* Rights

When a suspect responds to the *Miranda* warnings by invoking either his right to remain silent or his right to have an attorney present at questioning, an interrogator has basically three options: she can leave the suspect alone for a period of time, hoping that the latter will change his mind about asserting his rights; she can initiate further contact with the suspect, hoping that she can induce him to change his mind about invoking his rights; or she can simply proceed to question the suspect despite the fact that he has invoked his rights, a strategy that has been described as questioning "outside *Miranda*."[57] After presenting examples of each strategy, I will consider whether the strategy employed is legally permissible.

1. Leaving the Suspect Alone So He Can Change His Mind

When dealing with suspects who have invoked one of their *Miranda* rights, interrogators are sometimes advised simply to give the suspect an opportunity to change his mind. In advising interrogators as to when they should question a suspect "outside *Miranda*," an interrogator's training videotape provides the following advice: "Before you go 'outside *Miranda'* give him a chance to sit and stew in the cell for a little while and see if he changes his mind."[58] If the suspect initiates any further conversation relating to his case with the police, an officer will then seek to obtain a waiver and interrogate the suspect.

Is the strategy legally permissible? *Miranda* itself seemed to indicate that once the suspect invoked either of his *Miranda* rights, no interrogation would occur unless the suspect's attorney was present.[59] Once the suspect invoked his right to an attorney, the Court may have contemplated that the police would be required to provide him with a lawyer as soon as possible. In a post-*Miranda* case,[60] however, the Court indicated that the police are not obligated to respond to a suspect's request for counsel by providing him with an attorney.[61] Rather, under *Edwards v. Arizona,*[62] the police are simply prohibited from interrogating the suspect without the presence of an attorney unless the suspect "initiates" further communications with the police.[63] If, after "stewing in his cell," the suspect "initiates" further communications with the police and then waives his *Miranda* rights, the waiver will be valid.

Oregon v. Bradshaw,[64] another post-*Miranda* case, indicated, moreover, that a court may easily find that a suspect "initiated" further communications with the police. In *Bradshaw,* an officer gave the suspect *Miranda* warnings and the latter invoked his right to an attorney. The officer immediately terminated the conversation. A few minutes later, the suspect said to the officer, "Well, what is going to happen to me now?" *Bradshaw* held that the suspect's question legitimated the officer's subsequent attempts to obtain a *Miranda* waiver.[65] The Court's pivotal plurality opinion stated that the suspect's question constituted "initiation" within the meaning of *Edwards* because "although ambiguous . . . [it] evinced a willingness and a desire for a generalized discussion about the investigation."[66]

Under *Edwards* and *Bradshaw,* the strategy of allowing a suspect who invokes either of his *Miranda* rights to "sit and stew in the cell" so that he may change his mind about talking to the police is certainly permissible. Even if the suspect invokes his right to an attorney, the police are simply prohibited from interrogating him without the presence of an attorney unless he "initiates" further communications with them. In practice, moreover, the suspect's "initiation" will not be difficult to establish. If the suspect says anything that may be reasonably interpreted by the police as showing a willingness to discuss any aspect of the investigation,[67] the police may properly seek to obtain a valid *Miranda* waiver.

2. Prompting the Suspect to Change His Mind

When a suspect invokes his right to remain silent, an interrogator may initiate further contact with the suspect in the hope that she will thereby lead him to change his mind and make a statement.[68] When the suspect invokes his right to have an attorney present, the interrogator has to be careful lest she violate *Edwards*'s prohibition. Some interrogators, however, have developed subtle strategies for prompting a suspect to waive his rights even after the suspect has invoked his right to an attorney.

In one case, for example, the police gave the suspect his *Miranda* warnings after arresting him for rape and assault. The suspect, who was seventeen at the time, invoked both his right to remain silent and his right to have an attorney present. The police then placed him in a cell at the police station. Several hours later, a detective went to his cell. She introduced herself to the suspect and informed him that she had interviewed the victim and obtained her story of what happened. She then told the suspect that "she knew he had advised the police earlier that he did not wish to discuss the facts of the case with the police, but, if he changed his mind, she would be willing to speak with him."[69] The suspect decided that he wanted to tell the detective his side of the story. After some further discussion, the detective went over a form with a printed version of the *Miranda* warnings; the suspect signed the form waiving his rights and made incriminating statements.

Is the strategy legally permissible? The suspect could argue that the detective's initial statements to him violated *Edwards* for two reasons: first, she interrogated the suspect at that point; second, the detective rather than the suspect "initiated" the exchanges that took place after the suspect invoked his right to have an attorney present, and, therefore, under *Edwards*, the detective was prohibited from interrogating the suspect even after she gave him a new set of *Miranda* warnings and received a signed waiver of his rights.

The suspect could argue that the detective's statement to the effect that she would be "willing to speak" with the suspect if he changed his mind about invoking his rights constituted interrogation because this statement was made for the purpose of getting the suspect to tell his story to the police. In explaining the test for interrogation, *Innis* said that when a "police practice is designed to elicit an incriminating response from the accused, it is unlikely that the practice will not" meet the test.[70]

Why would the detective tell the suspect she would be willing to talk to him if he changed his mind about talking to the police? In view of the fact that the detective first stated that she had interviewed the victim and obtained her story, the detective's strategy seems obvious. In stating that she was "willing to talk" to the suspect, she was hoping to entice him into telling her his story in the hope that he could thereby counterbalance whatever she had heard from the victim. In her presentation of this option, moreover, the detective was using a variation of the reverse psychology described by Mark Twain in *Tom Sawyer*.[71] By minimizing her own apparent interest in hearing the suspect's story, she hoped to make the option of giving a statement seem irresistibly attractive.

Although this argument seems quite persuasive, lower courts deciding these issues are not likely to engage in subtle analysis that will result in excluding statements on the basis of *Edwards*. Not surprisingly, the lower court deciding this case concluded that the detective's initial statements to the suspect did not constitute interrogation.[72] Using *Innis*'s basic test for interrogation,[73] the court concluded that the detective's remarks did not imply a question or demand a response.[74] Rather, they merely constituted "an expression of her availability if [the suspect] wanted to talk."[75] Thus, even though her comments obviously "struck a responsive chord,"[76] they did not constitute interrogation.

Even if the detective's remarks did not constitute interrogation, the suspect could argue that the detective rather than the suspect "initiated" further exchanges within the meaning of *Edwards*. Once the suspect invokes his right to an attorney, *Edwards* requires no interrogation unless the suspect "initiates further exchanges, communications or conversations." Arguably, the detective initiated further communications relating to the case when she stated that she would be willing to hear the suspect's story.[77] If the detective initiated further communications with the suspect at that point, it should follow that the suspect did not initiate further communications with the detective at any subsequent point because the detective's remarks to the suspect precipitated the flow of conversation that led to the suspect's waiver of his rights. Based on this argument, the suspect's waiver would be invalid.

Although this argument seems even more persuasive than the previous one, a court could reject it on the ground that the detective's remarks to the suspect did not initiate further communications with the suspect. Rather, these remarks constituted "an expression of her availability" if the suspect changed his mind about invoking his rights. Viewed in this light, the detective's remarks did not initiate further communications because they did not call for a communication from the suspect.[78]

3. Questioning "Outside *Miranda*"

Questioning "outside *Miranda*" is a relatively new interrogation strategy that is apparently used only in discrete situations.[79] An interrogator employing this strategy will typically tell a suspect who has invoked his *Miranda* rights that he wants to talk to him "off the Record."[80] By putting his request in these terms, the interrogator hopes to convince the suspect that he can receive the benefits of telling his story to the police without being concerned about the possibility that his words may be used against him.

In employing this strategy, interrogators differ with respect to what they tell suspects concerning the admissibility of their statements. In one case, the interrogator promised the suspect only that the suspect's statement would not be used against him in the government's case in chief. When viewed in context, however, this promise would be unlikely to alert a typical suspect to the fact that his statement would be admissible against him in other circumstances. After the suspect invoked his right to an attorney, the dialogue between the interrogator and suspect proceeded as follows:

> DETECTIVE TALBOT: Okay, now, let me, let me explain to you what's happened. You've basically invoked your right to have an attorney . . .
>
> McNALLY: Right.
>
> DETECTIVE TALBOT: . . . At this point, nothing that you say can be used against you in Court . . . in California because you have invoked your right to have an attorney.
>
> McNALLY: Right.
>
> DETECTIVE TALBOT: I still would like to know what happened now because—well, I'll tell you where I come from. I don't trust anything that anybody tells me after they've talked to an attorney and the D.A. that will be working with us on this case doesn't either.[81]

After some further conversation, the officers persisted:

DETECTIVE TALBOT: [I]f you were in our place, would you trust something that somebody told you after they talked to an attorney? . . . [T]he deal is here. It's up to them . . . to talk about it. The only thing is, everything that falls after this—we'll go in one direction based on the physical evidence and the statements that we have. If we don't have anything to the contrary, that's the direction we're gonna' go and we're gonna push it.

McNALLY: Right.

DETECTIVE TALBOT: Okay, and fuck your attorney. It's just—I don't care about him anymore.

McNALLY: Yeah.

DETECTIVE TALBOT: Okay. As far as I'm concerned, you know, they really mess up the system. I wanna' know now what you're gonna tell me later. It can't be used against you. We . . .

DETECTIVE COOPER: This is your opportunity.

DETECTIVE TALBOT: . . . told you that.

DETECTIVE COOPER: And it's—this is your opportunity and it's not gonna' be used against you . . .

McNALLY: . . . Alright. I'll . . . and this can't be used against me?

DETECTIVE COOPER: No, absolutely . . . [W]e're promising you, it's not gonna' be used against you—in the case in chief—against you, okay? Just, this is for our edification of what happened.

McNALLY: Well, anyway, he picked me up outside, outside the Oar House, okay? He asked me if I wanted to go have some beers . . .[82]

Although the interrogators' last statement to the suspect accurately described the extent to which his statements would be inadmissible, a typical suspect would be unlikely to understand that statements inadmissible in the "case in chief" might still be admissible for some other purpose.

In other cases, interrogators clearly communicate to the suspect that their "off-the-record" statements cannot be used by the police for any purpose. In one case, the interrogator repeatedly stated this point and emphasized it with the aid of graphic examples:

> INTERROGATOR: I mean everything you tell us right now I'm not gonna be able to use any way, James, because you've already said you're gonna, you want an attorney. Okay? So what, whatever you tell me right now, it's not gonna be admissible anyway. You know what I'm saying. You're smart enough to realize that and I'm being up front with you anyway right now as we're speaking. Okay? You've already said you wanted an attorney and you've been, you've been in court before where, where you know where you said, where they said, "Will this evidence, this testimony is not admissible because my client already went ahead and said he wanted an attorney."[83]

> SUSPECT: So what I don't understand if, whatever I say right now is, you know, you can't use because I said I wanted to talk to a lawyer?

> INTERROGATOR: No, no you, unless you say, unless you say "Detective I want to go on the record," okay? I mean everything you say right now is not gonna be used against you. I'll tell you that right now. I already know, I already know that you are the person responsible. Okay, that's my, that's my feeling okay? That is my, that's just my feeling. I'm being very up front with you, okay. Ah if I was to say, "No I don't think it's you. I think it's somebody else," well I'd be bullshitting you. I'm just telling you straight.

> SUSPECT: Yeah, I know.

> INTERROGATOR: Okay, all I'm interested is finding out the facts. You can tell me off the record, that's fine. I can't use that. I would like it to be on record but that would only be with, with, with, with you saying, "Fine, I will go ahead and tell you and I want it on the record and I realize, I realize that I don't have, that I can have an attorney." But I want to tell you, I mean you know without that, I mean you know whatever you tell me right now doesn't mean a hill of beans. You can tell me that you've murdered 50 people here and that they're buried here, here and there. So what? You know, so what?[84]

After hearing this interrogator's speech, even a cautious suspect would be convinced that his statements to the interrogator could not be used against him in any way. Predictably, the suspect eventually made incriminating statements to the interrogator.

Is the strategy legally permissible? In *Harris v. New York*,[85] the Court established the impeachment exception to *Miranda,* holding that statements obtained from a defendant in violation of *Miranda* are admissible for the purpose of impeaching the defendant's credibility in the event that he testifies in his own defense at trial.[86] In *Hass v. Oregon*,[87] the Court extended *Harris,* holding that the impeachment exception applies even when the police violate *Miranda* by interrogating a suspect after he responds to the *Miranda* warnings by invoking his right to have an attorney present at questioning.[88] In both *Harris* and *Hass,* the Court indicated that the impeachment exception would not apply if the evidence the government sought to introduce was obtained in violation of the due process voluntariness test.[89] Thus, when interrogators employ the strategy described in the examples above, the question presented is whether the suspect's statements should be excluded for all purposes because they were obtained in violation of due process.

When an interrogator misleads a suspect as to the admissibility of statements given during questioning "outside *Miranda,*" the suspect could argue that the statements were obtained in violation of due process because the interrogation practice employed to obtain them was fundamentally unfair.[90] This strategy constitutes a particularly pernicious form of misrepresentation because it essentially turns *Miranda* inside out. Instead of informing suspects that they are confronted with an adversary situation, which was one of *Miranda's* purposes,[91] interrogators are able to use the *Miranda* warnings in a way that allows them to deceive suspects into believing that it is not against their interest to talk when it really is.

Based on the Court's expressed concern for prohibiting interrogation practices "offensive to a civilized system of justice,"[92] this argument would appear to have force. If *Miranda* retains any vitality, using *Miranda* to deceive a suspect as to the admissibility of his statements should be viewed as a reprehensible police practice. At least when the interrogator affirmatively misrepresents the extent to which the statements obtained in violation of *Miranda* will be admissible, the suspect would appear to have a strong argument that the statements are involuntary.

The argument might be rejected, however, on the ground that the interrogator's deception does not exert coercive force and, therefore, would not be enough in itself to render the suspect's resulting statement involuntary. In *Colorado v. Connelly*,[93] a post-*Miranda* due process case, the Court stated that "coercive police activity is a necessary predicate to the finding that a confession" is involuntary.[94] Based on this language, a court could plausibly conclude that deceiving a suspect with respect to the circumstances under which the suspect's statement may be admitted against him will not be enough in itself to render the statement involuntary. In fact, a majority of the lower courts addressing the issue have essentially taken this approach.[95]

Miranda's Present Effect on Law Enforcement

In view of the data showing how interrogators have adapted to *Miranda*, employing sophisticated methodologies for the purpose of gauging *Miranda*'s past effect on law enforcement is a futile enterprise. Data relating to *Miranda*'s past impact on interrogators' ability to obtain confessions tells us little or nothing about *Miranda*'s present effect on interrogators' ability to solve crimes through obtaining incriminating statements from suspects. Because interrogators have shaped their strategy in accordance with post-*Miranda* decisions weakening *Miranda*'s safeguards, *Miranda*'s effect on law enforcement will inevitably be a moving target that varies depending not only on the nature of the interrogation strategies employed but also on the frequency and sophistication with which those strategies are utilized.

The data does show that modern interrogators have developed sophisticated strategies for circumventing *Miranda*'s obstacles to a successful interrogation. Indeed, in important respects, the strategies employed for the purpose of obtaining *Miranda* waivers parallel the strategies that the *Inbau Manual* advises interrogators to use to obtain statements from reluctant suspects. In both situations, the underlying strategy is essentially to convince the suspect that it is not only expected but also advantageous for him to waive his rights and make a statement. When the most effective strategies for obtaining *Miranda* waivers are employed, moreover, there is little reason to believe that interrogators will be any less effective in obtaining waivers than they are in eliciting statements. Thus, when these strategies are employed, *Miranda*'s costs to law enforcement are likely to be negligible. If the interrogator can persuade the suspect to make a statement, she can also persuade him to waive his *Miranda* rights.

Interrogators do not always employ the most effective strategies for obtaining *Miranda* waivers. As the examples presented indicate, some interrogators deliver the *Miranda* warnings in a neutral manner. Others seek to de-emphasize the warnings, but without employing sophisticated strategies that would lead suspects to believe that waiving their rights is in their own best interests. It is not clear, of course, why different interrogators adopt different strategies. From examining a limited sample of interrogation transcripts, however, it appears that interrogators are more likely to employ sophisticated strategies in serious cases where obtaining incriminating statements will be most important to the authorities.[96] If this is true, then it supports the hypothesis that interrogators are able to minimize *Miranda*'s impact most effectively when it is most important for them to do so.

Although seeking to quantify *Miranda*'s costs to law enforcement is a dubious enterprise, the data relating to interrogators' strategies for circumventing *Miranda*'s requirements does support two general conclusions: first, *Miranda* imposes some costs on law enforcement; second, the costs imposed are slight. The fact that police are able to obtain statements admissible for impeachment from suspects who respond to the *Miranda* warnings by invoking their rights indicates that *Miranda*'s safeguards lead to the loss of statements that would otherwise be admissible in the government's case in chief. If *Miranda*'s safeguards were replaced by the due process voluntariness test, statements presently admissible only for the purposes of impeachment would also be admissible in the government's case in chief.* From the government's perspective, statements admissible in their case in chief will generally be more valuable than statements admissible solely for the purpose of impeachment.[97]

But how often does *Miranda* result in lost statements for the police? There are undoubtedly a core of suspects—professional criminals—who are not going to make statements under any circumstances.[98] For these suspects, the presence or absence of *Miranda* warnings makes no difference. For other suspects, *Miranda* will generally not impose a serious impediment to obtaining incriminating statements. Based on the most recent studies, it appears that in most jurisdictions at least 80 percent of

---

* To the extent that interrogators obtain these statements through deceiving suspects as to whether they will be admissible for any purpose, it might be argued that the suspect's knowledge of *Miranda*'s protections assists interrogators' misrepresentation. This argument seems dubious, however. Even if *Miranda* were abolished, interrogators could undoubtedly be subtle enough to deceive suspects with respect to whether the statements made to the police would be admissible against them. In many cases, simply stating to the suspect that his statements to the officer would be "off the record" would be likely to be sufficient.

all suspects waive their *Miranda* rights and make statements to the police. When the police employ their most sophisticated strategies for obtaining *Miranda* waivers, moreover, the percentage of suspects who waive their rights undoubtedly increases. Indeed, if obtaining *Miranda* waivers were a significant problem for law enforcement, interrogators would presumably be often advised to question suspects "outside *Miranda*" so that they could be sure of obtaining incriminating statements useful for some purpose. In fact, however, interrogators are advised to question "outside *Miranda*" only as a last resort. The fact that interrogators sometimes obtain statements through questioning "outside *Miranda*" shows that *Miranda* does impose some costs on law enforcement; the fact that interrogators rarely employ this strategy indicates that those costs—at least in terms of percentage of incriminating statements lost—are quite small.

NOTES

1. See Paul G. Cassell & Bret S. Hayman, *Police Interrogation in the 1990's: An Empirical Study of the Effects of Miranda*, 43 UCLA L. REV. 839, 859 (1996) (83.7 percent of suspects from a sample of 129 waived their rights); Richard A. Leo, *Inside the Interrogation Room*, 86 J. CRIM. L. & CRIMINOLOGY 266, 276 (1996) (78.3 percent of suspects from a sample of 175 waived their rights).

2. A Westlaw search conducted on May 13, 2000, indicated that, as of that time, the Court had decided approximately thirty-five cases that applied *Miranda* (including interpreting it, narrowing it, or carving out exceptions to it). See Westlaw: Keycite, May 13, 2000. For an illuminating discussion of some of these cases, see Geoffrey R. Stone, *The Miranda Doctrine in the Supreme Court*, 1977 SUP. CT. REV. 99.

3. See *supra* chapter 6.

4. *Miranda,* 384 U.S. at 476.

5. *Id.*

6. See 384 U.S. at 477.

7. *See* Oregon v. Hass, 420 U.S. 714 (1975); Harris v. New York, 401 U.S. 222 (1971).

8. See 470 U.S. at 307–08 (1985).

9. Mincey v. Arizona, 437 U.S. 385, 401–02 (1978); *Elstad,* 470 U.S. 298, 304 (1985).

10. *See* Anthony G. Amsterdam, *The Supreme Court and the Rights of Suspects in Criminal Cases*, 45 N.Y.U. L. REV. 785, 790–91 (1970).

11. In advocating that the police be required to record interrogations when feasible, Kamisar explained why police officers will naturally be inclined to slant their testimony so that it will favor a ruling of admissibility:

    It is not because a police officer is more dishonest than the rest of us that we should demand an objective recordation of the critical events. Rather, it is because we are entitled to assume that he is no less human—no less inclined to reconstruct and interpret past events in a light most favorable to himself—that we should not permit him to be "a judge in his own cause."

KAMISAR, ESSAYS, *supra* chapter 1, note 24, at 137 (*quoting* Felix S. Cohen, *Field Theory and Judicial Logic,* 59 YALE L.J. 238, 242 (1950)).

12. 441 U.S. 369 (1979).
13. 441 U.S. at 373.
14. An exception may apply when the suspect is so mentally handicapped that he lacks the capacity to understand the meaning of the *Miranda* warnings. In practice, however, courts have generally held that a suspect's mental handicap is only one of many factors to be weighed in determining the validity of a *Miranda* waiver. *See, e.g.,* United States v. Gaddy, 894 F.2d 1307, 1312 (11th Cir. 1990) ("Mental illness is only a factor to be weighed in determining the validity of a waiver"); Dunkins v. Thigpen, 854 F.2d 394, 398–99 (11th Cir. 1988) (finding suspect's waiver valid despite evidence of mental retardation).
15. Interrogation Transcript of Dante Parker, Maricopa County, Ariz., Sheriffs Office in Phoenix, Ariz. (Sept. 12, 1991).
16. Richard A. Leo, *Miranda's Revenge: Police Interrogation as a Confidence Game,* 30 L. & SOC'Y REV. 259, 272 (1996).
17. *Miranda,* 384 U.S. at 475.
18. 479 U.S. 564 (1987).
19. 479 U.S. at 567.
20. 475 U.S. 412 (1986).

21. 475 U.S. at 422.
22. Peter Carlson, *The Seduction: Cops, Suspects, and the New Art of Interrogation,* WASH. POST, Sunday Magazine, Sept. 13, 1998, at 6, 11.
23. Interrogation Transcript of Kentrick McCoy, Sacramento, Cal., Police Dep't 14–15 (Sept. 1, 1996).
24. Interrogation Transcript of McConnell Adams, Oakland County Sheriff Department, Pontiac, Mich. 3–15 (Dec. 31, 1996), *State v. Adams,* Circuit Court for the County of Oakland, State of Michigan, Case No. 97–150765-FC.
25. *Id.* at 14.
26. *Miranda,* 384 U.S. at 476.
27. *Cajole* is defined as "to persuade with deliberate flattery, esp in the face of reasonable objection or reluctance." WEBSTER'S THIRD NEW INTERNATIONAL DICTIONARY OF THE ENGLISH LANGUAGE 313 (Philip Babcock Gove ed., Merriam-Webster 1981).
28. Spring v. Colorado, 479 U.S. 564, 572 (1987); Moran v. Burbine, 475 U.S. 412, 421 (1986).
29. *See* Colorado v. Connelly, 479 U.S. 157, 169 (1986); Fare v. Michael C., 442 U.S. 707, 724–25 (1979); *cf.* Michigan v. Mosley, 423 U.S. 96, 108 (1975) (White, J., concurring) (arguing that, even after a suspect initially asserts his right to remain silent, voluntariness is the appropriate standard for determining the validity of a *Miranda* waiver).
30. See *supra* chapter 4.
31. No cases after 1990 yielded such holding based on federal law. Search of Westlaw, Allfeds Library (June 13, 2000).

32. *See, e.g.,* United States v. Anderson, 929 F.2d 96, 100 (2d Cir. 1991) (finding waiver invalid when DEA agent told suspect he would forfeit chance to cooperate with agents if he invoked his right to an attorney); United States v. Morgan, 911 F. Supp. 1340, 1350–51 (D. Kan. 1995) (finding waiver invalid when postal inspector told suspect that he would not be permitted to invoke his Fifth Amendment privilege at trial).

33. United States v. Anderson, 929 F.2d 96 (2d Cir. 1991).

34. The court indicated, however, that the agent's misrepresentation would not have been sufficient to render the suspect's waiver involuntary if the suspect had been "knowledgeable about *Miranda* waivers." 929 F.2d at 99. Rather, the court stated that the question to be determined was whether, based on the totality of circumstances, "the defendant's will was overborne by the agent's conduct." *Id.*

35. Rhode Island v. Innis, 446 U.S. 291 (1980).

36. See 446 U.S. at 300–301.

37. The government might argue, of course, that prior to reading Adams his *Miranda* rights, the interrogators did not make any statements to Adams that seemed to call for an immediate answer. Rather, their statements suggested that Adams would *later* answer their questions relating to why the killings occurred etc. Thus their statements to Adams should not constitute interrogation under the *Innis* test because they were not the functional equivalent of direct questions.

38. *Miranda*, 384 U.S. at 478–79.

39. 470 U.S. 298 (1985).

40. 470 U.S. at 309.

41. *Id.* at 318.

42. *Id.*

43. Most courts would find that both Adams's waiver and his subsequent statement were voluntary because neither was induced by coercive police pressure. In addition, they would find that Adams's *Miranda* waiver was valid because, prior to making the waiver, he was informed of his *Miranda* rights.

44. As Justice Brennan explained in his *Elstad* dissent, the suspect's first incriminating admission makes it much easier for interrogators to obtain subsequent admissions because "[s]tandard interrogation manuals advise that '[t]he securing of the first admission is the biggest stumbling block.'" 470 U.S. at 328 (Brennan, J., dissenting) (quoting from A. AUBRY & R. CAPUTO, CRIMINAL INTERROGATION 290 (3d ed. 1980)).

45. In *Elstad,* an officer who had an arrest warrant for the suspect failed to give him *Miranda* warnings prior to asking him questions in his living room. 470 U.S. at 300–301. Since the officer did not inform the suspect at that time that he was under arrest, the officer might have believed that the suspect was not yet in custody because a reasonable person in his position would not have been aware that his "freedom of action [was] curtailed to a 'degree associated with formal arrest.'" Berkemer v. McCarty,

468 U.S. 420, 440 (1984) (quoting from California v. Beheler, 463 U.S. 1121, 1125 (1983) (per curiam)).

46. Interrogation of Russell Stone, Salt Lake City Police Dep't, Utah 2–4 (Dec. 5, 1995).

47. Midkiff v. Commonwealth, 462 S.E.2d 112, 114 (Va. 1995).

48. Interrogation Transcript of Prudencio Sanchez, Monterey County, Cal., Sheriff's Office 37–38 (Oct. 1997).

49. Interrogation Transcript of Vince Yarborough, Vallego, Cal., Police Dep't 3 (1994), Case No. 94-02881.

50. *See, e.g.,* The King v. Warickshall, 168 Eng. Rep. 234 (K.B. 1783) (excluding confessions induced by the "flattery of hope").

51. See Lynum v. Illinois, 372 U.S. 528, 534 (1963); Leyra v. Denno, 347 U.S. 556, 559–60 (1954).

52. 553 A.2d 409 (Pa. 1989).

53. 553 A.2d at 411.

54. See United States v. Pinto, 671 F. Supp. 41, 60 (1987) (holding that a police promise to keep suspect out of jail if he cooperated vitiated suspect's *Miranda* waiver).

55. Collazo v. Estelle, 940 F.2d 411, 416 (9th Cir. 1991) (finding waiver invalid because of police admonition that it "might be worse" if the suspect did not cooperate).

56. United States v. Rutledge, 900 F.2d 1127 (7th Cir. 1990); United States v. Bye, 919 F.2d 6, 9–10 (2d Cir. 1990).

57. For a full analysis of the strategy of questioning "outside *Miranda*," see Charles D. Weisselberg, *Saving Miranda*, 84 Cornell L. Rev. 109, 132–40 (1998).

58. See Weisselberg, *supra* note 57, at 189.

59. See *Miranda,* 384 U.S. at 444–45: "If . . . [a suspect] indicates in any manner and at any stage of the process that he wishes to consult with an attorney before speaking there can be no questioning. Likewise, if the individual is alone and indicates in any manner that he does not wish to be interrogated, the police may not question him."

60. Duckworth v. Eagan, 492 U.S. 195 (1989).

61. 492 U.S. at 204.

62. Edwards v. Arizona, 451 U.S. 477 (1981).

63. 451 U.S. at 484–85.

64. 462 U.S. 1039 (1983).

65. 462 U.S. at 1043–44 (plurality opinion of Rehnquist, J.).

66. *Id.* at 1046.

67. The plurality observed that suspects' routine requests—for food, a drink, or to use the phone, for example—could not be viewed as initiation within the meaning of *Edwards. Id.* at 1045.

68. See Michigan v. Mosley, 423 U.S. 96, 103 (1975) (holding that interrogator may make further efforts to interrogate a suspect who invokes his right to remain silent so long as she "scrupulously honors" the suspect's assertion of his right).

69. Commonwealth v. D'Entremont, 632 N.E.2d 1239, 1240 (Mass. App. Ct. 1994).

70. *Innis,* 446 U.S. at 302.

71. As punishment for playing hooky, Tom Sawyer's Aunt Polly ordered him to whitewash her fence. Tom, however, conned his playmates into doing the job for

him by convincing them that whitewashing the fence was a desirable activity rather than a chore. He accomplished this by pretending that he enjoyed the activity so much that he would not allow his friends to do any of the whitewashing for him. See SAMUEL CLEMENS, THE ADVENTURES OF TOM SAWYER 18–23 (1876). As the author explained, "Tom . . . had discovered a great law of human action, without knowing it—namely, that in order to make a man or boy covet a thing, it is only necessary to make the thing more difficult to attain." *Id.* at 23.

72. *D'Entremont*, 632 N.E.2d at 1241.

73. See *Innis*, 446 U.S. at 300–301.

74. *D'Entremont*, 632 N.E.2d at 1242.

75. *Id.* at 1242–43.

76. *Id.* at 1242 (quoting *Innis*, 446 U.S. at 301).

77. In *Bradshaw*, the pivotal plurality opinion stated that a suspect's statement would constitute "initiation" if it "evinced a willingness and a desire for a generalized discussion about the investigation." 462 U.S. at 1046 (plurality opinion of Rehnquist, J.). Based on this definition, the detective's comment to the suspect would appear to constitute "initiation": the interrogator stated that she was willing to talk to the suspect about his case; under the circumstances, this statement would constitute strong evidence of her desire to engage in such a conversation.

78. In *D'Entremont*, the lower court did not even consider this issue. This failure may indicate that the lower court believed that its conclusion that the detective's first statement to the suspect did not constitute interrogation within the meaning of *Miranda* disposed of the suspect's *Edwards* argument. In other words, if the detective's first statements to the suspect did not constitute interrogation, then the suspect's later statements to the detective constituted "initiation" within the meaning of *Edwards.*

79. Weisselberg does not say when interrogators first began to employ this strategy. The training video, cited in his article, that advises interrogators as to how to employ the strategy was apparently made in 1990. See Weisselberg, *supra* note 57, at 189.

80. *Id.* at 160.

81. *Id.* at 54–55.

82. *Id.* at 56–58.

83. Interrogation Transcript of James Nimblett, San Diego, Cal., Police Dep't 36 (July 30, 1990).

84. *Id.* at 45.

85. 401 U.S. 222 (1971).

86. *See* 401 U.S. at 226.

87. 420 U.S. 714 (1975).

88. In *Hass*, the defendant was given the *Miranda* warnings after he was arrested for burglary. *See* 420 U.S. at 715. While en route to the police station, the defendant told the arresting officer that he wanted to call his lawyer. *See id.* The officer told the defendant that he could do that after they arrived at the police station. *See id.* at 715–16. While still en route to the station, the defendant asked the officer if he had to locate some of the stolen property. The officer replied that defendant wasn't obligated to do

so, but he "wanted to get the matter cleared up that night." Defendant then revealed the location of the stolen property to the officer. See Weisselberg, *supra* note 57, at 183, referring to *Hass* appendix at 21–23, Oregon v. Hass, No. 73-1452 (Oct. Term, 1974).

89. *See Hass,* 420 U.S. at 723 ("If, in a given case, the officer's conduct amounts to an abuse, that case, like those involving coercion or duress, may be taken care of when it arises, measured by the traditional standards for evaluating voluntariness and trustworthiness"); *Harris,* 401 U.S. at 224 (observing that the defendant did not claim that his confession was involuntary under the traditional due process test).

90. See Colorado v. Connelly, 479 U.S. 157, 163 (1986) (reiterating that "certain interrogation techniques . . . are so offensive to a civilized system of justice that they must be condemned"); Miller v. Fenton, 474 U.S. 104, 109 (1985) (same).

91. See *Miranda,* 384 U.S. 436, 469 (1966).

92. See *supra* note 90.

93. 479 U.S. 157 (1986).

94. 479 U.S. at 167.

95. See People v. Peevy, 953 P.2d 1212, 1214 (Cal. 1998); State v. Favero, 331 N.W.2d 259 (Neb. 1983). *But see* Linares v. State, 471 S.E.2d 208, 211–12 (Ga. 1996) (holding defendant's confession involuntary on the ground that

police told defendant that any information he provided would not be used against him).

96. Of the interrogation transcripts collected by Leo and Ofshe that reveal interrogators employing sophisticated psychological strategies, nearly all of the interrogations took place in connection with murder or other high-profile cases. See transcripts on file with Richard A. Leo. While Leo and Ofshe's collection does not, of course, constitute a randomly selected sample of interrogation transcripts, concluding that the police are more likely to employ their most sophisticated strategies in high-profile cases accords with intuition. As Professor Samuel Gross has pointed out, in less important cases the police are unlikely to expend the time necessary to conduct an interrogation in which a range of sophisticated psychological strategies may be employed. See Samuel R. Gross, *The Risks of Death: Why Erroneous Convictions Are Common in Capital Cases,* 44 BUFF. L. REV. 469, 485 (1996).

97. Statements admissible for impeachment will be admissible only if the suspect testifies in his own defense, and even then, only for the limited purpose of impeaching his credibility. *See, e.g.,* Harris v. New York, 401 U.S. 222 (1971).

98. See SIMON, HOMICIDE, *supra* chapter 3, note 52, at 198: "The professionals say nothing."

In *United States v. Dickerson*,[1] the Court considered the constitutionality of 18 U.S.C. § 3501, the statute that Congress had passed in response to the *Miranda* decision thirty-two years earlier.[2] In place of *Miranda*'s warnings and waiver requirements, 18 U.S.C. § 3501 provides that voluntary confessions shall be admitted into evidence.[3] The statute does go on to list factors that the trial judge "shall take into consideration" in deciding whether the confession is voluntary, including whether the suspect was warned of his right to remain silent and his right to the "assistance of counsel";[4] the statute specifies, however, that "the presence or absence of any of [these] factors . . . need not be conclusive on the issue of the voluntariness of the confession."[5] As Kamisar has pointed out,[6] all of the factors specified in the statute, including those relating to whether the suspect was warned of his rights, were factors that were taken into account in applying the pre-*Miranda* voluntariness test. Thus 18 U.S.C. § 3501 was clearly designed to overrule *Miranda*, replacing it with the due process test.

Over the next thirty-two years, the Justice Department generally declined to use 18 U.S.C. § 3501,[7] viewing it as "unconstitutional in the light of *Miranda*."[8] In 1999, however, the Fourth Circuit—accepting Cassell's argument on behalf of the Washington Legal Foundation—held that § 3501 was constitutional because the *Miranda* warnings were not themselves constitutionally protected rights but only judicially created rules that could be overridden by Congress.[9] This ruling set the stage for the Court's decision in *Dickerson*.

The genesis for the argument accepted by the Fourth Circuit was an article by Grano published in 1985.[10] In his article, Grano attacked *Miranda*'s warnings and waiver requirements on the ground that in adopting and maintaining those safeguards the Court was improperly promulgating prophylactic rules.[11] In *Miranda* itself, the Court stated, "Unless adequate protective devices are employed to dispel the compulsion inherent in custodial surroundings, no statement obtained from the defendant can truly be the product of his free choice."[12] In order to dispel the compulsion, the Court required either the safeguards provided by *Miranda* or others that would be "at least as effective in apprising accused persons of their right of silence and in assuring [them] a continuous opportunity to exercise it."[13] As Grano admitted, this language seemed to mean that, in the absence of safeguards, a statement produced by custodial interrogation has actually been "compelled" within the meaning of the Fifth Amendment.

Based on *Miranda's* overall analysis, however, Grano asserted that the Court did not really mean that every statement obtained as a result of custodial interrogation would in fact be compelled. In his *Miranda* dissent, Justice White posed a hypothetical in which a police officer asked a suspect who had just been taken into custody whether he had anything to say. The Court made no attempt to refute Justice White's "common sense" conclusion that "an incriminating response to such a simple question cannot really be viewed as 'compelled.' "[14] In addition, the Court conceded that the statements in the cases before it "might not be involuntary in traditional terms."[15] It added, however, that this did not diminish its "concern for adequate safeguards to protect precious Fifth Amendment rights."[16] In justifying the prescribed safeguards, moreover, it stated that "when an individual is taken into custody . . . and is subjected to questioning, the privilege against self-incrimination is jeopardized."[17] Grano maintained that "[s]uch reasoning is the language of prophylaxis,"[18] adding that post-*Miranda* decisions that refer directly to "*Miranda's* prophylactic requirements"[19] remove any doubt concerning *Miranda's* "prophylactic nature."[20] Grano then concluded that *Miranda's* prophylactic rules are constitutionally illegitimate because the Court lacks power to impose prophylactic rules not mandated by the Constitution.[21]

Whatever *Miranda* itself may have intended,[22] post-*Miranda* cases make it clear that *Miranda's* safeguards are prophylactic in the sense that they are designed to exclude confessions that are not necessarily compelled within the meaning of the Fifth Amendment privilege.[23] In at least two cases, the post-*Miranda* Court has made it clear that the due process voluntariness test supplies the standard for determining whether a confession has been compelled within the meaning of the privilege.[24] Given this interpretation, *Miranda's* conclusion that, in the absence of safeguards, custodial interrogation necessarily produces compulsion is not empirically accurate. Based on the pre-*Miranda* voluntariness cases, custodial interrogation by itself does not create such coercive pressure as to mandate a conclusion that a suspect's resulting statement would necessarily be involuntary under the due process test.[25] Indeed, in *Miranda* itself, the Court admitted that the confessions in the cases before it might not be found to be involuntary under that test.[26] In the sense that they are designed to exclude statements that would not necessarily be determined to be constitutionally inadmissible, *Miranda*'s rules are prophylactic.

One of the central issues in *Dickerson* would thus appear to relate to the Court's authority to promulgate prophylactic rules. If *Miranda*'s safeguards are prophylactic rules and the Court lacks the authority to promulgate constitutional prophylactic rules, then *Miranda*'s safeguards should be treated as nonconstitutional rules that could be overridden by a federal statute.[27] As Justice Scalia observed in his dissent,[28] however, the *Dickerson* majority did not address the Court's authority to promulgate constitutional prophylactic rules. In holding that 18 U.S.C. § 3501 was unconstitutional, the majority simply characterized *Miranda* as "a constitutional decision of this Court," which "may not be in effect overruled by an Act of Congress."[29]

The *Dickerson* majority did observe that the Fourth Circuit justified its conclusion as to *Miranda*'s safeguards' nonconstitutional status by pointing to the fact that post-*Miranda* cases "have created several exceptions to *Miranda*'s warnings requirement and . . . have repeatedly referred to the *Miranda* warnings as 'prophylactic.'"[30] The majority's response to the Fourth Circuit's reasoning was cryptic: "We disagree with the Court of Appeals' conclusion, although we concede that there is language in some of our opinions that supports the view taken by that court."[31] Did the majority mean that its references to *Miranda*'s safeguards as prophylactic rules supported the conclusion that the safeguards are not constitutionally required? Did its holding that *Miranda*'s safeguards are constitutionally required indicate that the safeguards should not be viewed as prophylactic rules? Or did its holding indicate that the safeguards should be viewed as constitutionally appropriate prophylactic rules? Instead of addressing these questions, the Court simply supported its conclusion that *Miranda*'s safeguards are constitutionally required by demonstrating that in *Miranda* itself the majority clearly intended to establish a constitutional rule.[32]

In response to Justice Scalia's criticism of its holding, the *Dickerson* majority obliquely referred to *Miranda*'s promulgation of prophylactic constitutional rules. It explained that *Miranda* concluded that "the traditional totality-of-the-circumstances test resulted in a risk of overlooking an involuntary custodial confession, . . . a risk that the Court found unacceptably great when the confession is offered in the case-in-chief to prove guilt."[33] Although the majority thus recognized that *Miranda* had adopted a conclusive presumption that amounted to a prophylactic constitutional rule, it provided no analysis relating to the Court's authority to adopt such rules. Rather, in its next paragraph, it simply stated that whether or not it agreed with *Miranda,* it would not overrule it.[34]

As Justice Scalia observed in his dissent, *Dickerson*'s holding implicitly reaffirmed the Court's power to promulgate prophylactic constitutional rules.[35] Justice Scalia further observed, however, that he applauded the majority's refusal to base its reaffirmance of *Miranda* specifically on the ground that the Court has the constitutional authority to promulgate such rules.[36] Citing Grano's article, Justice Scalia vehemently asserted that granting the Court the power to promulgate constitutional prophylactic rules is a pernicious doctrine that undermines the balance of power established by the Constitution.[37]

Neither Justice Scalia's view of the Court's power to promulgate prophylactic rules nor his assessment of the rules promulgated in *Miranda* is correct. As Professor David Straus has said, conclusive presumptions or prophylactic rules are "a central and necessary feature of constitutional law."[38] The Court was justified in adopting the conclusive presumption adopted in *Miranda,* moreover, because, as Professor Stephen Schulhofer has explained, the presumption that, in the absence of safeguards, custodial interrogation would produce compulsion was "a responsible reaction to the problems of the voluntariness test, to the rarity of cases in which compelling pressures are truly absent, and to the adjudicatory costs of case-by-case decisions in this area."[39]

In order "to minimize the sum of error costs and administrative costs,"[40] the Court will often establish rules that are "prophylactic" in the sense that they establish conclusive presumptions that minimize the necessity for case-by-case adjudication.[41] In *Gideon v. Wainwright,*[42] for example, the Court's holding that indigent defendants are entitled to the assistance of counsel at a felony trial was predicated on the conclusion that, in the absence of such assistance, the indigent defendant cannot receive a fair trial.[43] But, as the Court tacitly acknowledged in a subsequent opinion,[44] some indigent defendants would in fact be able to represent themselves with sufficient ability to secure a fair trial. Thus *Gideon*'s rule was prophylactic in the sense that it applied a conclusive presumption that could not be empirically verified.

As Schulhofer has pointed out, moreover, at least one of the Court's Fourth Amendment cases[45] adopted what might be characterized as a "reverse prophylactic rule,"[46] holding that, following the arrest of an occupant of an auto, searches conducted within the passenger compartment of the auto will be viewed as searches "incident to an arrest" (and, therefore, reasonable), regardless of whether the justifications that properly authorize a "search incident to arrest" are actually present.[47]

In assessing *Miranda,* the focus should thus not be on whether the Court lacks the power to promulgate prophylactic rules. Promulgating such rules is in fact an indispensable part of constitutional adjudication. Through reaffirming *Miranda,* moreover, *Dickerson* implicitly recognized that the Court has the power to adopt such rules for the purpose of providing suspects subjected to custodial interrogation with appropriate constitutional safeguards.

Another significant issue in *Dickerson* concerned a legislature's power to replace *Miranda*'s warnings and waiver requirements with alternative safeguards. In seeking to uphold the Fourth Circuit's decision, Cassell argued that, when evaluated in the context of our present system, § 3501 provides a constitutionally acceptable alternative to *Miranda.* During the thirty years since the statute was enacted, new remedies for redressing "abusive police conduct" have become available. In view of these additional remedies, Cassell argued, § 3501 "complies with the requirement that a legislative alternative be equally as effective in preventing coerced confessions."[48]

The Court summarily rejected this argument. While admitting that there are more remedies for abusive police conduct in 2000 than there were in 1968, the majority stated that, even if these remedies are taken into account, § 3501 did not meet the "constitutional minimum" because "*Miranda* requires procedures that will warn a suspect in custody of his right to remain silent and which will assure the suspect that the exercise of that right will be honored."[49]

Significantly, the Court rejected Cassell's claim that a legislative alternative to *Miranda* only needs to be as effective as *Miranda* in preventing the introduction of involuntary confessions. Instead, the test applied by the Court adhered to *Miranda* by reiterating that any legislative alternative to *Miranda* would at least have to assure that the suspect was warned of his right to remain silent and to provide some mechanism for assuring that the suspect would have a meaningful opportunity to exercise that right.[50] Through stating the test in this way, the Court did nothing to encourage legislatures to adopt Cassell's proposal, under which *Miranda*'s most significant safeguards would be replaced by a requirement that the police electronically record custodial interrogations.[51] As in *Miranda,* the Court emphasized that the safeguards adopted should be designed to assure that the suspect is aware of his rights, not to assist the court in deciding the voluntariness of the suspect's confession. The Court thus seemed to indicate that either the *Miranda* warnings themselves or something very similar to them would be necessary to satisfy the minimum constitutional standard.

Cassell's final argument was that the Court should overrule *Miranda*. Specifically, he argued that the Court should replace *Miranda's* conclusive presumption—that in the absence of *Miranda's* safeguards, custodial interrogation results in compulsion—with a rebuttable one under which the government would have the burden of proving that a confession obtained in violation of *Miranda* was voluntary (and, therefore, not compelled). In support of this position, Cassell asserted that there is a "lack of congruence and proportionality between *Miranda's* rules and Fifth Amendment violations."[52] In response to the claim that overruling *Miranda* would erode public confidence in the criminal justice system, moreover, he argued, "Public confidence in the criminal justice system cannot be enhanced by a rule that conceals from the jury truthful and voluntarily given confessions."[53]

In view of the present Court's generally conservative orientation, these arguments might have been expected to resonate with enough of the justices to produce a favorable decision. By a seven-to-two majority, however, the Court succinctly dismissed Cassell's argument. The majority's stated reasons for rejecting the invitation to overrule *Miranda* related primarily to stare decisis and to society's acceptance of *Miranda*. In *Dickerson's* most memorable line, the majority stated that the *Miranda* "warnings have become part of our national culture."[54]

As Justice Scalia stated in dissent, however, if the majority believed that *Miranda* was wrongly decided, neither considerations of stare decisis nor the warnings' place in our "national culture" provided a sufficient basis for refusing to overrule it. In the next chapter, I will probe more deeply into the reasons why the *Dickerson* majority was disinclined to overrule *Miranda*. Examining this question will lead to a clearer understanding of *Miranda's* role in regulating modern police interrogation practices.

NOTES

1. 120 S. Ct. 2326 (2000).
2. See *supra* chapter 5.
3. 18 U.S.C. § 3501(a).
4. 18 U.S.C. § 3501(b).
5. *Id.*
6. Yale Kamisar, *Can (Did) Congress "Overrule" Miranda?* 85 Cornell

L. Rev. 883, 926–36 (2000).
7. For a full account and analysis of the Department of Justice's use of 18 U.S.C. § 3501, see Paul G. Cassell, *The Statute That Time Forgot,* 85 Iowa L. Rev. 175, 197–225 (1999).

8. Peter Brooks, Troubling Confessions: Speaking Guilt in Law and Literature 33 (2000).

9. United States v. Dickerson, 166 F.3d 667, 672 (1999).

10. Joseph D. Grano, *Prophylactic Rules in Criminal Procedure: A Question of Article III Legitimacy,* 80 Nw. U. L. Rev. 100 (1985) (hereinafter Grano, *Prophylactic Rules*).

11. See Grano, *Prophylactic Rules, supra* note 10, at 106–11.

12. *Miranda,* 384 U.S. at 457.

13. 384 U.S. at 467.

14. Grano, *Prophylactic Rules, supra* note 10, at 109, quoting from *Miranda,* 384 U.S. at 533–34 (White, J., dissenting).

15. *Miranda,* 384 U.S. at 457.

16. *Id.,* quoted in Grano, *Prophylactic Rules, supra* note 10, at 108.

17. *Id.* at 478, *quoted in* Grano, *Prophylactic Rules, supra* note 10, at 108 (emphasis added).

18. Grano, *Prophylactic Rules, supra* note 10, at 108.

19. *Id.* at 110.

20. *Id.* at 109–10.

21. *Id.* at 106–11.

22. In *Miranda* itself, the Court provided considerable evidence that a compelled confession was not the same as an involuntary one. Taken in context, the Court's dictum to the effect that the statements before it might not be found to be "involuntary in traditional terms," 384 U.S. at 457, suggested that the Fifth Amendment, which the Court was now applying to custodial interrogation, provided a stricter standard than the due process voluntariness test. Moreover, as Schulhofer has pointed out, if the concepts of "involuntariness" and "compulsion" are not distinct, *Miranda*'s waiver requirements seem incoherent. Whereas waiver of the Fifth Amendment privilege is a meaningful concept that has been applied at trial and in other contexts, it seems nonsensical to suggest that a person would waive her right to be free of pressure that "breaks the will" so as to produce an involuntary confession. See Stephen J. Schulhofer, *Reconsidering Miranda,* 54 U. Chi. L. Rev. 435, 444–45 (1987).

23. *See, e.g.,* Oregon v. Elstad, 470 U.S. 298, 306 (1985): "The *Miranda* exclusionary rule, however, serves the Fifth Amendment and sweeps more broadly than the Fifth Amendment itself. It may be triggered even in the absence of a Fifth Amendment violation."

24. See Oregon v. Elstad, 470 U.S. 298, 307–8 (1985); New York v. Quarles, 467 U.S. 649, 655 n.5 (1984).

25. See *supra* chapter 4.

26. *Miranda,* 384 U.S. at 457.

27. Based on a long line of precedent, "the power to judicially create and enforce nonconstitutional 'rules of procedure and evidence for the federal courts exist[s] only in the absence of a relevant Act of Congress.'" *Dickerson,* 120 S. Ct. at 2332 (citing Palermo v. United States, 360 U.S. 343, 353 (1959)).

28. 120 S. Ct. at 2343–46.

29. *Id.* at 2329.

30. *Id.* at 2333.

31. *Id.*

32. *Id.* at 2334. As the *Dickerson* majority indicated, there was

abundant evidence that the *Miranda* majority intended to establish a constitutional rule. Most importantly, *Miranda's* rule was applied to "proceedings in state courts," and the Court lacks authority to apply nonconstitutional rules to state court proceedings. 120 S. Ct. at 2333. In addition, *Miranda's* majority opinion was "replete with statements indicating that it thought it was announcing a constitutional rule," and "the Court's ultimate conclusion was that the unwarned confessions obtained in the four cases before the Court in *Miranda* 'were obtained from the defendant under circumstances that did not meet constitutional standards for protection of the privilege.'" *Id*. at 2333–34 (quoting from *Miranda*, 384 U.S. at 491). As *Dickerson* observed, moreover, even *Miranda's* "invitation for legislative action" to protect the Fifth Amendment privilege showed that the decision was constitutionally based because *Miranda* provided that legislative alternatives that "differed from the prescribed *Miranda* warnings" would have to be "'least as effective in apprising accused persons of their right of silence and in assuring a continuous opportunity to exercise it.'" 120 S. Ct. at 2334 (quoting *Miranda*, 384 U.S. at 467).

33. 120 S. Ct. at 2335.
34. *Id*. at 2336.
35. *Id*. at 2343–46 (dissenting opinion of Scalia, J.).
36. *Id*. at 2345.
37. *Id*. at 2343.

38. David A. Strauss, *The Ubiquity of Prophylactic Rules*, 55 U. Chi. L. Rev. 190 (1988).
39. Schulhofer, *supra* note 22, at 453.
40. Strauss, *supra* note 38, at 193.
41. *Id*.
42. 372 U.S. 335 (1962).
43. 372 U.S. at 344.
44. Faretta v. California, 422 U.S. 806 (1975).
45. New York v. Belton, 453 U.S. 454 (1981).
46. Schulhofer, *supra* note 22, at 449.
47. In *Chimel v. California*, 395 U.S. 752, 763 (1969), the Court held that a search incident to a suspect's arrest extended only to the suspect's person and the area "'within his immediate control'–construing that phrase to mean the area from within which he might gain possession of a weapon or destructible evidence." Although the justification for allowing the search of the area within the suspect's "immediate control" was solely to protect the officer and to prevent the suspect from destroying evidence, in *Belton* the Court nevertheless held that following the arrest of an occupant of an auto, the police would be permitted to search the passenger compartment of the auto, regardless of whether that area would be within the "immediate control" of the suspect at the time of the search. The Court's justification for establishing this per se (or prophylactic) rule was that it was needed "to establish the workable rule this category of cases requires." 453 U.S. at 460.
48. *Dickerson*, 120 S. Ct. at 2335.
49. *Id*.

50. In place of *Miranda*'s requirement that the warnings would have to assure the suspect a "continuous opportunity to exercise the right," the Court stated that the warnings would have to assure the suspect that his "exercise of that right will be honored." 120 S. Ct. at 2335. It is not clear whether the altered statement of the requisite standard was intended to have significance.

51. Under Cassell's proposal, police would not be required to inform the suspect of his right to have counsel present at the interrogation or to obtain an affirmative waiver of rights from the suspect before questioning him. Cassell, *Miranda's Social Costs, supra* chapter 1, note 26, at 496–97.

52. Amicus brief on behalf of the Washington Legal Foundation filed by Paul G. Cassell in the case of *United States v. Dickerson,* p. 33.

53. *Id.* at 34.

54. *Dickerson,* 120 S. Ct. at 2336.

CHAPTER 9

Miranda's Limitations

One of the most interesting aspects of the *Dickerson* decision was the Court's response to the request that *Miranda v. Arizona*[1] be overruled. In a revealing portion of the majority opinion, Justice Rehnquist seemed to indicate that the Court would not "agree with *Miranda*'s reasoning and resulting rule" if it "were . . . addressing the issue in the first instance."[2] In rejecting the constitutional attack on *Miranda,* however, he stated that "principles of stare decisis weigh heavily against overruling it now."[3]

But if a majority of the Court disagreed with *Miranda*'s constitutional holding, why should it reject an opportunity to overrule or at least modify the Warren Court's landmark decision? As the majority itself acknowledged,[4] stare decisis has not been an impediment to overruling other constitutional decisions. Did *Dickerson* refuse to consider overruling *Miranda*'s constitutional holding simply because, as Justice Rehnquist put it, the *Miranda* "warnings have become a part of our national culture"?[5] Or, as another commentator has asserted, should *Miranda*'s survival more appropriately be attributed to the fact that the Court considered the constitutionality of the statute overruling *Miranda* "at the very moment when the Court's interest in protecting its constitutional turf against Congressional incursions was at a peak unmatched in recent years"?[6]

Identifying the precise reasons for *Dickerson*'s rejection of the constitutional assault on *Miranda* is, of course, impossible. In my judgment, however, a major reason for the Court's disinclination to overrule *Miranda* relates to *Miranda*'s limitations. By the time the Court confronted the issue in *Dickerson,* it had become obvious that, regardless of what the Warren Court may have intended, *Miranda*'s safeguards today provide very limited restraints on police interrogators.

To some extent, of course, *Miranda*'s limitations may be attributed to post-*Miranda* decisions. As I explained in chapter 6, decisions by the Burger and Rehnquist Courts substantially weakened *Miranda*'s protections.[7] Indeed, as interpreted by the present Court, *Miranda* essentially provides suspects with two safeguards: first, the suspect will be informed of his four *Miranda* rights prior to police questioning; and, second, through invoking either his right to remain silent or his right to have an attorney present at questioning, the suspect has at least a theoretical opportunity to either forestall police questioning entirely or to bring it to a halt at any point after it commences.

These safeguards are not insignificant. As I indicated in chapter 7, there is probably a small group of suspects who choose to remain silent as a result of hearing the *Miranda* warnings. In addition, the warnings may lead some suspects to invoke their rights at some point during the interrogation, thereby reducing the extent of their incriminating statements to the police. In the great majority of cases, however, the *Miranda* safeguards do not provide significant restraints on police interrogating suspects.

For constitutional purposes, of course, the question is whether *Miranda*'s safeguards combined with the Court's other constitutional restrictions on interrogation practices provide a constitutionally appropriate accommodation between promoting law enforcement's interest in obtaining reliable incriminating statements and protecting suspects from pernicious interrogation practices. In addressing this question, I will consider both the effectiveness of the safeguards *Miranda* does provide and the significance of *Miranda*'s failure to address two critical areas of concern. First, I will consider the extent to which *Miranda*'s core protections—providing suspects with knowledge of their constitutional rights prior to interrogation and with an opportunity to forestall or halt the interrogation by invoking their rights—provide individuals with protection from pernicious interrogation practices. And then, I will consider two critical issues that *Miranda*, as interpreted by the present Court, fails to address: providing for accurate fact-finding in police interrogation cases; and providing restrictions on interrogation practices following a suspect's valid waiver of *Miranda* rights.

The Efficacy of *Miranda*'s Core Protections

The current Court would apparently maintain that in most instances interrogators' iteration of the *Miranda* warnings provides suspects with adequate protection from the effect of abusive or overreaching interrogation practices. In *Davis v. United States*,[8] the Court stated that "the primary protection afforded suspects subjected to interrogation is the *Miranda* warnings themselves."[9] It added, "Full comprehension of the rights to remain silent and request an attorney [is] sufficient to dispel whatever coercion is inherent in the interrogation process."[10] Based on this language, the Court seems to believe that the suspect's awareness of her rights provides her with the means to counter the coercive effect of interrogation practices. If the suspect believes she lacks the resources to deal with the pressures generated by custodial interrogation practices, she can invoke one of her rights, thereby forestalling interrogation. Moreover, if she decides to waive her *Miranda* rights but, thereafter, concludes that her interrogators are subjecting her to undue pressure, she again has the opportunity to invoke one of her rights, thereby halting the interrogation.

In the context of twenty-first-century interrogation practices, however, the idea that a suspect's awareness of her rights provides an antidote to the coercive effect of custodial interrogation is either naive or disingenuous. In *Miranda* itself, the Court said, "The circumstances surrounding in-custody interrogation can operate very quickly to overbear the will of one merely made aware of his privilege by his interrogators."[11] The same point applies, of course, even if the suspect is given the four *Miranda* warnings rather than merely informed of her right to remain silent. As the length of a custodial interrogation increases, the practical significance of the suspect's knowledge of her rights decreases.

Even if the Warren Court underestimated the effect of a "once stated warning,"[12] moreover, the practices employed by seasoned interrogators will often have the effect of undermining a suspect's sense that he will be able to assert rights. As excerpts from interrogations presented in a later chapter will indicate,[13] police interrogators are often so overwhelmingly in control of the interrogation—dictating the pace of the questioning and the topics under discussion—that the suspect subjected to questioning may have no practical opportunity to invoke his rights. And even when this is not the case, the interrogator's ability to connect with the suspect—through establishing a close rapport with him, for example— makes it extremely unlikely that the suspect will have either the ability or the inclination to break the connection by asserting his rights. In most cases, therefore, its seems fanciful to believe that suspects would have the capacity to escape the mounting pressures generated by sophisticated interrogators by simply insisting on their right to remain silent or to have an attorney present.

Miranda's Failure to Address Critical Issues

When the police seek to interrogate a suspect, the great majority of suspects waive their *Miranda* rights and submit to interrogation.[14] In this category of cases, where the need to provide constitutional protections for suspects seems most obvious, *Miranda*'s failure to address critical issues is most apparent. When a suspect waives his rights and is subjected to custodial interrogation, *Miranda*'s safeguards neither address the problem of determining what happened during the interrogation nor provide guidelines for determining what restraints should be imposed on the police conducting the interrogation.

Miranda's failure to address the critical limitations of the fact-finding system was apparent even at the time the case was decided. In his *Miranda* dissent, Justice Harlan observed that *Miranda*'s safeguards were "not designed to guard against police brutality or other unmistakably banned forms of coercion" because "[t]hose who use third-degree tactics and deny them in court are equally able and destined to lie as skillfully about warnings and waivers."[15] Since the post-*Miranda* Court has taken no steps toward requiring that the government satisfy its "heavy burden" of showing a suspect's intelligent waiver of his *Miranda* rights though producing "corroborated evidence"[16] from a neutral source,[17] the government is able to establish the admissibility of confessions given during secret interrogations solely on the basis of police testimony.[18] In weighing the credibility of police officers' and suspects' conflicting versions as to what transpired during an interrogation, moreover, judges are as inclined to credit the police today as they were in the pre-*Miranda* era.[19] Thus, when police willing to engage in abusive interrogation practices are also willing to deny using them in court, *Miranda*'s safeguards provide no protection against the likelihood that the police testimony will be accepted.

Miranda also fails to impose meaningful restrictions on police interrogation practices. Once a suspect waives his *Miranda* rights, *Miranda* provides only one further significant barrier to police interrogators. *Miranda*, as interpreted in *Edwards* and its progeny,[20] does specify that the police will have to end the interrogation when a suspect invokes his right to have an attorney present.[21] This rule does impose some restraint on police interrogators. An interrogator who wants to obtain incriminating statements must not employ practices that will lead a suspect to break off the interrogation by invoking this right. In theory, this might lead interrogators to avoid employing abusive interrogation practices because of a concern that the suspect might respond to such practices by halting the interrogation.

As I have already indicated, however, the suspect's right to halt an interrogation by invoking his right to an attorney does not provide a significant safeguard in practice. Once the suspect has waived his *Miranda* rights, the pressures generated by the resulting interrogation are likely to obliterate whatever awareness he might have had as to the meaning or significance of the *Miranda* warnings. Moreover, since *Miranda* provides no restrictions on the interrogation practices that the police may employ once the suspect has consented to the interrogation, there is nothing to prevent the police from structuring the interrogation so that the pressures generated by their practices will effectively preclude the suspect from invoking her rights.[22] If the interrogator perceives that the suspect has a compliant or nonassertive personality, the interrogator can assume control of the interrogation, dictating its pace in a way that effectively precludes the suspect from seeking to halt it by invoking her right to counsel. Similarly, if the interrogator perceives that the suspect is eager to gain the interrogator's acceptance, the interrogator can structure the interrogation so as to build a rapport that the suspect would be unwilling to sever by halting the interrogation.

Miranda, of course, could have been interpreted to impose restrictions on postwaiver interrogation practices. *Miranda* itself stated that "the fact of lengthy interrogation . . . before a statement is made is strong evidence that the accused did not validly waive his rights."[23] This language could have been interpreted to mean that lengthy interrogations are generally impermissible. The *Miranda* decision's apparent disapproval of interrogation techniques described in various interrogation manuals,[24] moreover, could have been interpreted to prohibit interrogators from employing those techniques. And *Miranda*'s language imposing a heavy burden of waiver on the government[25] could have been interpreted to preclude interrogators from employing interrogation practices that pressure suspects to give up their right to remain silent through pressing them to reveal information they are reluctant to disclose.

But post-*Miranda* cases have not interpreted *Miranda* in these ways. Neither the Supreme Court nor any lower court has ever indicated that the length of the interrogation, the interrogation tactics employed during the interrogation, or pressure exerted on the suspect to reveal information he is reluctant to disclose has any bearing on the validity of the suspect's *Miranda* waiver. On the contrary, once the suspect validly waives his *Miranda* rights, he is deemed to have consented to an interrogation, and the due process voluntariness test provides the only restrictions on the police conducting the interrogation.[26]

The restrictions provided by that test, moreover, are insubstantial. Over the past two decades, the Rehnquist Court has indicated that the post-*Miranda* due process test is essentially similar to the pre-*Miranda* test.[27] As under the old test, confessions induced by force,[28] threats of force,[29] promises of protection from force,[30] or excessively lengthy continuous interrogations[31] are involuntary. When interrogators do not employ one of these extreme techniques, however, the voluntariness of a confession is determined on the basis of the pre-*Miranda* totality of circumstances test under which a court must assess both the interrogators' practices and the suspect's individual characteristics for the purpose of determining whether the suspect's will was overborne.[32]

As the pre-*Miranda* due process cases demonstrated,[33] this test provides interrogators with considerable leeway. When extreme tactics—such as force or threat of force—are not employed, interrogators will have few, if any, guidelines as to what practices are prohibited. Indeed, an interrogation practice that contributes to a finding that a suspect's confession was involuntary in one case may be permissible when employed in another case involving a different set of circumstances.[34] When provided with such insubstantial guidelines, the police will generally feel that they may err on the side of promoting law enforcement interests, employing any combination of interrogation techniques that have not been specifically determined to be impermissible.[35]

Miranda may, indeed, have had the unintended effect of reducing the extent to which the due process test is applied to restrain pernicious interrogation practices. In *Dickerson,* the Court asserted that the pre-*Miranda* due process voluntariness test, which 18 U.S.C. § 3501 sought to revive, was "more difficult than *Miranda* for law enforcement officers to conform to."[36] The significant number of Supreme Court cases excluding suspects' confessions on the basis of the pre-*Miranda* due process test indicated that, even if that test was ultimately ineffective in controlling the police or providing guidance for lower courts, the test did have some teeth. In applying the test, lower courts at least had to confront difficult questions relating to whether police subjected suspects to abusive or overreaching interrogation practices. In a considerable number of cases, moreover, lower courts did conclude that police-induced confessions were involuntary.[37]

Since *Miranda,* there is considerable reason to believe that lower courts are less inclined either to address these questions or to resolve them in favor of a suspect claiming his confession is involuntary. During the post-*Miranda* era, the Court has equated a confession involuntary under the due process test with one that is compelled under the Fifth Amendment privilege.[38] In *Dickerson,* the Court observed that when the police have "adhered to the dictates of *Miranda,*" a defendant will rarely be able to make even "a colorable argument that [his] self-incriminating statement was 'compelled.'"[39] Lower court cases support this view. An analysis of recent decisions suggest that when the police have complied with *Miranda,* it is, in fact, very difficult for a defendant to establish that the confession following the *Miranda* waiver was involuntary.[40] The similarity between the tests for establishing a valid *Miranda* waiver and a confession admissible under the due process test may partially explain this phenomenon. In both instances, a court must assess the totality of circumstances for the purpose of determining whether the suspect's action was voluntary.[41] Although lower courts do generally consider the two issues separately,[42] some courts may tend to view them as inextricably intertwined, believing that if the defendant voluntarily waived his *Miranda* rights his subsequent statements should also be viewed as voluntary. In addition, the Supreme Court's disinclination to decide the admissibility of confessions under the due process test during the post-*Miranda* era has undoubtedly enhanced lower courts' tendency to reject such claims.[43]

Addressing *Miranda*'s Failures

The constitutional restrictions imposed by *Miranda* and the post-*Miranda* due process voluntariness test thus fail to provide rules or guidelines that will regulate police interrogation practices. Except for prohibiting extreme tactics, such as violence or threats of violence, the post-*Miranda* constitutional limitations impose virtually no limit on police interrogation practices. Safeguards that prohibit interrogation practices viewed as pernicious by society are thus extremely limited.

Should the Court address this problem? Or should the Court leave it to other institutions such as legislatures or state courts? According to the Court's interpretation of both the Fifth Amendment privilege and the Fourteenth Amendment due process clause, "interrogation techniques . . . offensive to a civilized system of justice"[44] are unconstitutional. Since this is so, the Court has a constitutional obligation to address this issue. In order to fill the gap left by *Miranda* and the post-*Miranda* due process test, the Court should formulate rules that reduce the likelihood that police will engage in pernicious interrogation practices.

But what interrogation practices should society view as pernicious? Most responsible members of society would agree that one guiding principle against which police interrogation techniques should be measured relates to an interrogation technique's propensity to produce untrustworthy statements. If there is a sufficient likelihood that the government's employment of a particular interrogation technique will produce false or untrustworthy statements, then that interrogation technique should be improper.

Support for this principle stems not only from our historical concern for guarding against wrongful convictions resulting from government-induced confessions but also from a strong perception that both guilty and innocent individuals should be protected against the suffering—in terms of both psychological damage and impairment of autonomy—that results from overreaching or coercive interrogation practices. Empirical data shows that modern jurors are likely to give great weight to suspects' confessions, whether or not they are reliable;[45] the concern for protecting against wrongful convictions stemming from government-induced false confessions is, therefore, just as great today as it was when the Anglo-American rule excluding government-induced untrustworthy confessions evolved. In many cases, moreover, there will be considerable equivalence between the pressure generated by an interrogation technique and the likelihood that the technique will produce untrustworthy statements. As Professor George Thomas has pointed out, in most instances, a suspect would not falsely "admit guilt unless she found the pressure to confess overwhelming."[46] Accordingly, there is ample justification for accepting some prohibition on interrogation methods likely to produce false or untrustworthy statements.

Miranda's most important limitations thus relate to its failure to address the problem of inadequate fact-finding in interrogation cases and its failure to provide restrictions on police interrogation methods that are likely to produce untrustworthy statements. To what extent, though, do *Miranda*'s limitations create real problems for society? In order to explore this question, empirical data relating to both inadequate fact-finding in interrogation cases and false confessions produced by modern interrogation practices would be helpful. If neither of these problems are widespread, then the need for the Court to fill the gaps produced by *Miranda*'s limitations is obviously less pressing. If, on the other hand, empirical data shows that either of these problems are of significant magnitude, it seems appropriate to further consider the nature of the problems and the means that should be taken to address them.

Chapter 10 provides insight into the magnitude of the problem of inadequate fact-finding. That chapter examines a pattern of cases in which police from a particular department systematically perpetrated extraordinarily abusive interrogation practices over a prolonged period. The safeguards provided by *Miranda* obviously provided no meaningful protection to the suspects subjected to these practices. As chapter 10 will show, in order to insure that safeguards designed to protect against abusive interrogation practices will be effective, the Court needs to implement reforms that directly address the problem of enhancing accurate fact-finding.

Chapters 11 and 12 address the problem of determining the extent to which police interrogation practices produce false confessions and wrongful convictions resulting from such confessions. Chapter 11 assesses this problem from a broad perspective, utilizing various approaches to estimate the likelihood that standard interrogation practices produce either false confessions or resulting wrongful convictions. Although it is impossible to produce precise estimates of these phenomena, examination of the existing data clearly demonstrates that standard interrogation methods produce both false confessions and resulting wrongful convictions with sufficient frequency to provoke societal concern.

Chapter 12 seeks to explore the particular dynamics through which interrogation practices produce false confessions that may or may not result in wrongful convictions. Through examining a small number of police-induced false confessions in considerable detail, this chapter provides at least a starting point for identifying the particular set of circumstances that are likely to produce either false confessions or resulting wrongful convictions. Taken together, these three chapters identify some of the problems that the Court needs to address if it is to impose appropriate restraints on police interrogation practices.

Finally, chapters 13 and 14 consider some of the ways the Court might address these problems. Chapter 13, which addresses the problem of insuring accurate fact-finding in police interrogation cases, considers whether there is a constitutional basis for imposing a mandatory audio- or videotaping requirement in police interrogation cases. Chapter 14 considers some of the ways in which the Court might refurbish the due process voluntariness test to impose appropriate restraints on police interrogation practices.

NOTES

1. 384 U.S. 436 (1966).
2. Dickerson v. United States, 120 S. Ct. 2326, 2335 (2000).
3. *Id.*
4. See 120 S. Ct. at 2336.
5. *Id.*
6. Linda Greenhouse, *A Turf Battle's Victim: Opposition to Miranda Ruling Fell Prey to Justices' Desire to Win a Bigger War*, NEW YORK TIMES, June 28, 2000, § A, p. 1.
7. *See supra* chapter 6.
8. 512 U.S. 452 (1994).
9. 512 U.S. at 460–61.

10. *Id.,* quoting from Moran v. Burbine, 475 U.S. 412, 427 (1980).
11. *Miranda,* 384 U.S. at 469.
12. *Id.*
13. *See infra* chapter 12.
14. *See supra* chapter 7.
15. 384 U.S. at 505 (dissenting opinion of Harlan, J.).
16. *Id.* at 475.
17. *See supra* chapter 6.
18. *See, e.g.,* North Carolina v. Butler, 441 U.S. 369 (1979) (defendant's waiver of *Miranda* rights can be inferred by his words and actions, regardless of whether he signs *Miranda* waiver form).
19. *See supra* chapter 4.
20. *See* Minnick v. Mississippi, 496 U.S. 146 (1990); Arizona v. Roberson, 486 U.S. 475 (1988); Edwards v. Arizona, 451 U.S. 477 (1981).
21. *See Edwards,* 451 U.S. at 484–85. The Court added, moreover, that the police would not be permitted to reinterrogate a suspect who invoked his right to counsel unless the suspect "himself initiate[d] further communication, exchanges, or conversations with the police." *Id.* at 485.
22. Based on *United States v. Davis,* 512 U.S. 452 (1994), moreover, interrogators need not respond to a suspect's ambiguous request for an attorney. In order to invoke his right to counsel under *Edwards,* the suspect "must articulate his desire to have counsel present sufficiently clearly that a reasonable police officer in the circumstances would understand the statement to be a request for an attorney." 512 U.S. at 459.
23. 384 U.S. at 476.
24. *See id.* at 448–54.
25. *See id.* at 475.

26. *See, e.g.,* Colorado v. Connelly, 479 U.S. 157 (1986).
27. *See supra* chapter 7.
28. *See, e.g.,* Brown v. Mississippi, 297 U.S. 278 (1936).
29. *See, e.g.,* Beecher v. Alabama, 389 U.S. 35 (1967).
30. *See* Payne v. Arkansas, 356 U.S. 560 (1958).
31. *See, e.g.,* Ashcraft v. Tennessee, 322 U.S. 143 (1944) (holding that thirty-six hours of continuous interrogation is "inherently coercive").
32. *See generally* Welsh S. White, *What Is an Involuntary Confession Now?* 50 Rutgers L. Rev. 2001, 2008–20 (1998).
33. *See supra* chapter 4.
34. In *Spano v. New York,* 360 U.S. 315 (1959), for example, the Court expressed disapproval for the deceptive strategy employed by the interrogators, thus suggesting that certain categories of police trickery might constitute improper interrogation practices. See *supra* chapter 4. In *Spano* itself, however, the Court stated that the trickery employed was simply "another factor which deserves mention in the totality of circumstances." 360 U.S. at 323. If the same trickery were employed on another suspect under different circumstances, a lower court could thus properly hold that employing the trickery in those circumstances would not render the suspect's confession involuntary.
35. *Cf.* Brinegar v. United States, 338 U.S. 160, 182 (1949) (dissenting opinion of Jackson, J.) (observing that "the extent of any privilege of search and seizure without

warrant which we sustain, the officers interpret and apply themselves and will push to the limit").

36. *Dickerson,* 120 S. Ct. at 2336.

37. *See generally Developments in the Law—Confessions,* 79 Harv. L. Rev. 938, 958 (1966) (observing that the "expanding scope of Supreme Court decisions" affected state court decisions, making them more inclined to hold a suspect's confession involuntary).

38. *See, e.g.,* New York v. Quarles, 467 U.S. at 655 n.5 (1985) (observing that, in order to show his confession was compelled within the meaning of the Fifth Amendment privilege, the defendant would have to show that "his statement was coerced under traditional due process standards").

39. *Dickerson,* 120 S. Ct. at 2336, quoting from Berkemer v. McCarty, 468 U.S. 420, 433 n.20 (1984).

40. Based on a Westlaw search examining all federal and state cases decided during the years 1999 and 2000, it appears that, out of all the cases in those years in which the police obtained valid *Miranda* waivers, there were only four cases in 1999 and five cases in 2000 in which courts held the suspect's postwaiver confession involuntary. See Search of Westlaw, Allfeds and Allstates Library (Oct. 15, 2000) (on file with the author). In at least four of these cases (two in 1999 and two in 2000), moreover, this holding was based on state constitutional law rather than the due process

clause of the Fourteenth Amendment. *See id.*

41. *See, e.g.,* State v. Murray, 510 N.W.2d 107, 110 (N.D. 1994) (applying due process voluntariness test to determine the validity of a *Miranda* waiver). *See generally* Richard A. Leo & Welsh S. White, *Adapting to Miranda: Modern Interrogators' Strategies for Dealing with the Obstacles Posed by Miranda,* 84 Minn. L. Rev. 397, 418 (1999).

42. *See, e.g.,* United States v. Anderson, 929 F.2d 96, 98 (2d Cir. 1991) (observing that, even if suspect's *Miranda* waiver is valid, the court must still decide whether the officer's statement "coerced [him] into confessing").

43. After pointing out that the Court reversed twenty-three convictions during the quarter century prior to *Miranda* but only two in the quarter century since, Professor Louis Michael Seidman suggests that "this silence at the top" has led lower courts to treat voluntariness claims less seriously. See Louis Michael Seidman, *Brown and Miranda,* 80 Cal. L. Rev. 673, 745 (1992).

44. *Connelly,* 479 U.S. at 163 (quoting Miller v. Fenton, 474 U.S. 104, 109 (1985)).

45. *See, e.g.,* Gerald R. Miller & F. Joseph Boster, *Three Images of the Trial: Their Implications for Psychological Research, in* Psychology in the Legal Process 19–38 (Dennis Sales ed., 1977) (discussing empirical data showing that in a mock trial experiment subjects exposed to three types of evidence of suspect's guilt—identification evidence, circumstantial

evidence, and the suspect's confession—were "significantly more likely" to view the suspect's confession as establishing guilt than either of the other two types of evidence). *See generally* EDWARD W. CLEARY, MCCORMICK'S HANDBOOK OF THE LAW OF EVIDENCE § 148, at 316 (2d ed. 1972) ("[T]he introduction of a confession makes the other aspects of a trial in court superfluous, and the real trial, for all practical purposes, occurs when the confession is obtained").

46. George C. Thomas III, *Justice O'Connor's Pragmatic View of Coerced Self-Incrimination*, 13 WOMEN'S RTS. L. REP. 117, 125 (1991).

CHAPTER 10

The Third Degree Redux

The reduction of physical coercion in obtaining confessions has been characterized as one of the "the success stories of human rights in the United States."[1] Even in *Miranda*, the Court stated that interrogation practices involving "physical brutality and violence . . . are undoubtedly the exception now."[2] Over the next three decades, as the police increasingly resorted to psychologically oriented techniques, physically abusive interrogation practices became even rarer. In 1995, a knowledgeable observer stated that "the third degree has largely disappeared from the American scene."[3]

Or has it? Although it may be true that we have developed "a societal norm against coercing confessions,"[4] there is at least one pocket of the country in which allegations that the police have systematically extracted confessions through torture have been documented by defense attorney groups, citizen's coalitions, an internal police review agency, and Amnesty International.[5] Examination of this pattern of abusive interrogation techniques illuminates the circumstances that are likely to precipitate this behavior. The courts' response to the claims of abuse, moreover, reveal the inherent limitations in *Miranda* and the other Supreme Court cases designed to eliminate offensive interrogation practices

The Pattern of Abusive Interrogation Practices

For more than a decade during the 1970s and 1980s, black suspects interrogated in the Area 2 police station on Chicago's South Side claimed that several officers extracted confessions from them by torture.[6] Since the suspects were invariably gang members who had extensive criminal records,[7] their claims were given little credit; when the police denied they had physically coerced the suspects' confessions, judges refused to suppress the suspects' confessions,[8] and suspects' complaints about police brutality before the Office of Professional Standards were dismissed as unfounded.[9] Nevertheless, the nature of the suspects' allegations was disturbing: "Certain types of torture . . . were alleged over and over—suffocation with a typewriter cover, electroshock with a specially constructed black box [likely a field telephone mechanism], hanging by handcuffs for hours, a cattle prod to the testicles, Russian roulette with a gun in the suspect's mouth."[10] Even assuming that each suspect's credibility was dubious, why would even one of them fabricate such unusual forms of abuse rather than simply a more credible example of police brutality? And why would so many of them make the same bizarre false accusations?

In most cases, individual suspects claiming their confessions were extracted by physical coercion were not able to present evidence of Area 2 officers' prior practices because the courts barred past allegations against the particular officer or against other Area 2 officers on relevance grounds.[11] The strikingly similar nature of different suspects' allegations began to emerge, however, after Andrew Wilson brought a federal civil rights suit against the officers involved in his interrogation and the City of Chicago.[12] Wilson was charged with the murder of two police officers in 1982. After his pretrial motion to suppress his confession was denied, he was convicted of murder and sentenced to death.[13] While his appeal was pending in the Illinois Supreme Court, Wilson brought a civil suit under the 1979 federal civil rights act.[14]

In his civil suit, Wilson accused Commander John Burge, who was then in charge of Area 2 investigations, of orchestrating a series of abusive interrogation practices: "It was charged that various policemen beat Wilson after his arrest and arrival at Area 2; that they put a plastic bag over his head so he could not breathe; that they burned him, first with a cigarette and later on a radiator."[15] In addition, Wilson alleged that, using two different devices, officers administered electric shock "to his genitals, his nose, and his fingers."[16] The device was a small black box. Wires from the box were attached with clamps to Wilson's right ear and nostril, and one of the officers turned the crank, causing Wilson excruciating pain.[17] "After examining the physical evidence, the deputy chief medical examiner, initially a skeptic, became a believer."[18] Wilson also alleged that "after the electroshock was finished, he was taken to another police station for a lineup, and that there he got a mouthful of the lieutenant's gun."[19]

During Wilson's trial, his attorneys at the People's Law Office began to get anonymous letters in police department envelopes suggesting other leads, and eventually they compiled a list of more than sixty men who claimed to have been abused by Burge and his detectives.[20] These allegations not only strengthened Wilson's civil suit but also precipitated further investigations into the interrogation practices employed by Burge and the Area 2 detectives serving under him.

Prior to these investigations, Burge had been one of the department's rising stars. After serving in Vietnam, Burge "joined the force in 1970. . . . He made sergeant in just five years, lieutenant in ten, and in the early 1980's became one of the youngest officers to take over a detective unit—Area 2 Violent Crimes on the South Side."[21] Moreover, Burge and the detectives working under him got results: "They won confessions, closed cases, and got convictions."[22]

In the wake of Wilson's civil suit, however, it became apparent that Burge's results had come at a price. As a result of the allegations that were made in connection with that suit, Michael Goldston, a police investigator, investigated allegations of misconduct by Area 2 personnel. The Goldston report, which was presented to the police department's Office of Professional Standards,[23] concluded that Burge and the detectives under him systematically employed abusive interrogation practices. According to Goldston's report, "The time span involved cover[ed] more than ten years. The type of abuse described was not limited to the usual beating, but went into such esoteric areas as psychological techniques and planned torture."[24] The report also concluded that "[p]articular command members were aware of the systematic abuse and perpetuated it either by actively participating in same or failing to take any action to bring it to an end."[25]

The Office of Professional Standards charged Burge with misconduct in the *Wilson* case. Although Burge denied any wrongdoing, a Police Board decision in 1993 concluded that he was guilty of physical abuse in that case and should be removed from the force. After Burge's dismissal, the city changed its strategy in Wilson's civil suit. It admitted that Wilson had been subjected to torture, but claimed that Burge alone was responsible, and that, when he tortured Wilson, he was acting outside the scope of his employment. This argument was rejected, however, and Wilson was eventually awarded damages of over one million dollars.[26] Subsequently, the city settled civil claims with several other suspects who claimed that Area 2 detectives extracted their confessions through torture.[27]

As a result of the Area 2 detectives' abusive interrogation practices, Illinois courts continue to consider issues arising from cases that are now nearly two decades old. Most significantly, ten Illinois defendants now on death row have alleged that Area 2 detectives extracted their confessions through torture. These defendants, whom the media have alternatively characterized as the "death row ten" or the "Jon Burge ten,"[28] have claimed that their convictions and death penalties should be reversed because the confessions precipitating their convictions were involuntary.

In some of the "death row ten" cases, there is not only substantial basis for crediting the defendant's allegations of police brutality but also considerable reason to doubt the truth of the defendant's confession. In Stanley Howard's case, for example, Howard's confession stated that shortly before dawn on May 20, 1984, he approached a parked car in which a man and a woman were sitting. He asked the man in the driver's seat for a match, and shot the man after the man told him to move along.[29] Howard's confession stated that he did not know either the victim, Oliver Ridgell, nor the woman next to him, Tecora Mullen. Since Ridgell and Mullen, who were both married to other people, had been involved in an extramarital relationship for some time, the disclosure that their death resulted from a random shooting was itself surprising. Intuitively, it seemed more likely that the perpetrator of this early morning shooting would have had a motive for his act. Nevertheless, although Mullen was at first only able to say that Howard "looked like" the killer, she positively identified Howard as the killer at trial. The jury convicted Howard of murder and sentenced him to death.

Aside from Howard's confession, the evidence of his guilt seemed weak. At trial, the prosecution presented no physical evidence, such as the murder weapon or fingerprints at the scene of the crime. Although Mullen's testimony might have seemed persuasive to the jury, the value of her identification was dubious, especially in view of her initial uncertainty.[30] After Howard was convicted, moreover, tenants in an apartment near the scene of the killing testified that, at the time of the shooting, they heard conversation that indicated the killing was not a random act of violence—as Howard's confession indicated[31]—but rather that the killer knew the two people in the car. Thus one witness testified that before shooting the man in the driver's seat, the killer said, "I told you I'd get you."[32] Based on this evidence, Howard's confession that he committed a random act of violence on a victim involved in an extramarital relationship seemed implausible.

Howard was also able to produce unusually strong evidence in support of his claim that the police brutally coerced his confession. In contrast to most defendants, he was able to produce medical reports that provided support for his allegations. Following a police chase that led to his arrest, Howard complained of injuries and was taken to a hospital. Burge's detectives then questioned him; Howard claimed that during the interrogation the detectives kicked him, punched him, and placed a plastic typewriter cover over his head. After he confessed, he was again taken to a hospital. "Medical records show[ed] that he had new injuries, including bruises on his left leg that match[ed] his description of police mistreatment."[33] Nevertheless, when Howard's attorney sought to suppress his confession, the judge denied the motion, refusing to credit Howard's claims in the face of three detectives' testimony that "they treated Howard well during questioning."[34] On appeal, the Illinois Supreme Court refused to disturb this ruling, concluding that based on the testimony of the detectives and a paramedic who testified that "he did not observe any injuries to [Howard's] head," the judge could properly find that the defendant incurred his injuries while "attempting to elude the arresting officers" rather than while being interrogated by the detectives.[35]

While Howard and the other members of the "death row ten" are still under sentence of death, they now have considerable cause for hope. Although Illinois courts have previously rejected the claims that their confessions were extracted by torture, higher courts are now not only "ordering judges to hear these claims,"[36] but also expressing considerable skepticism toward the government's opposition to granting defendants' relief. In granting one condemned inmate a hearing on his request for a new trial, for example, a federal judge wrote that it was "common knowledge" that Burge and the officers who worked with him "engaged in the physical abuse and torture of prisoners to extract confessions."[37] Although the fate of the "death row ten" has not yet been resolved, the pattern of abuse perpetrated by the Area 2 detectives will inevitably cast doubt on the validity of the convictions in these and other cases.[38]

Explaining the Pattern of Abuse

In seeking to explain the combination of circumstances that precipitated this extraordinary pattern of abusive interrogation practices, attention should be directed not only toward Jon Burge and the detectives who served under him but also the suspects who were subjected to these bizarre forms of torture. Burge's critics have claimed that Burge learned the exotic interrogation practices he later employed while serving in Vietnam.[39] If this is so, why did he decide to transport these extraordinary techniques to Area 2? Why did he and the detectives working under him choose to employ the techniques on some suspects but not others? And why were they able to employ them without significant problems for such an extended period?

Since Burge has never admitted employing abusive interrogation techniques, we can only speculate as to why he and other detectives chose to employ particular practices in particular cases. The reason the detectives may have elected to employ bizarre forms of torture in some Area 2 cases, however, seems fairly obvious. In contrast to ordinary forms of physical abuse—such as beating a suspect or burning him on a radiator, as was done in Wilson's case—the more exotic interrogation practices employed in later Area 2 cases—suffocating a suspect with a typewriter cover, for example, or hanging him by handcuffs for hours— were calculated to leave few or no signs of injuries on the suspects.

In determining whether a suspect will be able to sustain allegations of police brutality, the presence of injuries will often be critical. If the suspect has no discernible injuries, the judge hearing the suspect's motion to suppress his confession is likely to credit police denials of abuse rather than the suspect's claims that he was subjected to brutality that left no marks.* The Illinois Supreme Court has held, moreover, that a defendant claiming that his confession was extracted through police brutality will not be permitted to admit evidence showing that the police engaged in prior acts of brutality unless he could show that "in both the prior allegations of abuse and the case before the court, there was evidence of injury consistent with police brutality."[40] By engaging in torture that was calculated to leave no discernible injuries, the Area 2 detectives were thus shielding themselves from courtroom proceedings that would be likely to expose their systematic pattern of abusive interrogation practices.

In deciding when to extract confessions through torture, the Area 2 detectives were selective, reserving their abusive interrogation practices exclusively for poor black suspects and primarily for gang members with criminal records. This pattern indicates that the Wickersham Commission report's conclusion that abusive interrogation practices are more likely to be applied against the poorer and weaker members of society remains valid. Suspects with more influence or resources would have been in a better position to mobilize public opinion so as to focus attention on the pattern of abusive practices. In reserving their abusive interrogation practices for suspects viewed as societal outcasts, the Area 2 detectives showed a disdain for the rights of the weakest members of

---

* As the *Howard* case indicates, moreover, even if the suspect can show injuries that appear consistent with his claims of police abuse, police testimony establishing another plausible explanation for the suspect's injuries will provide trial judges with a sufficient basis for rejecting the suspect's allegations.

society. Their conduct evidenced a belief that suspects drawn from this segment of the population had no protection against abusive interrogation practices.

The detectives' success in obtaining admissible confessions indicated that, to a considerable degree, their belief was justified. When there was a conflict between the testimony of a black gang member with a criminal record and one or more Area 2 detectives, judges—not surprisingly—chose to believe the detectives. For an extended period, moreover, the class of suspects who were subjected to abusive interrogation practices were unable to combine their testimony so as to present a compelling case to the courts. In practice, therefore, courts afforded these suspects little or no protection against abusive interrogation practices.

The abuses perpetrated by Area 2 detectives were undoubtedly aberrational. The state courts' impervious reaction to the claims of abuse, unfortunately, is not. As Professor Susan Bandes has pointed out, there are institutional considerations that foster "credulousness" in state courts confronted with "brutality claims and rote official denials."[41] Most significantly, perhaps, state court judges are disinclined to credit claims of police brutality because judges, who are generally elected by the public, are likely to share the public's perception that the police are the good guys and the suspects—particularly when drawn from the lowest classes of society—the bad guys. Judges will thus not only be inclined to disbelieve suspects' claims of police brutality but also to believe that in the rare cases in which such brutality occurs, the police may have had adequate justification for employing it. In addition, judges know that the police have considerable political influence; they are, therefore, aware that, in most instances, a judge's finding that the police employed brutality during a suspect's interrogation will create unfavorable political repercussions for the judge.[42] Thus it is not surprising that, in the absence of compelling evidence, state court judges generally refuse to credit suspects' claims that their confessions were extracted through torture.

This phenomenon underlines a fundamental weakness in *Miranda* and other Supreme Court cases designed to regulate police interrogation practices. Even if the cases provide guidelines that will eliminate abusive interrogation practices, the guidelines will be effective in practice only if some mechanism is provided that will eliminate the inherent limitations of the fact-finding process. Police who are willing to employ abusive interrogation practices will generally also be willing to lie about employing them. When this occurs, the traditional litigation process cannot be expected to do an adequate job of determining what took place during a secret interrogation. In order to make the Court's restrictions on abusive interrogation practices meaningful, it is therefore necessary to develop some better means of determining the critical facts.

Addressing the Problem of Fact-Finding

The authors of the Wickersham Commission report were clearly aware of the problem of determining facts relating to abusive interrogation practices. One of the report's few specific recommendations was that the police should be required to set forth the facts relating to the suspect's detention and interrogation, providing documentation as to the time of the suspect's arrest, the places the suspect was taken, the length of interrogation, and the names of those who participated in it.[43]

This requirement would not, of course, insure that the information provided by the police would be accurate. So long as their interactions with the suspect were conducted in secret, the police would be able to misrepresent critical facts, such as the time of the arrest or the length of the interrogation. Requiring the police to record contemporaneously the significant facts relating to every interrogation, however, would be likely to reduce the possibility of falsification for two reasons. First, if the police perceived the recording obligation as routine, they would be likely in most cases to provide accurate information without giving much thought to the possibility of falsification. And, second, requiring that the police provide particular facts contemporaneously would reduce the possibility that the police would fabricate facts in anticipation of litigation. The principle underlying the report's recommendation, therefore, was that requiring the police to provide documentation as to objective facts relating to their interactions with the suspect would facilitate litigation by providing a generally accurate record of the salient facts of the interrogation.

Due to the technological advances that have occurred during the seventy years since the Wickersham Commission Report, there are now even more effective means of requiring the police to follow procedures that will provide a generally accurate record of the salient facts of the interrogation. Most significantly, as numerous commentators have recommended,[44] the police could be required to audiotape or videotape their interrogations, thereby providing a complete record of each interrogation. As with the Wickersham Commission report's proposal, implementing this recommendation would not thwart all possibility of police misrepresentation. Since it would be impossible to monitor all interactions between the police and suspects, the police could engage in abusive interrogation practices prior to commencing the taping of the interrogation. In most instances, however, mandating audiotaping or videotaping of police interrogations would provide an objective record that would facilitate fact-finding relating to the critical facts surrounding an interrogation.

In the wake of the controversy surrounding the Area 2 torture cases, the Illinois legislature considered and at one point seemed inclined toward adopting a statute that would require the police to video- or audiotape interrogations of suspects in most cases.[45] Before the bill could be passed, however, the Illinois law enforcement community generated an intensive public relations effort designed to alert legislators to the problems that mandatory taping of interrogations creates for law enforcement. Among other things, their "Legislative Alert" stated that mandatory videotaping provides new "hoops and hurdles" for law enforcement[46] and "reflects major expansion of rights of the accused at the expense of crime victims, public safety and law enforcement."[47] As a result, the videotaping bill's support diminished to the point where "its sponsors failed to introduce it for a vote by the full House of Representatives."[48]

Nearly seventy years ago, the Wickersham Commission observed that the "real remedy" for protecting suspects against abusive interrogation practices "lies within the will of the community."[49] The defeat of the legislation providing for mandatory videotaping of interrogations in Illinois indicates, perhaps, that the political "will" for implementing reforms designed to protect suspects from abusive interrogation practices will generally be too weak to withstand pressure generated by politically influential groups associated with law enforcement. Nevertheless, just as the Wickersham Commission's report precipitated a climate that produced meaningful constitutional restrictions on police interrogation practices, the documentation of abusive interrogation practices perpetrated by Chicago's Area 2 detectives during the 1970s and 1980s may eventually lead to constitutional restrictions designed to minimize the possibility of such practices by enhancing the accuracy of fact-finding in police interrogation cases.

NOTES

1. See 3 WIGMORE ON EVIDENCE, *supra* chapter 1, note 14.
2. *Miranda*, 384 U.S. at 447.
3. CRAIG M. BRADLEY, THE FAILURE OF THE CRIMINAL PROCEDURE REVOLUTION 37 (1993).
4. PAUL CHEVIGNY, EDGE OF THE KNIFE: POLICE VIOLENCE IN THE AMERICAS 133 (1995).
5. Susan Bandes, *Patterns of Injustice: Police Brutality in the Courts*, 47 BUFF. L. REV. 1275, 1277 (1999).

6. Michael Goldston, Chicago Police Department, Office of Professional Standards, History of Allegations of Misconduct by Area Two Personnel, Section I, at 24–25 (1980) (unpublished memorandum, on file with the author).

7. *See* Bandes, *supra* note 5, at 1292.

8. *See id.* at 1290.

9. See *id.* at 1295–96.

10. *Id.* at 1296–97.

11. *See id.* at 1296.

12. *See* JOHN CONROY, UNSPEAKABLE ACTS, ORDINARY PEOPLE 162–64 (2000) (hereinafter CONROY, UNSPEAKABLE ACTS).

13. See People v. Wilson, 506 N.E.2d 571, 572 (Ill. 1987). On appeal to the Illinois Supreme Court, Wilson's death sentence was reversed and remanded. See *id.* On retrial, Wilson was again found guilty of murder and "sentenced to a term of natural life in prison." *Wilson,* 626 N.E.2d at 1286 (Ill. 1993).

14. 42 U.S.C. § 1983 (2000).

15. John Conroy, *House of Screams,* CHICAGO WEEKLY READER, Jan. 26, 1990, at 8.

16. *Id.*

17. See *id.* at 18.

18. See *id.* at 8.

19. John Conroy, *Poison in the System,* CHICAGO WEEKLY READER, June 25, 1999.

20. See CONROY, UNSPEAKABLE ACTS, *supra* note 12, at 158.

21. Charles Nicodemus, *Cop Links Ten Capital Cases,* CHICAGO SUN-TIMES, Feb. 26, 1999, at 6.

22. *Id.*

23. See Goldston, *supra* note 6, at 3.

24. *Id.* at 3.

25. *Id.*

26. See CONROY, UNSPEAKABLE ACTS, *supra* note 12, at 235.

27. *See id.* at 237–38.

28. See Nicodemus, *supra* note 21, at 6.

29. *Id.*

30. See Steve Mills & Ken Armstrong, *A Tortured Path to Death Row Series: Tribune Investigative Report. The Failure of the Death Penalty in Illinois,* CHI. TRIB., Nov. 17, 1999, at 10.

31. There was no evidence that Howard had ever known the victim or the other person in the car prior to the shooting. *Id.*

32. *Id.*

33. *Id.* at 11.

34. *Id.* at 17.

35. People v. Howard, 588 N.E.2d 1044, 1055 (Ill. 1991).

36. Steven Mills, *Claims, Probes of Cop Brutality Getting New Life, Courts Revisit Charges Dating to '80s,* CHI. TRIB., Apr. 4, 1999, at 3.

37. *Id.*

38. In *People v. Cannon,* 688 N.E.2d 693 (Ill. 1997), one of the "death row ten" cases, an Illinois appellate court ruled that the trial judge erred in Cannon's suppression hearing by not allowing the defense to show systematic torture by Area 2 officers. Cannon was the first case permitting a suspect to introduce such testimony in the absence of evidence corroborating the claim that he was subjected to physical abuse.

39. See CONROY, UNSPEAKABLE ACTS, *supra* note 12, at 76–77.

40. People v. Hobley, 637 N.E.2d 1002, 1010 (Ill. 1994).

41. See Bandes, *supra* note 5, at 1307.

42. *See, e.g.,* Lou Cannon, *One Bad Cop,* NEW YORK TIMES, Oct. 1,

2000, N.Y. *Times Magazine* at 32, 62 (explaining that Los Angeles judges are disinclined to disbelieve police testimony relating to suppression of evidence in criminal cases because "[a] judge who doesn't seem tough enough can pretty much expect an election challenge from an ambitious prosecutor, a daunting prospect in Los Angeles County, where even a bare-bones campaign can cost $100,000").

43. See *supra* chapter 2.
44. *See generally* KAMISAR, ESSAYS, *supra* chapter 1, note 24, at 133–35 (identifying commentators).
45. Steven A. Drizen & Beth A. Colgan, Let the Cameras Roll: Mandatory Videotaping of Interrogations Is the Solution to Illinois' Problem of False Confessions (unpublished article on file with Steven Drizen).
46. *Id.* at 87.
47. *Id.* at 88.
48. *Id.* at 89.
49. Wickersham Report, *supra* chapter 2, note 5, at 191.

CHAPTER 11

**Police-Induced False Confessions:
The Scope of the Problem**

To some people the idea that "anyone would confess to a crime he did not commit" seems incredible.[1] Even if the police employ interrogation techniques that exert considerable pressure, most people believe that a normal suspect would not confess to something he did not do. A growing body of empirical data indicates, however, that a substantial number of police-induced false confessions have in fact occurred.[2] From a policy perspective, therefore, it is important to assess the magnitude of this problem.

Although it may be impossible to estimate *how frequently* police-induced false confessions occur,[3] determining whether they occur with sufficient frequency to create a problem for our system of justice is essential. If such confessions occur with extreme infrequency, they may properly be dismissed as aberrational accidents that, while unfortunate, should not be viewed as posing a problem of sufficient magnitude to mandate changes in our system of justice. But if they occur with greater frequency, additional questions relating to their impact on our system of justice at least need to be considered.

This chapter will assess the magnitude of the problems created by police-induced false confessions. Specifically, I will try to answer the following questions: Do false confessions resulting from widely employed interrogation practices occur often enough to create a problem that needs to be addressed? If so, in what kinds of cases are such confessions most likely to occur? And how often will they be likely to lead to wrongful convictions? My conclusion is that in a small but significant category of cases, widely employed interrogation practices create a significant risk of false confessions that, in turn, leads to an unacceptable risk of wrongful convictions resulting from such confessions.

The idea that a suspect, who is neither insane nor physically coerced, will be induced by the police to confess to a crime he did not commit seems counterintuitive. Even in 1940, when police interrogation methods were less humane than they are today, Wigmore asserted that police-induced false confessions were rare.[4] More than half a century later, Joseph P. Buckley, one of the coauthors of the *Inbau Manual's* most recent edition,[5] asserted that, when properly utilized, currently employed interrogation techniques will not produce false confessions.[6] A growing body of empirical evidence, however, sheds doubt on Buckley's conclusion.[7] For the most part, two types of evidence have been presented: first, specific cases in which suspects' confessions are claimed or determined to be false;[8] and, second, social psychologists' analysis of interrogation practices' psychological dynamics, showing that in certain circumstances such practices are likely to create a substantial risk of false confessions.[9]

Although this empirical evidence is sufficient to rebut Buckley's claim that currently employed interrogation methods will *never* produce false confessions, it is not sufficient by itself to demonstrate that widely employed interrogation methods produce false confessions with sufficient frequency to create a serious problem for our system of justice. As Cassell has observed, even if it can be established that a few dozen post-*Miranda* suspects have in fact been convicted on the basis of police-induced false confessions, "quantitatively speaking," these cases constitute "a few drops in [a] very large bucket."[10] If only a vanishingly small percentage of cases is involved, moreover, social psychologists' analysis of the dynamics that produced these aberrational results will be of limited interest. In order to estimate the frequency of police-induced false confessions, some effort must be made to view this phenomenon from a broader perspective.

To obtain such a perspective, at least two approaches may be employed. First, we can assess the frequency of police-induced false confessions in a relevant sample of cases and, from that data, attempt to estimate the extent to which such confessions are likely to occur in some broader population. Second, through examining known police-induced false confessions, we can seek to determine the extent to which the factors that appeared to produce these false confessions would be likely to produce similar results in other cases.

Drawing Inferences from a Sample of Cases

Under the first approach, selecting an appropriate sample of cases is critical. Although the sample need not be drawn from the universe of all police interrogation cases, it should represent a population that is relevant to the question at issue. In this case, the sample selected should represent a population that is large enough and important enough so that the conclusion that a significant number of police-induced false confessions occurred within that population would provoke concern.

Cassell has suggested that studies of police interrogation practices such as Richard Leo's observation of interrogations in the California Bay Area in 1993,[11] his own and Brett Heyman's observation of interrogations in Salt Lake City during 1994,[12] and students' observations of police interrogations in New Haven, Connecticut, in 1966,[13] could provide samples from which we could determine the extent to which false confessions occur in the population of confessions resulting from standard interrogation practices. He has asserted, moreover, that these studies' failure to turn up even "one clear cut case of a false confession" indicates that police-induced false confessions are very rare.[14]

Leo and Ofshe have attacked Cassell's conclusion on the ground that the investigators conducting the studies were not examining the truth or falsity of the confessions observed.[15] While this is a legitimate objection, there is an even more fundamental problem with Cassell's approach. If a researcher were investigating the phenomenon of lung cancer, she would not focus her attention on samples that included only nonsmokers under the age of thirty; if no case of lung cancer emerged from such a sample, moreover, she would not therefore conclude that lung cancer is a rare phenomenon.* Since no one seriously contends that standard interrogation practices are likely to precipitate false confessions during routine interrogations, the same principle applies in the present situation. A researcher interested in the phenomenon of police-induced false confessions would not focus her attention on a sample consisting mostly of relatively nonserious cases in which police were able to obtain incriminating statements following relatively short interrogations. Moreover, a finding that such a sample contained no "clear cut case of a false confession" would indicate only that police-induced false confessions are unlikely to occur during the relatively short interrogations that typically occur in routine cases; it would not support the conclusion that such confessions rarely occur in other contexts or that they do not occur with sufficient frequency to create a problem that mandates attention.

In order to select an appropriate sample of cases, what criteria should be employed? The existing literature indicates that police-induced false confessions are most likely to occur in serious high-profile cases[16] in which the police conduct a lengthy interrogation employing a

---

* If she were not even looking for lung cancer cases, this conclusion would be even more implausible.

range of tactics.[17] Based on this information, researchers seeking to study the phenomenon of police-induced false confessions should limit their sample to relatively high-profile cases where there is at least a fair probability that the police will conduct a lengthy interrogation in which a range of tactics will be employed. Possible samples could include a collection of cases in which interrogators obtained confessions only after conducting prolonged interrogations of a certain length or cases in which the suspects were charged with crimes involving very serious punishments, such as the death penalty or imprisonment in excess of twenty years.

Limiting the sample in this way will, of course, make it impossible to draw from the results any conclusions as to how frequently police-induced false confessions occur in all cases. At most, the results will provide conclusions relating to the extent to which police-induced false confessions will be likely to occur in the population from which the sample was drawn. These conclusions will be significant, however, so long as they indicate that a problem exists in a population that is of sufficient magnitude to warrant concern. If, for example, examination of a sample drawn from cigarette smokers over the age of sixty showed that a certain percentage of the sample had lung cancer, this result would provide no information relating to the frequency with which lung cancer occurs in the general population; the result would nevertheless be significant, however, because the population of cigarette smokers over sixty is large enough so that conclusions relating to that population's health warrant societal concern.

Examining a sample of wrongful convictions in high-profile or potentially capital cases could illuminate the extent to which police-induced false confessions precipitate wrongful convictions in such cases. If wrongful convictions in high-profile or potentially capital cases occur with sufficient frequency to provoke societal concern, a finding that police-induced false confessions precipitate a significant proportion of such wrongful convictions should be sufficient to show that police-induced false confessions is a problem that mandates attention.

In view of the criminal justice system's concern for avoiding the conviction of innocent defendants,[18] most people would agree that, throughout our history, wrongful convictions in serious cases have occurred too often.[19] Over the past few decades, moreover, the numerous instances in which defendants convicted of capital crimes have been shown to be innocent have convinced even supporters of capital punishment that wrongful convictions in capital cases is an extremely serious problem.

On January 31, 2000, Illinois Governor George Ryan, a Republican who favors the death penalty, declared a moratorium on capital punishment, citing concerns about his state's "shameful record of convicting innocent people and putting them on death row."[20] The problem identified by Governor Ryan is in fact a national problem rather than one that exists only in Illinois. Since the death penalty was reinstated in 1976, at least "87 death-sentenced inmates have been released on grounds of innocence,"[21] some "within hours" of the time set for their execution.[22] Although more defendants on death row have apparently been exonerated in Illinois[23] than in any other state, the most likely reason for this is that Illinois is one of only two states "that permits DNA tests after conviction."[24] In the great majority of death penalty states, it is thus extremely difficult for a convicted capital defendant to obtain evidence that will establish his innocence. As a result, most commentators believe that the documented cases of defendants on death row who have been exonerated not only significantly understate the extent to which defendants in capital cases have been wrongfully convicted but also indicate that "many . . . who were executed might also have been innocent."[25] Indeed, even the conservative columnist George Will has asserted on national television, "[A] reasonable inference is that innocent people have been executed."[26] Since most would agree that "[f]ew errors made by government officials can compare with the horror of executing a person wrongly convicted of a capital crime,"[27] this evidence suggests that one of our system of justice's highest priorities should be to identify the principal causes of such miscarriages so that measures may be taken to reduce their occurrence.

Although determining whether a case may properly be characterized as a miscarriage of justice will inevitably be problematic, a sample of probable miscarriages of justice in potentially capital cases provides a reasonable source for determining the extent to which various causes are likely to precipitate such miscarriages of justice. If it appears that police-induced false confessions contributed to a significant proportion of the probable miscarriages of justice contained in the sample, reducing such confessions should properly be identified as a priority of our criminal justice system.

Several collections of proven or probable miscarriages of justice exist.[28] In order to assist in determining the extent to which police-induced false confessions precipitate wrongful convictions in potentially capital cases, such a collection should meet several criteria: first, it should be limited to potentially capital cases; second, it should be large enough so that the causes of wrongful convictions within the sample are likely to be represented in roughly the same proportions as they are in the total population of wrongful convictions in potentially capital cases; third, the collection should be selected so that the most important causes of such wrongful convictions are unlikely to be either under- or overrepresented; and, finally, the causes of the probable wrongful convictions should be identified with sufficient clarity so that it can generally be determined whether a police-induced false confession played any significant part in precipitating the wrongful conviction. Among the collections of wrongful conviction cases, the Bedau-Radelet collection of probable miscarriages of justices in capital cases[29] comes closest to satisfying these four criteria.

Bedau and Radelet identified 350 potentially capital cases in which miscarriages of justice[30] occurred in America between the years 1900 and 1985.[31] In selecting these cases, they relied heavily on previous research, with the result that better-known and previously researched cases were most likely to be included.[32] In 10 of the 350 cases included in their collection, moreover, Cassell and his coauthor Stephen J. Markman have challenged their conclusions, asserting that defendants included in their collection were in fact guilty.[33]

These considerations do not seriously diminish the extent to which the Bedau-Radelet pool of cases provides an adequate sample of wrongful convictions in potentially capital cases. Because Bedau and Radelet's cases are better known and have been subjected to more intense scrutiny than other wrongful convictions, their pool of cases does not represent a random sample of wrongful convictions in potentially capital cases. There is no reason to believe, however, that better-known wrongful convictions result from significantly different causes than other wrongful convictions. Therefore, Bedau and Radelet's pool of cases would appear to provide a sample of cases that includes an accurate cross section of the causes precipitating wrongful convictions in potentially capital cases. Moreover, the fact that a small percentage of their cases may be inaccurately classified would have only a slight bearing on the extent to which their sample represents the relevant population. Since there is no reason to believe that the possible misclassifications are likely to include a disproportionate number of cases involving any particular precipitating causes of wrongful convictions, the misclassifications would simply have the effect of decreasing the size of the relevant sample,[34] without reducing the validity of generalizations relating to the wrongful convictions' causes.

In 14 cases of their 350-case sample, Bedau and Radelet concluded that the record was too slender to provide any basis for determining the wrongful conviction's cause.[35] Of the other 336 cases, they concluded that a police-induced false confession was the primary or contributing cause of the wrongful conviction in 49, or 14.3 percent, of the cases.[36] Of the causes that may be directly attributed to the police or prosecution, false confessions ranked third, trailing only perjury by prosecution witnesses (117, or 34.8 percent)[37] and mistaken eyewitness identifications (56, or 16.7 percent).[38] If the Bedau-Radelet sample is limited to probable wrongful convictions occurring after 1966, when the third degree and other coercive interrogation practices that flourished during the early part of the century had apparently been replaced by more humane techniques,[39] the percentage of wrongful convictions attributed to false confessions is reduced by only about 3 percentage points; 11.4 percent of the wrongful convictions during that era were found to result from false confessions,[40] a figure that may be compared with the 37.5 percent of cases resulting from perjured testimony[41] and 24.1 percent of cases resulting from mistaken eyewitness testimony.[42]

If it is accepted that reducing wrongful convictions in potentially capital cases should be a high priority, data indicating that more than 10 percent of such wrongful convictions may be attributed wholly or partially to police-induced false confessions provides helpful data relating to the magnitude of the problem of police-induced false confessions. Based on the Bedau-Radelet study's conclusions, it appears that a police-induced false confession contributes to at least one out of every ten wrongful convictions in potentially capital cases. If reducing wrongful convictions in capital cases should be a high priority, then reducing the principal causes of such wrongful convictions should also be a priority. Data showing that police-induced false confessions is one of the leading causes of such wrongful convictions should thus be sufficient to establish that, at least in potentially capital cases, such confessions occur with sufficient frequency to warrant concern.

Indeed, the Bedau-Radelet study's conclusion relating to police-induced false confessions' role in precipitating wrongful convictions was one of the study's most surprising findings. Since mistaken eyewitness identifications are generally viewed as by far the greatest cause of wrongful convictions,[43] the fact that the Bedau-Radelet study found that errors resulting from police-induced false confessions were comparable to those resulting from mistaken identification witnesses has been viewed by commentators as a striking phenomenon that requires further study and analysis.[44] As Professor Samuel Gross explained in a thoughtful article,[45] these results suggest that conventional wisdom relating to the causes of wrongful convictions in ordinary cases does not necessarily apply in capital or other high-profile cases. In typical felony cases, mistaken identification evidence is much more likely to precipitate wrongful convictions than police-induced false confessions. In high-profile cases, however, where the police have more time to investigate[46] and are under greater pressure to make an arrest, the possibility of a police-induced false confession is much greater than it is in ordinary cases. In that context, the chances of error resulting from police-induced false confessions are comparable to the chances of error resulting from mistaken identifications, the cause that in most contexts has been recognized as the most significant precipitator of wrongful convictions. In view of the paramount importance of preventing wrongful convictions in serious cases, this evidence suggests that the problem of police-induced false confessions is of sufficient magnitude to warrant concern.

Extrapolating from Data Relating to Police-Induced False Confession Cases

At the conclusion of his riveting account of the case in which Peter Reilly was wrongfully convicted of manslaughter on the basis of a police-induced false confession, Donald S. Connery states that to those associated with the case, Reilly's experience precipitates a disturbing question: "How many more Peter Reillys are there?"[47] The force of this question stems from the seemingly typical aspects of Reilly's case.[48] With respect to the circumstances that appeared most pertinent to the outcome—the evidence pointing toward Reilly's guilt prior to the interrogation, Reilly's personal characteristics, the interrogation techniques employed by the police, and the prosecution's use of Reilly's confession at his trial—the case did not seem in any way aberrational. Therefore, if a wrongful conviction resulting from a police-induced false confession could occur in Reilly's case, it would seem plausible to conclude that the same result might occur in many other cases.

Drawing upon this insight, the second approach involves an attempt to extrapolate from existing cases of police-induced false confessions to estimate the likelihood that such confessions will occur in other cases. If, for example, a particular set of circumstances can be shown to have produced the police-induced false confession and the resulting wrongful conviction in Reilly's case, assessing the extent to which those same circumstances exist in other cases might yield insight into the extent to which police-induced false confessions and wrongful convictions resulting from such confessions are likely to occur in the total population of criminal cases.

This approach has some obvious difficulties, however. First, there is the problem of obtaining an adequate collection of police-induced false confessions. If the collection is limited to indisputably false confessions, it may be too small to be useful. If the collection is expanded to include probably false confessions, what degree of certainty should be required and what criteria should be employed to determine whether the requisite standard is met? Second, there is the problem of identifying the causes of police-induced false confessions. The factors that produce such confessions are undoubtedly complex. In particular cases, myriad circumstances relating to the interrogation tactics employed by the police and the individual characteristics of the suspect may play a part in producing the result. Thus examination of a collection of police-induced false confessions can at best yield conclusions relating to factors that accompany such confessions. In most cases, it will be impossible to establish a causal connection between these factors and the confessions. And, third, there is a problem with extrapolating from results in known cases to estimate results in unknown cases. Since every case is unique, it cannot be assumed that factors that appear to precipitate false confessions in one situation will necessarily precipitate false confessions in other situations. Subtle differences between the cases may be sufficient to produce different outcomes. For these reasons, extrapolating from existing police-induced false confession cases cannot be expected to provide anything close to precise estimates of the extent to which this phenomenon occurs in the total population of police interrogation cases.

Examining a collection of police-induced confessions that most objective observers would view as false can, however, at least provide insight into whether police-induced false confessions *could* occur with sufficient regularity to provoke societal concern. If such confessions are shown to occur in situations that may be characterized as typical in the sense that both the circumstances of the interrogation and the characteristics of the suspect are likely to be frequently duplicated in the total population of cases in which suspects are interrogated, we can at least conclude that some widely used police interrogation practices have considerable potential for producing false confessions from innocent suspects. The extent to which these interrogation practices produce false confessions would then depend on the extent to which interrogators employ them when questioning innocent suspects. At the least, those who claim that police-induced false confessions do *not* occur with sufficient frequency to provoke concern should then have the burden of showing why the confluence of interrogation techniques and characteristics that produce false confessions in an identifiable group of cases will not be likely to have the same effect in other seemingly similar situations.

The first step in the process of extrapolating from existing police-induced false confession cases involves selecting an adequate collection of such cases. In a groundbreaking article,[49] Leo and Ofshe presented sixty arguably relevant cases. Using criteria relating to both the strength of the evidence establishing the suspect's innocence and the weakness of the evidence corroborating the suspect's confession,[50] they identified thirty-four "proven"[51] and twenty-six "probable"[52] police-induced false confession cases and discussed their consequences. If either all or a substantial segment of this collection would be accepted by neutral observers as containing accurately classified police-induced false confessions, then extrapolating from this collection of cases would be appropriate.

In response to Leo and Ofshe's article, Cassell presented a detailed examination of one of their "proven" false confession cases and eight of their "probable" ones;[53] in each case, he concluded that Leo and Ofshe's classification of the confession as false was erroneous.[54] Based on these conclusions, Cassell asserted that Leo and Ofshe's other conclusions were also suspect. Focusing exclusively on the twenty-nine cases in which Leo and Ofshe claimed that false confessions led to wrongful convictions, Cassell concluded that their conclusions should be accepted only in the nine cases in which law enforcement authorities would agree with their conclusions.[55] In response to Cassell's article, Leo and Ofshe wrote another article,[56] which, among other things, challenged Cassell's analysis of the nine cases, asserting that his analysis in each of these cases was analytically flawed and tenditious.[57]

Since I have not examined the records of any of the nine cases in which Cassell challenges Leo and Ofshe's classifications, I am unable to determine the accuracy of the classifications that have been disputed. Cassell's decision to challenge only one of the cases in which Leo and Ofshe classified the suspect's confession as "proven" false does, however, seem significant. Since Cassell is an extraordinarily skillful advocate, it seems likely that if he had had any plausible basis for attacking any of the other "proven" false confession cases in Leo and Ofshe's collection, he would have done so. Moreover, although his attack on Leo and Ofshe's conclusion in the one "proven" false confession case he chooses to attack—James Harry Reyos's confession to murder—is skillfully presented,[58] his conclusion seems dubious. In this case, Dennis

Cadra, the Texas prosecutor assigned to defend Reyos's conviction on appeal, "came to the firm conclusion that it was physically impossible for Mr. Reyos to have committed the crime."[59] Cadra outlined the basis for his conclusion in a letter to then-Texas Governor Ann Richards. The killing was alleged to have occurred between 7:00 P.M. and 12:00 A.M. on December 21. Based on a date-stamped gasoline receipt signed by Reyos as well as the uncontradicted testimony of David Myer, Reyos was in Roswell, New Mexico, until at least 8 P.M. on December 21 (some 200 miles from Odessa, Texas, where the killing occurred) and based on a traffic ticket issued to Reyos by an officer of the New Mexico Highway Patrol, he was 15 miles west of Roswell at 12:15 A.M. on December 22.[60] Thus, as Cadra stated in his letter:

> For Mr. Reyos to have killed the priest, he had to have left Roswell immediately upon leaving Mr. Meyer's home (no sooner than 8:00 P.M. Texas time on December 21), driven over two hundred (200) miles to Odessa, met the priest and murdered him, driven over two hundred and fifteen (215) miles to a point at least fifteen miles west of Roswell, turned around, and then got a speeding ticket at 12:15 A.M. Texas time—a total time span of not more than 4½ hours. Even assuming it took as little as thirty minutes (a very conservative estimate) to meet up with the priest, get into a fight, strip him, bind his hands behind his back and murder him, Mr. Reyos would have had to have averaged a driving speed of over 111 miles per hour.[61]

However strong Cassell's attacks on Leo and Ofshe's classification of "probable" false confessions may be, his attack on their cases of "proven" false confessions seems too weak to undermine the authors' conclusions. Based on the evidence discussed in these articles, most, if not all, objective observers would accept Leo and Ofshe's conclusions with respect to their thirty-four "proven" false confession cases: each of these confessions appear in fact to be false.

These thirty-four cases provide a sufficient collection from which we can draw significant inferences relating to the likelihood of police-induced false confessions. In all of these cases, the police obtained the suspects' confessions through interrogation methods that are apparently widely employed by the police in serious high-profile cases. The suspects who confessed, moreover, were not aberrational suspects. Although a disproportionate number of them were mentally handicapped,[62] the thirty-four suspects who falsely confessed were representative of suspects in serious criminal cases. And, finally, there is no reason to believe that the circumstances that prompted the police to accept these false confessions as true were extraordinary. On the contrary, in all thirty-four cases, the police were apparently willing to accept the suspect's confession despite the absence of evidence that would corroborate its truthfulness. Accordingly, some extrapolation from the results in this collection of cases seems appropriate. Absent some explanation, it may properly be inferred that the police have employed interrogation techniques that at least created a risk of producing false confessions in many other cases.

The subsequent history of Leo and Ofshe's thirty-four "proven" false confession cases is also significant. In many of these cases, the suspect's innocence was established by evidence that "[came] to light shortly after their confession."[63] As a result, the prosecutor dismissed the charges prior to trial in slightly more than half the cases (eighteen out of thirty-four).[64] Of the sixteen suspects whose cases were not dismissed, however, all but one were adjudicated guilty: ten were wrongfully convicted and five pled guilty.[65] Even though the sample of cases involved is small, this striking result—more than 90 percent of the suspects who went to trial were convicted on the basis of apparently false confessions—suggests that when police-induced false confessions are accepted as true by the police and prosecutor, there is a very high risk that such confessions will result in wrongful convictions.

Assessing the Evidence

The evidence discussed in the two previous parts of this chapter strongly suggests that the problem of police-induced false confessions is of sufficient magnitude to warrant concern. In itself, the evidence considered in each part indicates that such confessions are likely to occur with disturbing frequency. Analysis of the Bedau-Radelet collection of miscarriages of justice suggests that, during the era covered by the study, police-induced false confessions were the primary or contributing causes of approximately one-tenth of the wrongful convictions in potentially capital cases. And analysis of Leo and Ofshe's collection of "proven" police-induced false confessions suggests two significant points: first, within the population of serious high-profile cases, the conditions that have the potential for producing police-induced false confessions are frequently present; and, second, when such confessions are presented to juries in criminal cases, there is a significant risk that the juries will wrongfully convict an innocent person.

The evidence presented in each part of this chapter, moreover, completes gaps that exist in the evidence presented in the other part. The Bedau-Radelet collection of cases is arguably of limited utility because it includes no wrongful conviction cases occurring after 1985. Since interrogation techniques are constantly evolving, one might hypothesize that, over the past two decades, standard interrogation methods have been altered so that the likelihood they will produce false confessions has been substantially reduced. Leo and Ofshe's collection of false confession cases seems to rebut that hypothesis, however. Within their collection of thirty-four "proven" false confession cases, twenty-three occurred after 1985 and nineteen after 1990, numbers that suggest the problem of police-induced false confessions in serious cases has not diminished. In a separate article, moreover, Ofshe and Leo explore the psychological dynamics through which interrogators produce false confessions from innocent suspects.[66] Although they do not address the question of how interrogation methods have altered over the past two decades, their analysis of the techniques employed in relatively recent cases indicates that, while the police may have developed increasingly sophisticated interrogation techniques, they have not refined those techniques so as to diminish the possibility of eliciting false confessions from innocent suspects.[67] Based on this evidence, there is every reason to believe that the conclusions emanating from the Bedau-Radelet study continue to be valid: at the dawn of the twenty-first century, police-induced false confessions continue to precipitate wrongful convictions in potentially capital cases with disturbing frequency.

If, on the other hand, Leo and Ofshe's collection of thirty-four "proven" police-induced false confessions is considered by itself, there is a significant problem with extrapolating from the results in those cases to conclude that other police-induced false confessions frequently occur. All that the Leo and Ofshe data can establish is that when the police employ certain interrogation techniques on innocent suspects, the chances that the interrogation will produce a false confession are significant. The data does not and cannot provide any indication as to how often the suspects subjected to these techniques are *innocent*. Indeed, there is some basis for arguing that an interrogator's decision to employ these techniques on an innocent suspect will be extremely rare. Prior to conducting an interrogation, the police should be able to determine in most cases whether a suspect is likely to be guilty. If they follow the advice of the *Inbau Manual*, moreover, they will employ sophisticated interrogation techniques designed to produce a confession only when they are certain of the suspect's guilt.[68] Arguably, therefore, the police may be able to limit the possibility that standard interrogation methods will precipitate a false confession by making intelligent preinterrogation decisions as to which suspects are guilty.

The magnitude of miscarriages of justice in serious cases revealed in the first part of this chapter provides a sufficient rebuttal to this argument. The frequency with which convicted capital defendants have been exonerated over the past quarter-century provides stark evidence of the extent to which police and other government officials mistakenly determine that suspects in capital cases are guilty. The Bedau-Radelet collection of miscarriages of justice in 350 potentially capital cases augments this data, moreover, showing that mistaken convictions in potentially capital cases have been a pervasive feature of our system of justice for at least the past century. Based on this data, few would dispute that wrongful convictions in serious cases occur too often. Such wrongful convictions cannot occur, however, unless innocent suspects are wrongfully charged with serious offenses.[69] And, in the normal course of our justice system, suspects will be charged only when the police conclude they are guilty. Thus, if the frequency of wrongful convictions in serious cases is unacceptably high, it ineluctably follows that the police too often make mistaken judgments as to whether suspects are guilty of serious offenses. Accordingly, the claim that police-induced false confessions will be limited to an acceptably small number of cases because the police rarely decide to interrogate nonguilty suspects should be rejected.*

Conclusion

In analyzing data relating to police-induced false confessions and wrongful convictions resulting from such confessions, my goal has been to determine whether such confessions or convictions occur with sufficient frequency to create a problem that our system of justice needs to

---

* Based on the constitutional premises that undergird our system of justice, this argument should be rejected in any event. Even if it were assumed that the police can generally make valid pretrial determinations as to suspects' guilt, allowing the police to obtain confessions that are likely to be true *only* because the police made valid preinterrogation determinations of the suspects' guilt should not be permitted. Whether or not the great majority of the confessions are true (because the suspects who confessed are in fact guilty), the confessions obtained under these circumstances are inherently untrustworthy in the sense that the interrogation techniques employed by the police were likely to produce false confessions from innocent suspects. Confessions obtained under these circumstances should not be constitutionally admissible. For elaboration of this argument, see *infra* chapter 14.

address. In order to meet this goal, it is not necessary to provide even tentative estimates as to the frequency with which such confessions or convictions arise or to address all the methodological objections that might be raised to the studies assessing these phenomena. Rather, I need only to show that the phenomena under consideration are real and sufficiently large to warrant concern.

In view of the recent documentation of frequent miscarriages of justice in capital cases, most would agree that reducing the possibility of wrongful convictions in such cases should be of paramount importance. The Bedau-Radelet collection of miscarriages of justice in potentially capital cases suggests that police-induced false confessions are an important precipitator of such miscarriages of justice, contributing to more than one-tenth of such wrongful convictions not only during the period from 1900 to 1985 but also during the first eighteen years of the post-*Miranda* era (1967 to 1985). Leo and Ofshe's collection and analysis of recent police-induced false confession cases indicate, moreover, that the interrogation techniques employed by the police in serious high-profile cases are at least as likely to produce false confessions today as they were in the early 1980s, the last period covered by the Bedau-Radelet study.[70] Based on the implications of this data, it appears that police-induced false confessions not only occur with substantial frequency but also that they play a substantial part in precipitating wrongful convictions in serious or potentially capital cases, contributing to approximately one out of every ten wrongful convictions in such cases.

It could be, of course, that the figure of one in ten is too high. Since the Bedau-Radelet collection of cases does not represent a random sample of wrongful convictions in potentially capital cases, the percentage of wrongful convictions resulting from police-induced false confessions contained in their collection of cases could be higher than the percentage of such wrongful convictions in the total universe of wrongful convictions in potentially capital cases.* Another possibility is that, over the past twenty years, law enforcement has developed more sophisticated techniques—including DNA testing—that allow it to make more accurate determinations of suspects' guilt prior to trial.[71] If either of these hypotheses is true, the percentage of wrongful convictions that could

---

* It could be, for example, that wrongful convictions resulting from police-induced false confessions are more likely to receive media attention than wrongful convictions resulting from other sources. If so, then the fact that the Bedau-Radelet collection included a disproportionate number of better-known wrongful convictions in potentially capital cases would slant their collection toward including a higher proportion of wrongful convictions resulting from police-induced false confessions.

reasonably be attributed to police-induced false confessions would be reduced; if the first hypothesis is true, moreover, the reduction might be quite substantial.[72]

In determining whether a phenomenon is of sufficient magnitude to warrant societal concern, however, estimating the precise size of the phenomenon is not critical. If data showing that about 10 percent of the people suffering from a serious disease had been injected with a drug that appeared to contribute to the outbreak of that disease, for example, this would be enough to provoke concern. Hypotheses that might allow a different interpretation of this data, moreover, would not be sufficient to dissipate that concern. The present case is similar. Within the criminal justice system, wrongful convictions in serious or potentially capital cases is a particularly virulent disease. The existing data suggests that police-induced false confessions have contributed to producing that disease in about one-tenth of all cases. Although this data is certainly not conclusive, it is sufficient to show that the problems of police-induced false confessions and wrongful convictions resulting from such confessions are of sufficient magnitude to demand attention.

Bedau and Radelet's conclusions should be considered in conjunction with Leo and Ofshe's research relating specifically to police-induced false confessions. Leo and Ofshe's conclusions as to the circumstances under which false confessions are likely to occur and the effect that they are likely to have on fact-finder take on added significance because the Bedau-Radelet study shows that false confessions in potentially capital cases are not a highly aberrational phenomenon. Moreover, Ofshe and Leo's study can be used to expand the Bedau-Radelet study's conclusions. The Bedau-Radelet study indicates that, at least through 1985, police-induced false confessions were a major cause of miscarriages of justice in potentially capital cases. Ofshe and Leo's examination of the circumstances under which modern interrogation techniques produce false confessions indicates that, over the past fifteen years, interrogation techniques have not been altered so that they are likely to exert less pressure on innocent suspects to confess.[73] On the contrary, their examination of examples of police-induced false confessions that occurred during the past decade[74] indicates that, in high-profile cases where the stakes are highest, modern interrogators have developed new techniques that may exert even more pressure on suspects to confess, with the result that, if anything, the likelihood of police-induced false confessions in such cases has increased.

Leo and Ofshe's study of proven or probable false confessions' impact on the criminal justice system[75] provides additional support, moreover, for the conclusion that police-induced false confessions precipitate wrongful convictions in serious criminal cases with disturbing frequency. After selecting their sample of thirty-four proven and twenty-six probable false confession cases, Leo and Ofshe sought to confirm prior research indicating that jurors give disproportionate weight to defendants' confessions by assessing the likelihood that jurors will convict defendants on the basis of confessions that are proven or probably false.[76] Based on the cases in their sample, they concluded that of the eleven suspects giving proven false confessions who went to trial, ten (or 91 percent) were convicted, and of the nineteen suspects giving probable false confessions who went to trial, twelve (or 63 percent) were convicted. Even if it can be shown that Leo and Ofshe misclassified a few of these cases, their study still establishes that, when presented with the opportunity, jurors are extremely likely to convict criminal defendants on the basis of false confessions.[77] This finding is significant because it shows that the system does not have safeguards that will prevent the jury from giving disproportionate weight to such confessions. Taken in conjunction with the evidence suggesting that police-induced false confessions occur in serious cases with disturbing frequency, this finding lends support to the conclusion that such confessions also produce wrongful convictions in such cases with disturbing frequency.

NOTES

1. See 60 Minutes: Did He Do It? (CBS television broadcast, June 30, 1996), available in Westlaw 1996 WL 8064916 (quoting jurors in Richard LaPointe's murder trial).
2. See White, False Confessions, supra chapter 1, note 40, at 108–9 n.26.
3. For contrasting views relating to whether the number of police-induced false confessions can be estimated, compare, e.g., Paul G. Cassell, Protecting the Innocent from False and Lost Confessions— and from Miranda, 88 J. Crim. L. & Criminology 497, 505 (1998) (hereinafter Cassell, Protecting the Innocent) (estimating that the number of wrongful convictions resulting from false confessions "might fall somewhere in the range between 10 . . . to 394" per year) with Richard A. Leo & Richard J. Ofshe, The Consequences of False Confessions: Deprivations of Liberty and Miscarriages of Justice in the Age of Psychological Interrogation, 88 J. Crim. L. & Criminology 429, 431–32 (1998) (hereinafter Leo & Ofshe, Consequences) (explaining why it is impossible to provide even a rough estimate of either the number of police-induced false con-

fessions or the number of wrongful convictions resulting from such confessions).

4. 3 WIGMORE ON EVIDENCE, *supra* chapter 1, note 14, § 867, at 359.

5. INBAU ET AL., *supra* chapter 1, note 23.

6. *See* Brian C. Jayne & Joseph P. Buckley, *Criminal Interrogation Techniques on Trial*, PROSECUTOR: J. NAT'L DISTRICT ATT'YS ASS'N, fall 1991, at 23.

7. *See generally* Welsh S. White, *False Confessions, supra* chapter 1, note 40, at 108–9 (summarizing empirical evidence).

8. See Richard J. Ofshe & Richard A. Leo, *The Social Psychology of Police Interrogation: The Theory and Classification of True and False Confessions*, 16 STUDIES IN LAW, POLITICS, AND SOCIETY 189, 220–38 (1997) (hereinafter Ofshe & Leo, *Social Psychology*); Leo & Ofshe, *Consequences, supra* note 3, at 444–72.

9. See Ofshe & Leo, *Social Psychology, supra* note 8, at 203–7; GUDJONSSON, PSYCHOLOGY, *supra* chapter 3, note 2.

10. Cassell, *Protecting the Innocent, supra* note 3, at 507.

11. Richard A. Leo, *Inside the Interrogation Room*, 86 J. CRIM. L. & CRIMINOLOGY 266 (1996).

12. Paul G. Cassell & Bret S. Hayman, *Police Interrogation in the 1990's: An Empirical Study of the Effects of Miranda*, 43 UCLA L. REV. 839 (1996).

13. Note, *Interrogations in New Haven: The Impact of Miranda*, 76 YALE L.J. 1519 (1967).

14. Cassell, *Protecting the Innocent, supra* note 3, at 583.

15. Richard A. Leo & Richard J.

16. Ofshe, *Using the Innocent to Scapegoat Miranda: Another Reply to Paul Cassell*, 88 J. CRIM. L. & CRIMINOLOGY 557, 566 (1998).

16. See White, *False Confessions, supra* chapter 1, note 40, at 133–34.

17. See Samuel R. Gross, *The Risks of Death: Why Erroneous Convictions Are Common in Capital Cases*, 44 BUFF. L. REV. 469, 485 (1996) (hereinafter Gross, *Risks*); Leo & Ofshe, *Consequences, supra* note 3, at 222–38.

18. *See, e.g., In Re Winship*, 397 U.S. 358, 371–72 (1970) (concurring opinion of Harlan, J.) (observing that the requirement of proof beyond reasonable doubt in criminal cases is "bottomed on a fundamental value determination of our society that it is far worse to convict an innocent man than to let a guilty man go free").

19. *See generally* Hugo Adam Bedau & Michael Radelet, *Miscarriages of Justice in Potentially Capital Cases*, 40 STAN. L. REV. 21 (1987) (examining miscarriages of justice in potentially capital cases from 1900 to 1985) (hereinafter Bedau & Radelet, *Miscarriages*).

20. New York Times Editorial, *New Looks at the Death Penalty*, NEW YORK TIMES, February 19, 2000, at A14.

21. *Id.*

22. Vivian Berger, Review of ACTUAL INNOCENCE: FIVE DAYS TO EXECUTION AND OTHER DISPATCHES by BARRY SCHECK, PETER NEUFELD & JIM DWYER, NEW YORK LAW JOURNAL, May 2, 2000, The Lawyer's Bookshelve, 2.

23. At the time Governor Ryan established Illinois's moratorium on capital punishment, twelve

defendants on death row had been exonerated. See Berger, *supra* note 22.

24. BARRY SCHECK, PETER NEUFELD & JIM DWYER, ACTUAL INNOCENCE: FIVE DAYS TO EXECUTION AND OTHER DISPATCHES FROM THE WRONGLY CONVICTED 246–47 (2000).

25. New York Times Editorial, *supra* note 20, at 14.

26. Berger, *supra* note 22, at 2.

27. Bedau & Radelet, *supra* note 19 at 22.

28. See Edward Connors et al., *National Institute of Justice, Convicted by Juries, Exonerated by Science: Case Studies in the Use of DNA Evidence to Establish Innocence after Trial* (1996); JEROME FRANK & BARBARA FRANK, NOT GUILTY (1957); EDWIN BORCHARD, CONVICTING THE INNOCENT (1932); Bedau & Radelet, *Miscarriages, supra* note 19.

29. Bedau & Radelet, *Miscarriages, supra* note 19.

30. Bedau and Radelet define miscarriages of justice in potentially capital cases as "cases in which: (a) The defendant was convicted of homicide or sentenced to death for rape; and (b) when either (i) no such crime actually occurred; or (ii) the defendant was legally and physically uninvolved in the crime." *Id.* at 45.

31. *Id.*

32. *Id.* at 28.

33. See Paul G. Cassell & Stephen J. Markman, *Protecting the Innocent: A Response to the Bedau-Radelet Study*, 41 STAN. L. REV. 121 (1988). For a response to Cassell and Markman's claim, see Bedau & Radelet, *The Myth of Infallibil-*

ity: A Reply to Markman and Cassell, 41 STAN. L. REV. 161, 164 (1988). After reviewing the available evidence relating to eight New York cases in which Cassell and Markman disputed Bedau and Radelet's claim that convicted (and, in these cases, executed) capital defendants were innocent, a group of experts in capital cases concluded that, in all eight cases, "a majority of neutral observers, given the evidence at our disposal, would judge the defendant in question to be innocent." Acker et al., *Gone But Not Forgotten: Investigating Cases of Eight New Yorkers (1914–1939) Who May Have Been Innocent* at 137 (paper presented at the Annual Meetings of the American Society of Criminology, Nov. 11–14, 1998).

34. See Gross, *Risks, supra* note 17, at 470–71.

35. Bedau & Radelet, *Miscarriages, supra* note 19, at 64.

36. *Id.* at 173–79.

37. *Id.*

38. *Id.*

39. See CRAIG M. BRADLEY, THE FAILURE OF THE CRIMINAL PROCEDURE REVOLUTION 37 (1995) (observing that in the wake of *Miranda* and other Warren Court criminal procedure decisions "[t]he 'third degree' seems to have largely disappeared from the American scene").

40. Bedau & Radelet, *Miscarriages, supra* note 19, at 177–79.

41. *Id.*

42. *Id.*

43. See United States v. Wade, 388 U.S. 218, 229 (1967) (quoting Wall's assertion that "[t]he influ-

ence of improper suggestion upon identifying witnesses probably accounts for more miscarriages of justice than any other single factor—perhaps it is responsible for more such errors than all other factors combined"). *See generally* WALL, EYE-WITNESS IDENTIFICATION IN CRIMINAL CASES 26 (1965).

44. *See, e.g.,* Gross, *Risks, supra* note 17, at 485 (observing that the Bedau-Radelet data indicates that "false confessions are a much more common cause of errors for homicides than for other crimes").

45. See Gross, *Risks, supra* note 17.

46. *Id.* at 485–87.

47. DONALD S. CONNERY, GUILTY UNTIL PROVEN INNOCENT 377 (1977).

48. See *Reilly* case discussed in detail *infra* chapter 12.

49. Leo & Ofshe, *Consequences, supra* note 3.

50. *Id.* at 436–37 (for both categories, the suspect's statement "lacked internal indicia of reliability"; for proven false confessions, "the confessor's innocence was established by at least one dispositive piece of independent evidence," and for probable false confessions, no "physical or other significant credible evidence supported the conclusion the defendant was guilty" and "[t]here was evidence supporting the conclusion the confession was false").

51. *Id.* at 444.

52. *Id.* at 447.

53. Paul G. Cassell, *The Guilty and the "Innocent": An Examination of Alleged Cases of Wrongful Convic-*

tions from False Confessions, 22 HARV. J.L. & PUB. POL'Y 523, 564–68 (1999) (hereinafter Cassell, *The Guilty*).

54. *Id.* at 538–64, 568–75.

55. *Id.* at 581.

56. Richard A. Leo & Richard J. Ofshe, The Truth about False Confessions and Advocacy Scholarship (unpublished manuscript on file with Richard Leo) (hereinafter Leo & Ofshe, Truth).

57. Leo & Ofshe, Truth, *supra* note 56, at 28–102.

58. Cassell, *The Guilty, supra* note 53, at 564–68.

59. Letter from Dennis Cadra to Governor Ann Richards (Dec. 31, 1991) at 2, *quoted in* Leo & Ofshe, *supra* note 56, at 88–89.

60. Leo & Ofshe, *supra* note 56, at 89.

61. Cadra, *supra* note 59, at 6, *quoted in* Leo & Ofshe, *supra* note 56, at 89.

62. Five of the thirty-four suspects who gave "proven" false confessions are referred to by the authors as mentally handicapped (Case Identifications #26, 27, 30, 32) or mentally retarded (Case Identifications #19). See Leo & Ofshe, *Consequences, supra* note 3, at 446–49. Examination of the secondary sources cited by the authors indicates that several other suspects in this category also had serious mental problems. *See generally* Welsh S. White, *What Is an Involuntary Confession Now?* 50 RUTGERS L. REV. 2001, 2044 n.247 (1998).

63. Leo & Ofshe, *Consequences, supra* note 3, at 482.

64. *Id.* at 483.

65. *Id.*

66. Ofshe & Leo, *Social Psychology, supra* note 8.

67. In their 1997 article, Ofshe and Leo described police interrogators' lack of training as follows: "Generally, police in America are not trained how to avoid false confessions, how to recognize different types of false confessions, or how to identify the telltale characteristics of false confessions." Ofshe & Leo, *Social Psychology, supra* note 8, at 193.

68. INBAU ET AL., *supra* chapter 1, note 23, at 77.

69. *See generally* Daniel Givelber, *Meaningless Acquittals, Meaningful Convictions: Do We Reliably Acquit the Innocent?* 49 RUTGERS L. REV. 1317, 1336–46 (discussing other data that indicates innocent suspects are frequently charged with serious offenses).

70. In potentially capital cases, interrogation of a suspect would be likely to precede the suspect's trial by a substantial period. Thus it may be assumed that the Bedau-Radelet collection does not include any cases in which the suspect's interrogation took place after 1983.

71. For an example of a case in which DNA testing aborted the trial of a suspect who apparently gave a police-induced false confession, see the *Crowe* case discussed *infra* chapter 12.

72. If, for example, the Bedau-Radelet collection of cases included twice as many wrongful convictions resulting from police-induced false confessions as a random sample of wrongful convictions in potentially capital cases, the estimate as to the percentage of wrongful convictions resulting from police-induced false confessions would be reduced by 50 percent.

73. See Ofshe & Leo, *Social Psychology, supra* note 8, at 194–207.

74. See *id.* at 251 (eleven of the thirteen interrogations from which the authors drew their material took place from 1991–96; the other two took place in 1986).

75. Leo & Ofshe, *Consequences, supra* note 3, at 472–91.

76. In all of the sixty cases in their sample, Leo and Ofshe maintained that, aside from the defendant's confession, "no physical or other significant credible evidence supported the conclusion that the defendant was guilty." *Id.* at 437.

77. In their latest article, Leo and Ofshe discussed the minimal extent to which their misclassification of a few confessions would affect their conclusions relating to the likelihood of the introduction of a false confession at trial producing a wrongful conviction. Leo & Ofshe, Truth, *supra* note 56, at 17–19.

CHAPTER 12

Examples of Police-Induced
False Confessions

Why do so many police-induced false confessions occur
in serious criminal cases? In order to explore this question, this chapter
will examine several cases in which interrogation practices, not clearly
impermissible under current law, resulted in confessions that are of such
dubious reliability that objective observers of the criminal justice system
would be likely to view them as false. The cases selected were chosen for
several reasons: they occurred in different segments of the post-*Miranda*
era; they involved a range of suspects, including one who was mentally
handicapped, three who were youths, and three who appeared to be relatively capable of resisting police pressure; and they involved a range of
interrogation techniques, illustrating the variety of tactics employed by
the police in serious high-profile cases. In each case, moreover, the circumstances under which subsequent evidence cast doubt on the truthfulness of the suspect's confession and law enforcement's reaction to that
evidence illuminate some of the practical difficulties in assessing the reliability of police-induced false confessions, a problem that affects the difficulty of detecting and classifying such confessions.

In presenting these cases, I have drawn largely from secondary
sources, which in most cases provide relatively complete accounts of the
suspect's interrogation and the case's subsequent history. Whenever
possible, I have also reviewed the full transcript of the suspect's interrogation[1] and am, therefore, sometimes able to provide information that
assists in determining the efficacy of specific interrogation tactics
employed by the police.

Considering a small number of police-induced false confession
cases in detail is valuable because doing so illuminates the process
through which these confessions were obtained and determined to be
probably false, allowing a fuller examination of not only the interrogation methods that produced the confessions but also the dynamics that
led law enforcement officials to accept them as evidence that should be

used in criminal prosecutions and to defend their truthfulness even when other evidence suggested they were false. Accordingly, after presenting the cases, I will seek to draw conclusions relating to the characteristics of suspects who give police-induced false confessions, the interrogation tactics that produce these confessions, the difficulties in classifying wrongful convictions resulting from police-induced false confessions, and the relationship between police-induced false confessions and wrongful convictions.

Cases Involving Police-Induced False Confessions

Peter Reilly—1973

On the evening of September 28, 1973, eighteen-year-old Peter Reilly called the police and reported that his mother, Barbara Reilly, had been brutally attacked in their home.[2] At 10:02 P.M., the state police arrived and found that Barbara, who "had almost been beheaded," was dead.[3] Within twenty-four hours, Reilly confessed to his mother's killing. Subsequently, the police arrested him for murder, and he was incarcerated for 143 days before undergoing a trial in which he was convicted of voluntary manslaughter.[4]

The police commenced their interrogation of Reilly at 6:30 A.M., approximately nine hours after he had discovered his mother's dead body. Although Reilly was of above-average intelligence, he had low self-esteem and was easily influenced by others.[5] In addition, he was traumatized by his mother's death and by his realization that he was suspected of her murder.[6]

After about four hours of questioning, Reilly agreed to take a polygraph test. After the test, the polygraph examiner, who was also a detective, told Reilly the test indicated he was being deceptive.[7] Reilly initially responded that he "didn't do it."[8] The detective soon undermined Reilly's confidence in his own innocence, however, by emphasizing the infallibility of the lie detector test:

> DETECTIVE: No, the polygraph can never be wrong, because it's only a recording instrument, recording from you. It's the person interpreting it who could be wrong. But I haven't made that many mistakes in the twelve years, in the thousands of people who sat here, Pete.

REILLY: That's right.

DETECTIVE: Is there any doubt in your mind, right now, that you hurt your mother last night?

REILLY: The test is giving me doubt right now.[9]

Soon afterward, Reilly became even less convinced of his innocence. After the detective reiterated his confidence in Reilly's guilt and suggested various motives for the crime,[10] Reilly, who still had no clear memories of attacking his mother, said, "Gotta keep digging. Gotta dig. Gotta keep pushing. I believe I did it."[11] The detective responded, "I know you did it."[12]

Over the next six hours, the chief interrogating officer questioned Reilly about the crime, emphasizing that the police already had clear evidence of his guilt and that Reilly needed to show his trust for the police by confessing to the crime.[13] After several false starts in which Reilly reiterated that he did not remember attacking his mother,[14] he stated, "I remember slashing toward her throat."[15] Even after this admission, Reilly again professed not to remember, yet tried with almost pathetic eagerness to supply details that would please his interrogator:*

INTERROGATOR: You remember the knife?

REILLY: There may have been a knife but I don't recollect it as well. Why do you ask about a knife?

INTERROGATOR: Well, Pete, you know there was a knife.

REILLY: I mean, was there a knife mark?

INTERROGATOR: Pete, you know very well why I won't answer that question. Cause you're not being honest. You're being dishonest with me. You're trying to maneuver me and trick me into telling you facts that you already know. I know the facts.

REILLY: Well, if you could give me some hints.[16]

---

* Reilly, who was fatherless, came to view the interrogator as a father figure. At one point, he even asked if it might be possible for him to come and live with the detective and his family. *See* JOAN BARTHEL, A DEATH IN CANAAN 98 (1977).

During the lengthy interrogation, Reilly made additional incriminating statements, including the admission that he must have raped his mother, even though there was no evidence that his mother had ever been raped.[17] But even while making these admissions, he continued to express doubt as to whether any of his statements reflected reality. At one point, for example, he said, "[It's] almost like I'm making it up."[18] Eventually, the officers reduced Reilly's statements to a written confession, excluding, despite their promise to include it, Reilly's insistence that he was not really sure of the truth of his confession.[19]

Prior to trial, Reilly's counsel moved to suppress his confession. After an extensive pretrial hearing, however, the confession was introduced into evidence.[20] At a jury trial before Judge Speziale, the prosecution "base[d] its case almost entirely on [Reilly's] confession."[21] In addition to introducing Reilly's signed statement, the prosecutor presented testimony showing that he "had expressed or confessed his guilt to four different officers, in informal remarks as well as the formal interrogation, and had appeared to be remarkably calm and unremorseful to two more officers."[22]

In an effort to show that Reilly's confession was false, Reilly's defense counsel introduced the tapes of Reilly's interrogation so that the jury would understand the circumstances under which his confession occurred.[23] Following lengthy deliberations, the jury convicted Reilly of voluntary manslaughter. Judge Speziale sentenced him to six to sixteen years imprisonment.[24]

Following a hearing that occurred about one year after Reilly's conviction, however, Judge Speziale reversed Reilly's conviction and sentence on the basis of after-discovered evidence. After considering the new evidence, the judge ruled that Reilly's conviction for manslaughter was "a grave injustice" and that it was "more than likely" that a new trial would lead to a different result.[25] Although the prosecutor who prosecuted Reilly at the first trial stated that he was going to seek a retrial, he died before he could do so.[26] Subsequently, a new prosecutor discovered evidence in the prosecutor's file that further weakened the government's case. Two witnesses had stated that they had seen Reilly at a movie theater at about 9:45 P.M. on the evening of his mother's death. Since this evidence was inconsistent with the time sequence presented by the prosecutor at Reilly's trial, it cast serious doubt on whether Reilly would have been able to arrive at his home in time to kill his mother.[27] As a result, the charges against Reilly were dropped. Neither the prosecutor who charged Reilly nor the police who investigated his case ever acknowledged Reilly's innocence, however; on the contrary, some of the police involved in the case have stated that they still believe he is guilty.[28]

Melvin Reynolds—1979

Following the abduction and murder of four-year-old Eric Christogen in St. Joseph, Missouri, on May 26, 1978,[29] police questioned numerous people, including twenty-five-year-old Melvin Reynolds, who had been diagnosed "as exhibiting signs of 'mental retardation' and 'antisocial behavior.'"[30] Although Reynolds did not match the physical description provided by witnesses describing Eric's abductor,[31] the police questioned him because an anonymous caller told them that Reynolds was observed on the afternoon of May 26 on the mall, which was the area where the child was last seen.[32] When the police questioned Reynolds at his home, Reynolds denied being on the mall on May 26. Skeptical as to his response, the police brought him to police headquarters for more questioning the next day.

After interrogating Reynolds for two hours, Sergeant John Muehlenbacher asked him if he would take a lie detector test, and Reynolds agreed. During the test, Muehlenbacher asked Reynolds, "Did you kill the boy?" Reynolds replied, "No. But I'll say so if you want me to."[33] The polygraph test indicated that Reynolds's denial of killing the boy was truthful, and the police released him. With no other suspects, however, they repeatedly came back to him. Between June 2, 1978, and February 14, 1979, they questioned him nine times,[34] including one session in which he was hypnotized and another in which he was given sodium amytal.[35]

On February 14, 1979, three officers, Detective Anderson, Detective Jones, and Sergeant Muehlenbacher, questioned Reynolds from 10:30 A.M. to 1:00 A.M.[36] During this interrogation, Anderson asked Reynolds why he had lied about matters relating to the Christogen investigation. Reynolds replied that he had lied because he was scared and did not want to have the murder pinned on him.[37] Anderson then accused Reynolds of various thefts and told him he needed to come clean. He said, "[W]e want the truth about this and everything else. Just wipe the slate clean and be done with it. Let's don't come back to your place . . . and pick you up and bring you in. Do you understand?" After a long pause, Reynolds, who was terrified at the prospect of being picked up again for further questioning, responded with a question, "Do you think that I'll go to the penitentiary?"[38] Anderson replied that he did not know and asked Reynolds whether he thought he needed to go there. Reynolds answered, "No, I don't think I do. I think I need help at the state hospital."[39]

When Anderson further pressed Reynolds to tell the truth about what happened, Reynolds said it was "awfully hard to talk about it."[40] At the request of Detective Jones, Reynolds then agreed to write the answers to six questions presented by the police. In response to the six written questions, Reynolds wrote that the child died by accident after Reynolds had sodomized him. Subsequently, the police asked Reynolds to write the account of the murder in his own words and sign it. Reynolds agreed. In writing the statement, Reynolds "used many of the same words, terms and phrases that Jones and Anderson had used in their questions" and statements to him.[41] Although his confession contained some material discrepancies from the known facts,* the police believed the confession was accurate, especially because Reynolds's statement that the boy died while being sodomized seemed consistent with the pathologist's finding as to the cause of death.

At Reynolds's trial, the prosecution presented no eyewitness or forensic evidence, relying entirely on Reynolds's confession. In closing argument, the prosecutor presented a convincing argument that the confession was sufficient to establish the defendant's guilt:

> Melvin Lee Reynolds told you he abducted and sexually assaulted Eric Christogen. He told you things only the real killer would know. He described in minute, painful detail just exactly how he did it. And then Melvin Lee Reynolds showed exactly the spot where the body was found on May 27, 1978.[42]

Although Reynolds's defense counsel emphasized that the interrogators' tactics would have the potential for producing a false confession,[43] the jury convicted Reynolds of second-degree murder. The judge sentenced him to life imprisonment.[44]

Nearly four years later, Charles R. Hatcher, a serial killer who had been charged with the murder of Michelle Steele, an eleven-year-old girl, confessed to the murder of Eric Christogen.[45] Hatcher, who at one point indicated that he had killed sixteen people,[46] stated that he told Eric to give him oral sex; after Eric did so, Hatcher said, "I grabbed him around the neck with both hands and choked him until I was pretty sure he was

---

* Perhaps the most glaring discrepancy was that Reynolds stated he observed the child alone for thirty-five minutes after his mother entered the store. According to Eric's mother, "Eric had only been out of her sight for 5 minutes." TERRY GANEY, ST. JOSEPH'S CHILDREN: A TRUE STORY OF TERROR AND JUSTICE 41 (1989).

dead."[47] Although Hatcher closely fit the original description of Eric's abductor[48] and revealed startlingly precise details relating to the circumstances of the crime,[49] the prosecutor responsible for Reynolds's conviction was extremely reluctant to accept Hatcher's confession as accurate.[50] He initially claimed that Hatcher's confession contained "nothing . . . that Hatcher could not have learned from the newspapers."[51] Later, the prosecutor admitted that, since he had prosecuted Reynolds and obtained his conviction, he was "pretty reluctant" to believe a mistake had been made.[52] Even after Officer Holtslager, who had obtained Hatcher's confession, established that Hatcher's statements referred to details that only the perpetrator could know, the prosecutor refused to prosecute Hatcher.[53] Within the community, other law enforcement personnel were also upset with Officer Holtslager's efforts to overturn Reynolds's conviction, maintaining that the jury's verdict should be respected.[54] Finally, however, the prosecutor gave Hatcher an opportunity to plead guilty to the crime.[55] At the plea colloquy, the judge accepted Hatcher's plea after the prosecutor and Officer Holtslager introduced substantial evidence establishing the accuracy of Hatcher's confession.[56]

Following Hatcher's guilty plea, Reynolds was released from prison. Later, his conviction was reversed. When asked by a reporter why he would confess to a crime he did not commit, Reynolds said, "A person's got a breaking point. I just couldn't take it no more."[57]

Leo Bruce, Mark Nunez, and Dante Parker—1991

On August 10, 1991, nine people were murdered at the Wat Promkunaram Buddhist Temple west of Phoenix, Arizona.[58] About a month later, based on a confession received from Michael McGraw, an inpatient at the Tucson Psychiatric Institute, the police interrogated four suspects: Leo Bruce, Mark Nunez, Dante Parker, and Victor Zarate.[59] Three of the four confessed.[60] Bruce, Nunez, and Parker all provided detailed written confessions admitting their participation in the murders. Zarate, on the other hand, never confessed.

Bruce's interrogation began at 2:30 A.M. on September 12, three hours after his arrest. A half hour into the interrogation, an FBI agent explained that the police had evidence showing Bruce's involvement in the crime: "You are not here by accident and the deal is already cracked and there's already been statements taken and there's already evidence matched up. . . . This is a serious deal, man, and we're not gonna go away."[61] As time went on, the interrogators increasingly emphasized to

Bruce that they had positive evidence of his guilt.[62] Bruce, however, adamantly insisted on his innocence.[63] The interrogators then suggested that if Bruce did not cooperate, the other perpetrators would place more of the blame on him. FBI Agent Casey developed this theme as follows: "The best thing to do is to cooperate now. . . . Don't you think it's smart to get your version of the story down . . . before everyone else gives theirs?"[64] When Bruce continued to deny any involvement in the crime, Casey responded, "Well, if you stick with that, you're gonna end up being sorry, I think. You're making a mistake by not cooperating at this point."[65]

The interrogators took a break at 4:30 A.M. At 5:00 A.M., they took Bruce to a property room, showing him "photographs of the victims, . . . photographs of enlarged fingerprints and other items of trace evidence, a floor plan of the temple, and a chart listing the names of Bruce's alleged accomplices."[66] Over the next seven hours, Bruce was continually questioned by two officers.[67] According to the officers, sometime between 9:15 A.M. and 12:10 P.M., Bruce stopped protesting his innocence and merely stated that he did not "remember what happened."[68] According to Bruce, sometime after 12:10 P.M., one of the officers suggested that if he did not "own up to his responsibility and explain the relatively minor role he played in the events, he might go to the gas chamber."[69] At 3:15 P.M., after almost thirteen hours of intermittent interrogation, Bruce began incriminating himself. Over the next two hours, he gave a detailed confession in which he admitted shooting all of the victims in the back of the head with a .22-caliber Marlin.[70]

The interrogations of Dante Parker and Mark Nunez were generally similar to the interrogation of Leo Bruce. In each case, several officers questioned the suspects for prolonged periods, prodded them to confess by telling them the police had incontrovertible evidence of their guilt, and alternated between implied promises of leniency if they did confess and threats of dire consequences if they did not. Both of these suspects, however, admitted their guilt considerably sooner than Bruce did,[71] suggesting that, even within a relatively limited time frame, the effective use of sophisticated interrogation techniques can exert great pressure on innocent suspects to confess.

In Parker's case, the time between the interrogation's beginning and the suspect's initial admission of guilt may have been as little as four and one-half hours.[72] After Parker waived his *Miranda* rights, two detectives, Riley and Scofield, accused him of being at the scene of the murder and demanded that he acknowledge his guilt.[73] When Parker denied that he had been at the scene of the crime, the detectives falsely informed him that they had incontrovertible evidence of his guilt: his accomplices— who knew things that only the killers would know—had told them about Parker's role in the crimes; a witness had identified Parker in a photo lineup; the victim's blood had been found on his clothes and shoes; and his fingerprints would be in the getaway car.[74] When Parker continued to protest his innocence, the detectives explained the consequences of his failure to confess:

> SCOVILLE: Let me explain something to you, you're in an unfortunate situation okay, you're one of the last persons that we talk to, right, we already know the majority of the story, okay. You're hooked up on the fact that hey I wasn't there or anything, we already know it's not true. Without a doubt, there's no, let me finish, there's no doubt in our mind that you were there, okay, the only way that you can help yourself right now is to start telling the truth and the reason being if you want us to believe what happened inside there, you have to be honest with us as far as even being there. Okay? Other people are going to tell us that you did, it's already happened.

> PARKER: But that's the thing.

> SCOVILLE: That's not the thing.

> PARKER: That's the thing, you can—I was with Renee. I didn't . . . I didn't do anything, I've never been to Phoenix since I've been in Tucson in March, never came to Phoenix, never.

> SCOVILLE: How come we have everybody telling us you were there?[75]

As time went on, the detectives reiterated this theme. They suggested to Parker that confessing to the detectives would be the best way for to him to present his story to the jury in a favorable light:

> RILEY: Put yourself in a jury box, Dante, you listen to the story, okay, you listening to the story about the people that got killed, okay, you have to make a decision when all this is over and you have to say hey does this make sense, what about this person, is this person a real bad individual or is this person a person that has

needs or some other motive did something and unfortunately some people got hurt . . .

SCOVILLE: You've got the opportunity right now to make those people think that hey, Dante is a person who made a mistake instead of hey, Dante's a cold-blooded killer and that's a big difference and I think you know that's a big difference. When they make the decision what's gonna happen to you, which do you want them to think? You . . . you need to think about that cause, partner that's . . . that's the bottom line and that's gonna be your decision that you're gonna have to live with for a long time. How do those people that made a decision on what can happen to you, think about you? Cold-blooded killer or person who made a mistake?[76]

When Parker did not respond to these inducements, the detectives became more explicit in threatening the consequences of not confessing:

SCOVILLE: You've been sentenced before . . . you've been sentenced before for little things and you know that if that judge gets pissed off at you it's a lot different than if he's not. And you right now can make a decision to make a difference about how the judge feels about you and you need to take it.

RILEY: What if he might send you to the gas chamber, and I don't say that to scare you, Dante, but in this situation that's a real possibility and I'm not gonna sit here, Wayne's not gonna sit here and lie to you about these things cause that's not gonna serve us any purpose . . .

SCOVILLE: So you're sitting here thinking it's us against you, that's not the case. We're here to help you out. . . . You need to think ahead to that sentencing time and have you walk before that judge, that's something to think about. Because you've been there before, think about how it was, think about how it's gonna be.[77]

Despite the detectives' reference to a possible death penalty, however, Parker did not confess.

Later, two other detectives, Sinsabaugh and Troutt, added a new element to the consequences of not confessing, threatening to arrest Parker's brothers, Peter and T.C., if he did not admit his involvement in the crime:

TROUTT: Dante, if T.C.'s not involved in this man, give it up.

SINSABAUGH: Make some right out of it, Dante.

TROUTT: We need to get that stopped.

SINSABAUGH: Everyone's here Dante, the game's up. All I need to know is Dante.

PARKER: Leave T.C. out of it. T.C. don't have anything to do with this.

SINSABAUGH: Peter either.

PARKER: Peter either.

SINSABAUGH: He's being brought in. What happened Dante, did you pull the trigger?

PARKER: I didn't pull no trigger.

SINSABAUGH: But you were there. Dante, just get it out man, just get it out once and for all so we don't have to go over this again. Were you there? I know you were there, my man.

TROUTT: We're gonna . . .

SINSABAUGH: Right?

TROUTT: We're gonna be in Tucson, Dante . . .

SINSABAUGH: This is not a game, my man, this is your one chance, I mean that, like Larry told you, I just want to know if you're a killer, Dante.

TROUTT: They're gonna hit that house big time, T.C.'s gonna go down right in front of his kids.

SINSABAUGH: And . . . and it's . . . it's not a game Dante, I'm talking to you as a man, that's all I can do, I'm showing you the respect I can cause I'm . . . I'm praying that you're not a you know, a cold blooded killer and . . . and I'm asking for your help to sort this fucking thing out. If you get messed up with some punks I want to hear about it. What happened Dante?[78]

This additional threat precipitated Parker's false confession. Over the next several hours, Parker admitted "to being a minor accomplice who knew little about and did not participate in the planning or the commission of the Temple Murders."[79]

During the next phase of the investigation, the police sought to obtain physical evidence that would corroborate the confessions. Although Bruce had confessed to shooting the victims with a .22 caliber Marlin, a ballistics test showed that his .22 caliber Marlin was not the murder weapon. In order to find the murder weapon, the police conducted ballistics tests on other .22 caliber Marlins that had been collected in unrelated incidents throughout Arizona. About six weeks after the suspects' confessions, "they scored a hit with one that had been taken from three high school students from western Phoenix ten days after the murders."[80] This precipitated a dramatic turn in the case. As Roger Parloff explained:

> One of those youths, Alessandro Garcia, 16, then confessed. He said that a Thai friend of his, Jonathan Doody, 17, had tricked his brother—a novice monk at the temple—into providing information about its security and valuables. After planning the raid for about a month, Doody and Garcia drove there in Doody's Mustang, entered in combat camouflage uniforms, stole jewelry, cameras, stereo equipment, and $2,650 in cash, and then killed all the witnesses.[81]

Garcia added that he shot four shots from his 20-gauge shotgun and that Doody fired numerous shots with a .22 caliber Marlin, shooting the people a couple of times in the back of the head to make sure they were dead. Ballistics tests confirmed that Garcia's shotgun was the other weapon fired during the temple massacre.[82]

Investigators failed to find any connection between Garcia and Doody and the four suspects who had previously confessed. On November 22, 1991, county attorney Richard Romley dismissed the cases against the four. Even though the dismissal was without prejudice (allowing the prosecutor to recharge the four suspects if new evidence came to light), Tom Agnos, who was then sheriff of Maricopa County, "criticized Romley's action—insisting that the suspects should have been forced to stand trial."[83]

Michael Crowe and Joshua Treadway—1998

On January 21, 1998, twelve-year-old Stephanie Crowe was found stabbed to death on her bedroom floor.[84] Raymond Tuite, a twenty-eight-year-old drifter who had a prior criminal record and a history of mental problems, was known to have been knocking on doors and peering in windows in the Crowe neighborhood on the night of the killing. When the police questioned Tuite, however, they believed his statement that he had not entered any house on that night. In fact, based on the apparent lack of any forced entry into the Crowe house, the police believed from the beginning that the killing was an "inside job," perpetrated by a member of the Crowe family.[85] Within hours, they became suspicious of Stephanie's fourteen-year-old brother, Michael Crowe. In contrast to the rest of the family, who all seemed distraught over Stephanie's death, Michael seemed "curiously unemotional."[86] In addition, the police wondered how he could have failed to see his sister's bloody corpse when he left his room in the early morning to get a painkiller.[87]

The police first interviewed Michael at 4:30 P.M. on January 26, five days after his sister had been stabbed to death. Following some preliminary questions, Detective Claytor asked Michael if he was willing to take a lie detector test. After Michael agreed, Detective McDonough twice asked Michael fifteen questions for the purpose of administering a CVSA (Computer Voice Stress Analyzer) test.[88] After reviewing the results, McDonough told Michael that the results indicated he was showing deception in response to the question, "Do you know who took Stephanie's life?"[89] Although Michael vehemently denied he was lying, McDonough emphasized the accuracy of the lie detector test, insisting that "technology is on our side."[90] The detective then referred to hair that had been found in Stephanie's hand; he asked Michael, "What if that's your hair?"[91] Michael responded, "It couldn't be," but when McDonough referred again to the CVSA results, Michael said, "I don't know why it says that. I told the truth on every question . . . I mean, I've truly lost everything if I can't even believe myself."[92]

After Michael had been interrogated for nearly two and one-half hours, McDonough left; Detective Claytor returned and immediately began talking about the physical evidence. He told Michael that they had found blood in his room, a statement that was later determined to be untrue. As Michael became increasingly distraught, Claytor said to him:

> We know who did it. What we need to do now is get over the fact that it's been done, and get down to why it was done, and get on with our lives here. Nothing we can do is ever going to change the fact that Stephanie is not with us anymore.[93]

Michael, who was sobbing, continued to insist that he hadn't killed his sister.

Just as in Peter Reilly's case, however, the interrogator gradually convinced Michael that he couldn't trust his own memory:

> CLAYTOR: You need to help us understand what's going on here. You need to help us understand how to help you. Just because a person makes a mistake—just because a person does something bad . . .
>
> CROWE: Oh, God.
>
> CLAYTOR: . . . A, it doesn't mean that the world comes to an end, and B, it doesn't mean that you're a bad person.
>
> CROWE: Why are you doing this to me? I didn't do this to her. I couldn't. God. Why? I can't even believe myself anymore. I don't know if I did it or not. I didn't, though.
>
> CLAYTOR: Well, I think you're on the right track. Let's go ahead and think through this now.
>
> CROWE: I don't think—if I did this, I don't remember it. I don't remember a thing.
>
> CLAYTOR: You know what, that's possible.
>
> CROWE: What's going to happen to me now? Even though I don't even know that I did it. What's going to happen?
>
> CLAYTOR: I'm going to try everything . . . that the system can muster to help you through this. And you know what, it can be done.[94]

Shortly after that, the interrogation, which had lasted about three and one-half hours, ended. Michael was returned to the children's center where he was staying. A social worker there later recalled that he was "emotionally drained, so tired he could barely walk."[95]

The next day, Michael was taken to the police station for another interrogation, one that would last six hours. During this interrogation, Claytor continually referred to the possibility of helping Michael if he confessed. When Michael asked what would happen if the "bad Michael" had taken over and killed Stephanie, Claytor replied, "You're a child. You're 14 years old. Nobody's going to hold you to the same standards that they would some criminal on the street. You're going to need some help through this."[96] But then the detective added, "It's a two-way street. We put out that effort, we need that effort." Later, he was even more explicit. He told Michael there were two paths he could take: he could make the police prove their case, which would lead him to jail; or he could give a detailed confession to the killing, which would lead to him getting "help."[97] Michael stated that he wanted to take the path toward "help," but he couldn't supply the details. In response to questions, he made up details, which he said were lies.

After a thirteen-minute gap during which the interrogation was not recorded, however, Michael's demeanor changed. He became more animated and talked openly about his mounting hostility toward his sister. Although he was still unable to provide details relating to the killing itself, he now said he was "positive" that he had killed Stephanie. When asked about the details, he said, "I can't get into details because I don't remember details . . . just pure rage."[98]

A few days later, the police questioned fourteen-year-old Joshua Treadway after they received a report suggesting that Treadway had taken a knife belonging to his friend Aaron Houser. Based on their investigation, the police believed that the knife, which had the words "Best Defense" on it, might have been used to kill Stephanie. On January 27, Treadway admitted that he stole Houser's knife on January 16, five days before Stephanie's body was discovered. The police then arrested him on a charge of petty theft.

On January 28, police interrogated Treadway from 9:45 P.M. until 8:00 A.M. the next morning. During the interrogation, Detective Claytor pressed him to explain how he received the "Best Defense" knife, intimating that the knife was the murder weapon:

CLAYTOR: If this was the knife that was used, how can you explain it?

TREADWAY: I can't because I didn't do anything with it. It's been under my bed.

CLAYTOR: I know what you're telling me isn't the truth and you know what, Josh? I can prove it.

At this, Treadway went into "fits of crying and hyperventilation."[99]

Claytor then told Treadway again and again that he needed to tell the truth. The youth finally responded that Aaron Houser had given him the knife. Shortly after that, however, Treadway recanted his statement and said he wanted to see his mother. In response, Claytor pointed out the consequences of ending the interrogation:

> If you want to conclude this conversation, we can do that, OK? But now you're no longer faced with the possibility of getting the truth out. Cause what's gonna happen is once I leave here, the only possible conclusion is that you have a knife that was used to kill a 12-year-old girl and it was there in your bedroom, OK? That's what I can prove. Now you stop and think about what else I have to prove after that. Not much.[100]

Treadway, who was crying, then stated again that he had been given the knife. Shortly after that, Claytor met with Treadway's father, who was at the police station, and told him that his son was being set up as a "patsy" by Michael Crowe and Aaron Houser. Treadway's father then exhorted Joshua, "Listen, son. If Aaron gave you the knife and told you to get rid of it, don't hide it."[101] Joshua, however, told his father that that had not happened.

Later, the Treadways agreed that Joshua would take a CVSA test. When Joshua said he stole the knife from Houser, Detective McDonough told him the test showed he was lying. Joshua, who was exhausted, finally changed his story. At 8:00 A.M., he told the detective that Houser had given him the knife on Crowe's instructions and told him to "get rid of it."[102] At that point, McDonough told Joshua he had passed the test and permitted him to go home.

Thirteen days later, Treadway's father took him to the police station for a second interrogation. After some consideration, the police decided that they did not need to read Treadway his *Miranda* rights because they had read the rights to him prior to the previous interrogation.

During this interrogation, which lasted ten hours, Treadway

quickly reiterated that Houser had given him the "Best Defense" knife four days after the killing and told him to get rid of it. He also said that Houser had told him the knife was used to kill Stephanie Crowe. McDonough then asked Treadway whether he was there. Treadway said he was not there himself, but Houser had admitted to him that he was there and that "he helped Michael."[103]

After intimating that Houser and Michael Crowe were making statements that would incriminate him, McDonough pressed Joshua to admit that he had been present at the killing. He asked, "[W]hat if your role was just the lookout? Tell me the truth?" Treadway responded, "Is that what Michael told you?" McDonough reiterated that he was asking for the truth. Treadway repeated that he had not been the lookout. But when McDonough admonished him "to stop denying," he altered his story. He told McDonough that he never entered the house and did not help the others with anything. The interrogation then proceeded as follows:

McDONOUGH: I believe you. Keep going. Tell me what you did.

TREADWAY: I didn't kill anyone.

McDONOUGH: I know. You were waiting outside. Where were you? And I understand, that's hard enough in itself, am I right? . . . Let it out. Let it go. It's going to hurt. You've got to let it go. The more you think about it, Josh, the harder it hurts.

TREADWAY: I know.

McDONOUGH: . . . Where did you stand? Let's start there, OK?

TREADWAY: Outside.

McDONOUGH: OK. Where outside?

TREADWAY: In the driveway.

Treadway then elaborated as to his role in the crime. He stated that he sneaked out of his house around 11:00 P.M., arrived at Houser's house at 11:30 P.M., and he and Houser walked two miles to Crowe's house, arriving there about 12:30 A.M. He also said that Michael Crowe wanted to kill his sister "really bad" because he did not like her. He said that Crowe and Houser would meet during school breaks and plan her killing. Later, he admitted that he did enter the Crowe house that night and saw Michael Crowe wash off the knife in the kitchen sink.[104]

At 7:25 P.M., Treadway was placed under arrest and read his *Miranda* warnings. Over the next two hours, he related the details of the killing again:

> Michael Crowe and Aaron Houser plotted the slaying, and Tread-way reluctantly agreed to go along; they walked to the Crowe house and Michael Crowe let them in; Treadway waited in the kitchen as the other two "went about the business"; Crowe rinsed the knife in the kitchen sink for "six or seven minutes"; Treadway and Houser walked two miles to Houser's house, arriving at "uh . . . 1:30 to 1:40, maybe even 2 o'clock, depending on how fast we walked."[105]

Treadway also responded to a few additional questions. As to his motivation for participating in the killing, he said he was afraid of Houser.

Based on Treadway's statement, Houser was also arrested for murder. Unlike the other two boys, he never confessed to the crime. In response to the detectives' questioning, however, he did provide the police with a hypothetical version of how the three youths might have perpetrated the killing. The police viewed this statement as incriminating because they believed it contained details that matched some of the physical evidence relating to the crime.[106]

Based on the murder charges, Crowe, Treadway, and Houser were each incarcerated for approximately seven months.[107] During a month-long hearing in July and August 1998, their cases were considered by Superior Court Judge Laura Palmer Hammes for the purpose of determining whether they should be tried as adults. For the prosecution, the interrogating detectives testified as to how they obtained the confessions and what the boys had said. Videotapes of the confessions were also played and physical evidence that seemed to corroborate them was introduced. For the defense, Richard Ofshe testified about coerced confessions, explaining why the interrogation methods employed could lead to false confessions.[108] Relatives of Houser and Treadway provided alibis for both boys on the night of the slaying. The defense also presented evidence relating to Tuite's activities on the night in question. Although Judge Palmer found the youths' confessions "troublesome," she nevertheless concluded that the evidence was sufficient to show "strong suspicion" that the teens were involved in the killing; accordingly, she bound them for trial in adult court.[109]

The case was assigned for trial to Superior Court Judge John M. Thompson, who had the reputation for giving everyone a fair shot. The defendants filed a motion to suppress all three boys' statements. After a three-week hearing, Judge Thompson issued the following ruling: he excluded Michael Crowe's confession on the ground that Claytor's statements to the effect that Crowe would get "help" if he confessed but would go to jail if he did not rendered the confession involuntary;* he excluded Aaron Houser's statement on the ground that the detectives had not adequately advised Houser of his *Miranda* rights; as to Treadway, he excluded the statements obtained during the overnight January 27–28 interrogation as coercive, finding that the detectives had denied the boy sleep and food for several hours, excluded the first eight hours of the second interrogation on the ground that the police failed to rewarn Treadway of his *Miranda* rights, but ruled that Treadway's statements during the final two hours of the interrogation, in which he repeated how the killing was planned and executed, were admissible because Treadway was warned of his *Miranda* rights before making those statements.†

After Judge Thompson's ruling, the prosecution's position was weakened, but not destroyed. Prosecuting Crowe and Houser without their statements would probably be impossible. The government could prosecute Treadway on the basis of his final statement, however; and, if Treadway were convicted, the government might then be able to induce him to testify against Crowe and Houser in exchange for a promise of leniency.[110]

---

*In Judge Thompson's view, Claytor's threat that Crowe would go to jail (if the police were required to prove the case) combined with his promise that Crowe would receive "help" if he confessed exerted coercive pressure on the fourteen-year-old suspect. Based on the due process voluntariness test, Judge Thompson's conclusion was proper, but by no means inevitable. In other post-*Miranda* cases, courts have held that suspects' confessions are voluntary despite the fact that they were given in response to an interrogator's promise that he would receive "help" or treatment if he confessed. *See, e.g.,* Miller v. Fenton, 796 F.2d 598 (3d Cir. 1986) (holding suspect's confession voluntary despite the fact that it was given after the detective repeatedly told the suspect that he was not a criminal and he would see to it that he received "help" with his problem if he confessed).

†The fact that Treadway's later statement seemed to be derived from his earlier inadmissible statement would not be sufficient to render the later statement inadmissible. Under *Oregon v. Elstad,* 470 U.S. 298 (1985), the fact that a defendant's earlier statement is obtained in violation of *Miranda* will not preclude the admission of the defendant's later statement so long as the later statement is voluntary and the defendant waived his *Miranda* rights before giving it.

Trial was set for January 13, 1999. On that date, 250 people were summoned to fill out questionnaires the attorneys would use in connection with selecting the jury. One of the questions asked potential jurors whether they thought it was possible for someone to confess to a crime he did not commit. Treadway's attorney, Ellen Attridge, was disheartened when she saw the potential jurors' response: "No way, juror after juror wrote."[111]

In fact, however, Treadway's case was never presented to a jury. Ed Blake, a respected expert in DNA evidence, had been hired jointly by the defense and prosecution to test the clothing of Raymond Tuite, the transient who had been seen in the Crowe neighborhood on the night Stephanie was killed. Shortly after the trial began, Blake's tests produced definitive results: "Three areas of Tuite's red turtleneck sweat shirt indicated the presence of Stephanie Crowe's blood."[112] As a result, Judge Thompson halted Treadway's trial, allowing the prosecution an opportunity to investigate and explain the blood on Tuite's shirt. Unable to explain, the prosecutors dismissed the case against Michael Crowe, Joshua Treadway, and Aaron Houser on February 25. In doing so, however, they did not acknowledge the defendants' innocence. While admitting for the first time that Tuite might have killed Stephanie, they stated that they needed more time to investigate and reserved the right to try Crowe, Treadway, and Houser again.[113] To date, the prosecution has not charged anyone with Stephanie Crowe's murder.

Conclusions to Be Drawn from the Cases

Each of these cases presents situations in which interrogation techniques typical of those employed by police in high-profile cases produced probably false confessions from typical criminal suspects. If it is accepted that police-induced false confessions occur in an unacceptably high number of serious cases,[114] examination of these cases should provide insight into the dynamics that produce such confessions. Moreover, there is no reason to believe that the criminal justice system's decision makers, including police, prosecutors, and jurors, reacted differently in these cases than they would in other serious high-profile cases involving probably false confessions. Analysis of these cases, therefore, illuminates not only the circumstances under which police-induced false confessions are likely to occur but also the ways in which critical decision-makers within the system are likely to react to them.

Suspects Who Give Police-Induced False Confessions

Since the cases presented were selected partly to illustrate the range of suspects who falsely confess in response to standard interrogation techniques, the background of the seven suspects who falsely confessed—one mentally retarded, three teenagers, and three apparently normal adults—does not provide any indication as to the frequency with which suspects with these backgrounds would be likely to give police-induced false confessions. The circumstances under which the various suspects confessed, however, may provide insight into the dynamics that are likely to precipitate false confessions from suspects of different backgrounds. And the fact that suspects from such a wide variety of backgrounds confessed provides insight into the power of interrogation techniques employed by the police.

In contrast to the other suspects, Melvin Reynolds, the only one of the seven who was mentally handicapped, evidenced an immediate willingness to confess. During his first interrogation, he indicated that he would confess to killing the victim if the interrogating officer wanted him to. This response illustrates what is known as the "cheating to lose" syndrome. More than thirty years ago, the President's Panel on Mental Retardation explained that mentally retarded suspects are often so eager to "please authority" that, if they believe a confession will please an authority figure, they will gladly confess, without evaluating the consequences of that decision in the way that a normal person would.[115] Although Reynolds's final confession was not obtained until he had been subjected to several lengthy interrogations, his eagerness to provide a confession if it would please the interrogator indicates that even relatively benign interrogation methods can easily produce false confessions from mentally handicapped suspects, a conclusion that suggests that suspects from this population will be most inclined to confess falsely in response to police questioning.

The interrogations of the three teenagers—Reilly, Crowe and Treadway—suggest that suspects from this population may also be especially vulnerable to certain interrogation techniques, especially those that are designed to convince the suspect that there is no doubt as to his guilt. When confronted with false evidence that they had failed a lie detector test, the responses of Reilly and Crowe were strikingly similar. Reilly almost immediately said that the reported test results were making him "doubt" his innocence; and Crowe soon expressed a similar view, stating, "I've truly lost everything if I can't even believe myself." In both cases, the youths thus seemed extraordinarily susceptible to the interrogator's suggestions. When the interrogator forcefully expressed his view of the relevant events—stating, "I know you did it," in Reilly's case, for example—the youthful suspects were apparently willing to distrust their own memories of what happened and, at least temporarily, to accept the interrogator's view of reality.

It is not clear, of course, that either Reilly or Crowe ever really believed that they were guilty of the crime to which they confessed. Both youths were traumatized by the experience of being suspected of killing a beloved family member. Under these circumstances, they may have felt so overwhelmed by the interrogator's suggestions that they felt it was in their interest to confess: Reilly, so as to gain the interrogator's acceptance;[116] and Crowe so that he could receive "help" from the system rather than be treated as a criminal.

In the case of Joshua Treadway, moreover, it seems clear that the fourteen-year-old suspect never seriously believed that he had been involved in the crime to which he confessed. As with Crowe and Reilly, however, the interrogator's repeated assertions that evidence established Treadway's involvement seemed to overwhelm the youthful suspect, forcing him first to acquiesce in his interrogator's view of the events and then to elaborate on those events, making incriminating statements that he knew were untrue.

These three cases thus suggest that youthful suspects may be especially vulnerable to the powerful influences exerted by one of the most well established interrogation techniques. When interrogators forcefully suggest to suspects that there is no doubt as to their guilt and that some advantage—either tangible or psychological—may result from them admitting their guilt, there is a significant danger that youthful suspects—whether guilty or innocent—will yield to the interrogator's suggestion and admit their guilt.

Standard interrogation techniques will also precipitate false confessions from suspects who do not appear to be especially vulnerable. Bruce, Nunez, and Parker all appeared to be mature adults who would have at least normal capacity to resist the pressures exerted by standard interrogation practices. In some respects, of course, the interrogation practices employed in these cases were excessive. In Bruce's case, the length and time of the questioning—thirteen hours of intermittent questioning beginning after 11:00 P.M.—would, arguably, exert overwhelming pressure on any normal suspect. And in Parker's case, some of the interrogators' implicit threats—especially their threat to involve Parker's brothers if Parker did not confess—appeared coercive and improper. In practice, however, the techniques employed were not aberrational.

According to Parloff, "None of the techniques used against the [three suspects] were outrageous enough to give their lawyers much hope of suppressing their statements."[117] On the contrary, all of the techniques employed were at least derived from techniques "specifically recommended by standard interrogation handbooks."[118] The police-induced false confessions precipitated in these cases thus suggest that, at least when interrogators employ the recommended techniques with the type of zeal that might be expected in serious high-profile cases, the interrogation techniques will exert sufficient pressure to produce false confessions from normal suspects.

The Interrogation Tactics That Produced the Confessions

In each of the seven cases, the suspect's false confession was precipitated by myriad factors, including the interrogators' techniques, the suspect's psychological makeup, and the overall dynamics of the interrogation. Identifying the specific interrogation tactics that produced the confessions in these cases is thus impossible. Nevertheless, a close examination of these interrogations reveals interrogation tactics that clearly played an important role in producing the suspects' false confessions and, therefore, appear to have the potential for producing false or untrustworthy confessions in other situations.

First, the tactic of revealing to the suspect that the evidence clearly establishes his guilt sometimes seems to have a surprisingly powerful effect. As I have already mentioned, interrogators' assertions suggesting that lie detector results established the suspects' guilt played a significant role in precipitating false confessions from Reilly and Crowe. Similarly, in Treadway's case, the interrogator's suggestion that forensic evidence established the suspect's participation in the crime—through intimating that a knife in his possession was the murder weapon—seemed to prompt the youthful suspect's shift in his story, leading to his eventual acknowledgment of his participation. Even with more mature suspects, moreover, this tactic may have considerable efficacy. In dealing with Leo Bruce the interrogators' act of showing Bruce a room full of evidence—thereby intimating they had a strong case against him—may have played a part in weakening the suspect's resistance. Based on these interrogations, telling a suspect that his guilt has been established by convincing evidence—especially forensic or scientific evidence—has considerable potential for producing false confessions.

These interrogations also indicate that in some instances interrogators are very adept at exploiting suspects' perception that they are caught in a "prisoner's dilemma,"[119] leading each suspect to believe that, in order to counter stories told (or likely to be told) by other suspects, it is in his best interest to make a statement—even a false statement—about the events in question. In questioning Joshua Treadway, for example, interrogators emphasized to Treadway and his parents that Crowe and Houser were trying to make Joshua a "patsy," thus exerting pressure on Treadway to tell a story that would implicate his two friends. Similarly, when questioning suspects in connection with the Buddhist temple murders, interrogators were able to intimate to each suspect that others had already given stories implicating him, and to emphasize that his best means of countering these stories was to tell his own version of what happened. The interrogators' highly effective use of this tactic indicates that, when two or more suspects are involved, the tactic may have the effect of inducing innocent suspects to falsely admit to some culpability in order to limit the extent to which they will be unfairly blamed by others.

And, finally, interrogators' threats seemed to directly precipitate at least two of the confessions and to play a part in producing some of the others. Detective Claytor told Michael Crowe he could take one of two paths: make the police prove their case, which would lead toward jail, or confess to the crime which would lead toward him receiving "help"; Michael made it clear that he was confessing because he wanted to take the path toward "help." Similarly, interrogators intimated to Dante Parker that his brothers would be arrested if he did not admit his involvement. Parker's first incriminating admission followed almost immediately, suggesting that this threat was the triggering cause. In nearly all of the other cases, moreover, interrogators provided some inducement to the suspect to confess. To Melvin Reynolds, the inducement was that he would not be questioned again. Leo Bruce was told that if he continued denying his guilt he was going to end up being "sorry." And Joshua Treadway was told that it would be to his advantage to get the "truth out." The tactic of threatening the suspect with harmful consequence if he does not confess thus played a significant part in producing false confessions.

Classifying False Confessions

The accounts of these cases also illuminate the difficulties in determining when a police-induced confession should be classified as false. Cassell has suggested that, at least when dealing with police-induced confessions that result in convictions, a suspect's confession should not be viewed as indisputably false unless "there was a clear determination of [the suspect's] innocence, preferably from the prosecuting authority that originally charged the [suspect]."[120] The stories of these cases show why this is an inappropriate standard. Of the seven cases considered, four were prosecuted; the prosecution obtained convictions against two of those four suspects and dismissed charges against the other two. Based on Cassell's standard, however, only one of the four charged suspects' confessions would be classified as "indisputably false"; in Melvin Reynolds's case, the prosecutor reluctantly admitted that Charles Hatcher's subsequent confession to Eric Christogen's murder was factually accurate, thus implicitly admitting that Reynolds's prior confession was false. Despite the disclosure of exculpatory evidence that seemed to establish Peter Reilly's innocence, the law enforcement personnel involved in Reilly's prosecution have never admitted that Reilly was innocent; to the contrary, police officers involved in the case maintain their belief in his guilt. And in the cases of Michael Crowe and Joshua Treadway, the presence of DNA evidence pointing to the guilt of another suspect was not sufficient to convince the prosecutors of the suspects' innocence. Although the charges against these suspects were dropped, the prosecutor reserved the right to file new charges.

Indeed, the stories of these cases indicate that when charges are brought against a suspect who confesses, law enforcement personnel involved in the decision to bring charges are inordinately resistant to altering their belief in the truth of the suspect's confession. Even in Melvin Reynolds's case, where Cassell's criteria for establishing a false confession was eventually met, the prosecutor was extraordinarily unwilling to believe that Reynolds's confession was false. Once a prosecutor has committed to prosecuting a suspect, political considerations dictate that the prosecutor will be reluctant to admit that he made a mistake. When the charges are brought on the basis of a suspect's confession, moreover, the prosecutor may be especially unwilling to admit error because his admission that a charging mistake was made will inevitably reflect adversely on the police involved in obtaining the suspect's confession and evaluating its truthfulness. Finally, like most lay people, law enforcement personnel may genuinely believe that a suspect subjected to standard interrogation techniques would not confess unless he were in fact guilty. For these reasons, law enforcement personnel involved in prosecuting suspects on the basis of their confessions cannot be expected to make objective determinations as to whether the suspects' confessions are false.

Although no group's judgment as to whether a confession is false will be totally free from bias, opinions of scholars, such as social psychologists or criminologists, who have studied police-induced false confessions should be preferred over the opinions of prosecutors involved in the prosecution of the suspects who confessed. The scholars are able to make a comprehensive evaluation of all the evidence relating to the suspect's guilt, including evidence that was not presented at trial. Since they are trained in detecting false confessions, moreover, the scholars are able to evaluate the truthfulness of particular confessions through drawing on a body of knowledge that is not available to the general public.[121] And, most importantly, in contrast to the prosecutors whose decision to prosecute a suspect on the basis of a police-induced confession gives them an obvious incentive for maintaining that the suspect's confession was true, scholars who evaluate the truthfulness of suspects' confessions do not have a stake in determining that any particular confession is either true or false.

The Relationship between False Confessions and Wrongful Convictions

The stories of these cases indicate that as soon as a police-induced false confession is accepted as true by the police, the risk that the false confession will lead to a wrongful conviction is substantial. Four of the seven cases tend to confirm research indicating that a defendant's confession is the most persuasive type of evidence.[122] The *Reynolds* and *Reilly* cases provide direct evidence and the *Crowe* and *Treadway* cases indirect evidence that jurors are likely to convict defendants on the basis of their confessions even if the other evidence against them is weak or nonexistent. In *Reynolds* and *Reilly*, jurors actually convicted on the basis of such evidence. In *Crowe* and *Treadway*, the pool of eligible jurors expressed the belief that a person will not confess to a crime he did not commit, a view that has been echoed by at least one group of jurors who convicted a suspect on the basis of an allegedly false confession.[123] Moreover, even a judge who viewed the Crowe and Treadway confessions as "troublesome" after hearing testimony that cast doubt on the confessions' reliability, nevertheless concluded that the confessions were sufficient to establish "strong suspicion" that the youths were involved in the killing. In the five cases that were not presented to a jury, it thus appears that the likelihood of the suspects' convictions would have been high if exculpating evidence had not come to light.

Indeed, the principal difference between the five cases in which suspects were not convicted on the basis of their confessions and the two in which they were was the timing of the discovery of the exculpatory evidence; in the former cases, but not the latter, evidence sufficient to cast doubt on the suspect's guilt turned up before the cases were presented to a jury. In all of the five former cases, moreover, the timing of the exculpatory evidence's discovery, if not its actual discovery, was adventitious. In the cases of Bruce, Parker, and Nunez, there was no reason to believe either that the murder weapon would be found prior to trial or that its discovery would almost immediately precipitate a confession exonerating the suspects who had previously confessed. And in the cases of Crowe and Treadway, there was no reason to expect that exculpatory DNA evidence would come to light at all, much less that it would be discovered before the suspects' cases were presented to the jury.

Based on the accounts of these cases, there is thus no reason for drawing a sharp distinction between police-induced false confessions and wrongful convictions resulting from such confessions. So long as the police-induced false confessions are accepted as true by the police and prosecutor, whether they will lead to wrongful convictions seems more likely to depend on adventitious factors relating to the discovery of other evidence than the intrinsic trustworthiness of the confessions. Thus, even if the prime concern is preventing wrongful convictions resulting from police-induced false confessions, the focus should be on preventing police-induced false confessions that are likely to be accepted as true by the police and prosecutors.

Conclusion

The value of presenting detailed accounts of cases involving police-induced false confessions is that it provides an opportunity for a close analysis of the dynamics involved in such cases, showing not only the context within which police-induced false confessions have occurred but also the ways in which decision makers within the system have responded to them. The case histories, moreover, provide support in a microcosm for conclusions reached by studies that have examined police-induced false confessions from a broader perspective. Most significantly, it appears that interrogation methods likely to be employed by police in serious high-profile cases have the potential for producing false confessions in a range of situations and that the criminal justice system's most important decision makers, including police, prosecutors, judges, and jurors, are far too likely to accept these confessions as true.

NOTES

1. Interrogation transcripts relating to all of the cases recounted in this chapter except the cases of Melvin Reynolds and Mark Nunez are on file with Professor Richard Leo.

2. A similar account of the *Reilly* case is contained in Welsh S. White, *False Confessions, supra* chapter 1, note 40, at 125–27.

3. DONALD S. CONNERY, GUILTY UNTIL PROVEN INNOCENT 20, 32 (1977) (hereinafter CONNERY, GUILTY).

4. *Id.* at 21, 252.

5. *See* GUDJONSSON, PSYCHOLOGY, *supra* chapter 3, note 3.

6. *See* CONNERY, GUILTY, *supra* note 3, at 21.

7. *See id.* at 63; JOAN BARTHEL, A DEATH IN CANAAN 54 (1977) (hereinafter BARTHEL, A DEATH).

8. BARTHEL, A DEATH, *supra* note 7, at 54.

9. *Id.* at 59.

10. *See id.* at 69–70, 71.

11. *Id.* at 74.

12. *Id.*

13. *See id.*

14. *See, e.g., id.* at 71, 91.

15. *Id.* at 91.

16. *Id.*

17. *Id.*

18. CONNERY, GUILTY, *supra* note 3, at 75.

19. *See* BARTHEL, A DEATH, *supra* note 7, at 107.

20. CONNERY, GUILTY, *supra* note 3, at 133.

21. *Id.* at 223.

22. *Id.* at 211.

23. *Id.* at 239.

24. *Id.* at 267.

25. *Id.* at 326.

26. *Id.* at 335.

27. For a detailed explanation of the evidence's significance, see *id.* at 339–41.

28. See Joseph A. O'Brien, *Mother's Killing Still Unsolved, but Peter Reilly Puts Past Behind*, HARTFORD COURANT, Sept. 23, 1993, at A1.

29. A full account of the *Reynolds* case is contained in TERRY GANEY, ST. JOSEPH'S CHILDREN: A TRUE STORY OF TERROR AND JUSTICE (1989) (hereinafter GANEY, ST. JOSEPH'S CHILDREN).

30. GANEY, ST. JOSEPH'S CHILDREN, *supra* note 29, at 33–34. A later test showed that Reynolds's IQ was 76, indicating that he was mildly mentally retarded. *Id.* at 52.

31. *Id.* at 34.

32. *Id.* at 32.

33. *Id.* at 35.

34. *Id.* at 37.

35. *Id.* at 38.

36. *Id.* at 39.

37. *Id.*

38. *Id.* at 40.

39. *Id.*

40. *Id.*

41. *Id.* at 41.

42. *Id.* at 66.

43. *Id.*

44. *Id.* at 69.

45. *Id.* at 165–67.

46. *Id.* at 171.

47. *Id.* at 166.

48. *Id.* at 15. Hatcher also closely matched a profile of Eric's abductor constructed by the FBI.

49. *Id.* at 166–67. Hatcher's confes-

sion laid out a detailed narrative of the murder. He correctly described the boy's clothing, including his underwear, and accurately described where the murder occurred and how he reached that location, including the trouble he had walking up the hill.

50. *Id.* at 168, 179–84.

51. *Id.*

52. *Id.* at 179.

53. *Id.* at 183.

54. *Id.* at 184.

55. *Id.* at 188–89.

56. *Id.* at 199.

57. *Id.* at 203.

58. A similar account of the *Bruce* case is contained in Welsh S. White, *False Confessions, supra* chapter 1, note 40, at 129–31.

59. *See* Roger Parloff, *False Confessions,* Am. Law., May 1993, at 58 (hereinafter Parloff, *False Confessions*).

60. Like the others, Zarate was subjected to a lengthy interrogation. *See* Parloff, *False Confessions, supra* note 59, at 59.

61. *Id.*

62. *See id.*

63. *See id.*

64. *Id.*

65. *Id.* at 60.

66. *Id.*

67. *Id.*

68. *Id.*

69. *Id.*

70. *Id.* at 58.

71. According to Parloff, Parker's initial admission of guilt may have occurred in as little as four and a half hours. *Id.* at 60. Although no transcript of Nunez's interrogation is available, Richard A. Leo, who has studied the Buddhist temple

cases, concluded that Nunez's confession was obtained even more quickly than Parker's. Telephone interview with Richard A. Leo on July 16, 1999.

72. Parloff, *False Confessions, supra* note 59, at 60.

73. Ofshe & Leo, *Social Psychology, supra* chapter 11, note 8, at 226.

74. *Id.* at 227.

75. *Id.*

76. *Id.* at 228.

77. *Id.*

78. *Id.* at 229–30.

79. *Id.* at 230.

80. Parloff, *False Confessions, supra* note 59, at 61.

81. *Id.*

82. *Id.*

83. *Id.* at 58.

84. My account of the *Crowe* and *Treadway* cases is drawn primarily from Mark Sauer & John Wilkens, *Haunting Questions,* San Diego Union-Trib., May 11–16, 1999.

85. Mark Sauer & John Wilkens, *Haunting Questions; Part 1: The Night She Was Killed,* San Diego Union-Trib., May 11, 1999, at A1.

86. *Id.*

87. *Id.* Stephanie's room was directly across the hall from Michael's. Her body was found lying on its side with her head just outside the doorway. But her doorway was in an alcove about two feet from the hall. Michael had to walk past her room in order to get to the kitchen for an aspirin.

88. The CVSA test is designed to detect lying through analysis of human voice vibrations. See John Wilkens & Mark Sauer, *The*

Arrest, SAN DIEGO UNION-TRIB., May 12, 1999, at A1.

89. *Id.*
90. *Id.*
91. *Id.*
92. *Id.*
93. *Id.*
94. *Id.*
95. *Id.*
96. *Id.*
97. *Id.*
98. *Id.*
99. Mark Sauer & John Wilkens, *The Knife,* SAN DIEGO UNION-TRIB., May 13, 1999, at A1.
100. *Id.*
101. *Id.*
102. *Id.*
103. John Wilkens & Mark Sauer, *More Arrests,* SAN DIEGO UNION-TRIB., May 14, 1999, at A1.
104. *Id.*
105. *Id.*
106. *Id.* Houser's hypothetical was as follows: "I would grab her from the arm, place it behind her back. I would stand behind her, cover her mouth. I would take out the knife. Then I would cut her throat." Stephanie Crowe's autopsy revealed no evidence that her mouth had been covered or that her throat was cut in that way; nevertheless, the police believed the statement was incriminating because Stephanie's lethal wounds were on her back, chest and throat. *Id.*
107. John Wilkens & Mark Sauer, *In Court,* SAN DIEGO UNION-TRIB., May 15, 1999, at A1 (hereinafter Wilkens & Sauer, *In Court*).
108. Telephone interview with Richard Leo on June 26, 1999.
109. Wilkens & Sauer, *In Court, supra* note 107.
110. John Wilkens & Mark Sauer, *The*

Bombshell, SAN DIEGO UNION-TRIB., May 16, 1999, at A1.

111. *Id.*
112. *Id.*
113. *Id.*
114. See *supra* chapter 11.
115. President's Panel on Mental Retardation, *Report of the Task Force on Law* 33 (1963).
116. See note 1.
117. Parloff, *False Confessions, supra* note 59, at 58.
118. *Id.*
119. For a definition and explanation of the "prisoner's dilemma," see CHARLES J. GOETZ, LAW AND ECONOMICS: CASES AND MATERIALS 15–18 (1984).
120. Cassell, *The Guilty, supra* chapter 11, note 50, at 581.
121. *Cf.* United States v. Hall, 93 F.3d 1337, 1345 (7th Cir. 1996) (observing that expert testimony as to confession's trustworthiness might assist the jury: "Even though the jury may have had beliefs about the subject," expert testimony based on "[p]roperly conducted social science research often shows that commonly held beliefs are in error").
122. See Leo & Ofshe, *Missing the Forest for the Trees: A Response to Paul Cassell's "Balanced Approach" to the False Confession Problem,* 74 DENV. U. L. REV. 1135, 1142 (1997). LAWRENCE S. WRIGHTSMAN & SAUL M. KASSIN, CONFESSION IN THE COURTROOM 1–2 (1993).
123. See White, *False Confessions, supra* chapter 1, note 40, at 105 (referring to statements made by jurors who convicted Richard LaPointe of murder and rape).

CHAPTER 13

Providing Adequate Fact-Finding in Interrogation Cases

As many commentators have pointed out,[1] imposing some kind of a requirement that the police electronically record interrogations is the most readily available means for improving fact-finding in police interrogation cases. In this chapter, I will consider whether there is a constitutional basis for imposing an electronic recording requirement and, if so, what form such a requirement might take.

Dickerson, of course, does reaffirm the Court's authority to adopt prophylactic constitutional rules for the purpose of providing adequate Fifth Amendment protection. As Kamisar has shown,[2] moreover, even before *Miranda,* the Court adopted a prophylactic constitutional rule that was designed to enhance accurate fact-finding in confession cases. In *Jackson v. Denno,*[3] the Court invalidated the New York procedure—which allowed the jury determining the defendant's guilt or innocence to determine the voluntariness of his confession—on the ground that it "did not afford a reliable determination" of the confession's voluntariness.[4]

In concluding that the New York procedure did not meet the requisite standard of reliability, the Court based its analysis on assumptions relating to jurors' ability to evaluate evidence. It concluded that because the jury might "find it difficult to understand the policy forbidding reliance upon a coerced, but true confession,"[5] the jury's belief that the defendant's confession was true would skew their determination of the confession's voluntariness,[6] rendering that conclusion too unreliable to satisfy the Constitution.

In reaching this result, the Court emphasized that the evolving nature of the due process voluntariness test magnified the difficulties in determining a confession's voluntariness. It pointed out that "facts are frequently disputed, questions of credibility are often crucial, and inferences to be drawn from established facts are often determinative."[7] Because of the sensitive judgments involved, it concluded that determining the voluntariness of a confession "requires facing the issue squarely, in illuminating isolation and unclouded by other issues."[8] Under the New York procedure, the jury would not be able to face the voluntariness issue squarely because of its overriding concern with adjudicating the defendant's guilt or innocence. The judge or a different jury would thus be required to determine the confession's voluntariness.[9] Imposing this requirement would also facilitate appellate review because it would provide a clear-cut determination relating to the critical issue.[10]

As Kamisar has pointed out, *Jackson* did not say that the New York procedure would always or even more often than not deprive defendants of a "fair and clear-cut determination that the confession used against him was in fact voluntary."[11] Indeed, as Justice Black noted in dissent,[12] the majority provided no empirical data supporting its assumptions concerning jurors' difficulty in determining confessions' voluntariness. The majority simply concluded that the New York procedure "pose[d] substantial threats to a defendant's constitutional right to have an involuntary confession entirely disregarded and to have the coercion issue fairly and reliably determined."[13] In view of the alternative of having a judge determine the confession's voluntariness prior to trial, the Court held that the New York procedure did not meet the constitutional standard of reliability.

Jackson's analysis provides a basis for arguing that when a more reliable alternative is available, a procedure under which judges are permitted to determine a confession's voluntariness through examining uncorroborated police testimony results in voluntariness determinations that fail to meet the constitutional standard of reliability. As the material presented in chapter 10 demonstrates, there are certainly some interrogation cases in which judges find it difficult to assess the credibility of police testimony accurately. As under the New York procedure that the Court invalidated in *Jackson*, there thus appear to be factors that will sometimes distort a judge's assessment of the critical testimony relating to the circumstances of a suspect's interrogation.

As Justice Black intimated in his *Jackson* dissent,[14] judges will not necessarily be superior to juries in assessing the credibility of police testimony at suppression-of-confession hearings. Even though judges are considering the admissibility of a defendant's confession prior to trial, they will be keenly aware that excluding the confession will be extremely damaging to the government's case, perhaps resulting in the acquittal of a suspect who has given a seemingly trustworthy confession. Judges may be even more reluctant than jurors, moreover, to have their ruling on the voluntariness of a confession result in the acquittal of an apparently guilty defendant.

While empirical data relating to judges' or juries' assessment of credibility in suppression of confession cases is lacking, it is generally believed that at least in cases involving the classic "swearing" contest, where the confession's admissibility depends on whether the judge believes the police or the suspect's testimony, judges invariably believe the police.[15] The material presented in chapter 10 provides strong evidence, however, that these credibility determinations are frequently incorrect. Imposing an electronic recording requirement would thus enhance the reliability of voluntariness determinations through eliminating the sizable proportion of incorrect determinations that occur as a result of judges' distorted and erroneous assessments of police credibility.

Even when there is no credibility conflict, moreover, an electronic recording requirement would enhance the reliability of voluntariness determinations by providing a fuller record of the facts relevant to the voluntariness determination. In *Jackson*, the Court emphasized that the voluntariness determination involves complex judgments including "inferences to be drawn from established facts."[16] In determining whether confessions produced by current interrogation practices are involuntary, it is essential to have a full record of the relevant facts so that the judge will be in a position to draw the appropriate inferences from those facts and an appellate court will have a record that will allow review of the judge's findings.

Even if the focus is solely on whether the interrogators exerted coercive pressure on the suspect, electronically recording the interrogation will provide a record that will be indispensable to assessing the nature of the pressure exerted. Videotaping an interrogation allows the courts to take into account the way in which the interrogator conducts himself—including the loudness of his voice, the persistence of his questioning, his physical proximity to the suspect, the suspect's reactions to the interrogator—including signs of fear, resignation, or weariness, as well as other factors relating to "police overbearing that might not be revealed in dry testimony."[17]

When a confession is challenged on the ground that it was produced by interrogation practices likely to produce an untrustworthy confession, having a complete record of the facts so that a judge can assess the interrogation techniques' effect on the suspect is particularly critical. As the interrogations recounted in chapter 12 indicate, it is certainly easier to gauge the pressures generated by interrogation techniques when there is a record that provides not only a full account of the techniques employed but also the way in which the suspect responded to each technique.

To take just two examples: in Dante Parker's case, a judge would obviously be in a better position to determine whether the interrogators' statements relating to Parker's brothers T.C. and Peter constituted the kind of threat that is likely to induce a false confession if she were in a position to "parse the implicit promises and threats"[18] contained in the officers' statements rather than merely relying on their testimony as to the inducements used to produce the confession. Similarly, in Michael Crowe's case, the interrogator's testimony concerning the circumstances of Michael's two interrogations would probably be unlikely to lead a fact-finder to believe that the interrogation techniques described would be likely to produce a false confession; on the other hand, a videotape of the interrogation, showing the full range of the interrogation techniques employed, as well as the sobbing and distraught fourteen-year-old's reaction to them, would lead most people to conclude that Michael's statement was designed to please his interrogator rather than to reflect his own view of the salient events.

The issue in *Jackson* differs from the mandatory electronic recording issue in that the former issue deals with identifying the constitutionally required fact-finder in confession cases and the latter with mandating the quality of evidence that should be produced to decide such cases. As to both issues, however, the ultimate focus should be on whether, given the availability of a viable alternative, the fact-finding mechanism at issue—in this case, the traditional procedure under which the judge is permitted to determine the constitutional admissibility of a confession on the basis of police testimony, without the aid of recording or other corroborative evidence—poses such "substantial threats to a defendant's constitutional right to have . . . the coercion issue fairly and reliably determined" as to render the mechanism unconstitutional. Given the vastly improved fact-finding likely to be produced by some form of electronic recording requirement, there is thus a strong argument in favor of constitutionally mandating such a requirement.

If this argument is accepted, what form should the electronic recording requirement take? Under the traditional procedure, where judges make the voluntariness determinations without the aid of electronic recording, the risk that the judge's determination will be unreliable is most apparent in cases where there is a conflict between uncorroborated police testimony and the suspect's testimony or where there is a lengthy interrogation in which the police employ a range of interrogation techniques. As a first step, therefore, the Court could hold that whatever electronic recording requirement is adopted should be applicable only to these types of cases.

This approach, however, would lead to unnecessary administrative difficulties. In practice, it would be very difficult to determine when the issues presented in an interrogation case would lead to the danger of unreliable voluntariness determinations. Just as *Jackson* invalidated the New York procedure in all cases, opting for a procedure that would generally result in more reliable voluntariness determinations, the electronic recording requirement should also be generally applicable. In deciding whether such recording is required, a court should not stop to consider whether such recording would *actually* be necessary to allow a factfinder to make a reliable determination of a particular confession's voluntariness.

Since electronically recording interrogations is not always feasible, however, there should be some exceptions to the recording requirement. In defining the boundaries of permissible exceptions, the decision in *Stephan v. State*[19] is instructive. In *Stephan*, the Alaska Supreme Court held that, in the absence of an excuse, the police failure to electronically record a "custodial interrogation conducted at the place of detention" violates the due process clause of the Alaska state constitution.[20] As examples of acceptable excuses, the court mentioned "an unavoidable power or equipment failure, or a situation where the suspect refused to answer any questions if the conversation is being recorded."[21] Based on the rule adopted, mandatory recording would also not be required if the interrogation did not occur at the "place of detention." Although the court did not clearly define this term, it probably meant to exempt interrogations occurring outside the police station—an interrogation conducted on the street, for example, or in an officer's automobile. The court added, moreover, that additional exceptions could be established if the government were able to prove "by a preponderance of the evidence, that recording was not feasible under the circumstances."[22]

Prior to *Dickerson*, Cassell proposed that the Court replace *Miranda*'s safeguards with alternative safeguards that would include a requirement that the police electronically record interrogations.[23] The *Miranda* safeguards and an electronic recording requirement serve different purposes, however; whereas the former are intended to assure that the suspect's awareness of his constitutional rights provides him with protection from being compelled to incriminate himself, the latter is designed to enhance the accuracy of the judge's fact-finding and legal determinations in confession cases. The former safeguards thus help to define the substance of interrogated suspects' protection from abusive or overreaching interrogation practices and the latter to provide a procedural mechanism through which interrogated suspects' substantive protections can be effectively enforced. There is, therefore, no reason why any of the *Miranda* safeguards should be replaced by an electronic recording requirement. On the contrary, an electronic recording requirement should be adopted so that the protections afforded by substantive protections (including those provided by *Miranda*) will be effective.

NOTES

1. *See, e.g.,* Cassell, *Miranda's Social Costs, supra* chapter 1, note 26, at 486–89. *See generally* KAMISAR, ESSAYS, *supra* chapter 1, note 24, at 135 (advocating "recording" of interrogations and recounting similar proposals made by other commentators, including the American Law Institute and the National Conference of Commissioners on Uniform State Laws).
2. Yale Kamisar, *Can (Did) Congress "Overrule" Miranda?* 85 CORNELL L. REV. 883, 946 (2000) (hereinafter Kamisar, *Congress*).
3. 378 U.S. 368 (1964).
4. 378 U.S. at 377.
5. *Id.* at 382.
6. *Id.* at 381. As an alternative ground for its holding, it added that, even if the jury found the defendant's confession involuntary, there was an unacceptable risk that the jury would consider the confession in determining the defendant's guilt. *Id.* at 388–89.
7. *Id.* at 390.
8. *Id.*
9. *Id.* at 395.
10. *Id.* at 391.
11. Kamisar, *Congress, supra* note 2, at 947.
12. 378 U.S. at 403 (dissenting opinion of Black, J.).
13. *Id.* at 389.
14. 378 U.S. at 401 (1964) (dissenting opinion of Black, J.).
15. See Anthony G. Amsterdam, *The Supreme Court and the Rights of Suspects in Criminal Cases,* 45 N.Y.U. L. REV. 785, 806–08 (1970).
16. *Jackson,* 378 U.S. at 390.
17. Cassell, *Miranda's Social Costs, supra* chapter 1, note 26, at 488.
18. *Id.*
19. 711 P.2d 1156 (Alaska 1985).
20. 711 P.2d at 1158. In a footnote, the court added that "alternative methods, such as the preparation of a verbatim transcript by a certified shorthand reporter, in lieu of an electronic device would also satisfy the requirements of state due process." 711 P.2d at 1159 n.11.
21. *Id.* at 1162.
22. *Id.* at 1162.
23. Cassell, *Miranda's Social Costs, supra* chapter 1, note 26, at 486–92.

CHAPTER 14

Regulating Interrogation Practices in the Twenty-first Century

In order to strike an appropriate balance between accommodating law enforcement's interest in obtaining reliable statements and protecting suspects from overreaching interrogation practices, what constitutional rules should the Court adopt? The major problem with the Court's current constitutional restraints on interrogation practices is that they fail to prohibit the police from employing pernicious interrogation practices. As I explained in chapter 9, pernicious interrogation practices can generally be equated with those that are substantially likely to produce untrustworthy statements. Is there a constitutional basis for prohibiting such interrogation practices? If so, what new constitutional rules should the Court establish to prohibit them? I will address the first of these questions in the next section, and the second in the succeeding section.

The Constitutional Basis for Adopting Rules That Protect against the Admission of Untrustworthy Confessions

The due process clause has been interpreted to require that the government employ procedures that will protect the innocent from wrongful convictions. Thus the government has been required to use fair identification procedures,[1] to disclose material exculpatory evidence to the defendant,[2] and to provide reciprocal discovery to the defense.[3] Although it is difficult to state the underlying constitutional principle with precision, in general the government has been prohibited from obtaining convictions with the aid of suggestive procedures that have a tendency to skew results unfairly in favor of the prosecution.

Starting with this premise, confessions resulting from police interrogation methods substantially likely to produce untrustworthy statements should be excluded on the ground that—given jurors' tendency to view confessions as convincing evidence of guilt[4]—such statements are too unreliable to be properly evaluated by the jury. This traditional basis for excluding police-induced confessions was reflected in the Court's due process voluntariness cases, including some that were decided shortly before *Miranda*.[5] Indeed, in 1963, Kamisar asserted that "in 99 cases out of 100," a confession's voluntariness would be determined on the basis of whether the "interrogation methods employed . . . create[d] a substantial risk that a person subjected to them will falsely confess— whether or not this person did."[6] Thus, in applying the pre-*Miranda* due process test, the Court seemed to accept the view that confessions resulting from interrogation methods likely—or substantially likely—to produce untrustworthy statements would be excluded as involuntary.

Since *Miranda*, the Court has decided only three voluntariness cases: *Mincey v. Arizona*,[7] *Arizona v. Fulminante*,[8] and *Colorado v. Connelly*.[9] Although all three cases purported to apply the pre-*Miranda* voluntariness test,[10] some commentators have read the *Connelly* case to mean that the Court is no longer concerned with applying the voluntariness test to exclude untrustworthy confessions. A close reading of *Connelly* indicates, however, that the decision was not intended to effect such a fundamental shift in constitutional doctrine. Although *Connelly* does indicate that the Court has shifted the due process voluntariness test so that it provides fewer safeguards against the introduction of some untrustworthy confessions, *Connelly* should not be read as altering the basic role of the due process test.

In *Connelly*, the suspect approached a police officer and said he wanted to confess to a murder.[11] The officer immediately advised the suspect of his *Miranda* rights; the suspect stated that he understood those rights but wanted to talk to the police.[12] Shortly thereafter, a homicide detective questioned the suspect, who admitted committing a murder.[13] Although the detective perceived no indication that the suspect was suffering from any sort of mental illness, a psychiatrist later testified that the suspect suffered from chronic schizophrenia and was in a psychotic state at the time he approached the police officer.[14] According to the psychiatrist, the suspect's condition caused him to receive command hallucinations that led him to confess.[15] On the basis of the psychiatric testimony, the state courts concluded that the suspect's confession was involuntary.[16]

The Supreme Court reversed, holding that the suspect's confession should not be excluded as involuntary because it was not a product of "police overreaching."[17] Justice Rehnquist's majority opinion acknowledged that "'certain interrogation techniques, either in isolation or as applied to the unique characteristics of a particular suspect, are so offensive to a civilized system of justice that they must be condemned.'"[18] The majority concluded, however, that the suspect's mental condition "can never conclude the due process inquiry."[19] Observing that in this case the police were unaware of the suspect's deeply disturbed mental condition,[20] the majority distinguished earlier cases holding that insane[21] or disoriented[22] suspects' confessions were involuntary on the ground that in those cases "police overreaching" exploited the suspects' known weaknesses.[23] Finding that the police did not engage in any coercive tactics in *Connelly*, the majority concluded that the suspect's confession was voluntary.[24]

The *Connelly* majority stated that "[a] statement rendered by one in the condition of [the suspect] might be proved to be quite unreliable, but this is a matter to be governed by the evidentiary laws of the forum . . . not by the Due Process Clause of the Fourteenth Amendment."[25] Focusing on this language, some commentators have interpreted *Connelly* as modifying the due process test so that it no longer provides protection against the introduction of unreliable confessions.[26]

Connelly need not be read as significantly altering the due process voluntariness test, however. The Court's opinion suggests that a suspect's special vulnerabilities will often be relevant in determining the voluntariness of his confession. Indeed, the Court reiterated that the legitimacy of an interrogation method will sometimes be evaluated on the basis of the way in which it is "'applied to the unique characteristics of a particular suspect,'"[27] thus indicating that interrogation methods legitimate in some contexts will be impermissible when employed against suspects with known vulnerabilities. The *Connelly* case was unusual, however, in at least two respects. First, the police exerted no pressure whatsoever on the defendant to confess. The interrogating detective merely asked him "'what he had on his mind.'"[28] After that, the suspect gave an unsolicited confession. Under these circumstances, the Court could properly conclude that the suspect's confession was not the product of police conduct that exerted any pressure on the suspect to confess.

Moreover, the Court concluded that the police who dealt with the *Connelly* suspect were not aware that he was suffering from a serious mental disability at the time he confessed. Although the suspect told the first officer he approached that "he had been a patient in several mental hospitals,"[29] neither that officer nor the detective who subsequently spoke to the suspect perceived that the suspect "was suffering from any kind of mental illness."[30] Under these circumstances, the Court could properly distinguish *Connelly* from cases in which interrogating officers exploited a suspect's known weaknesses.

When considered in conjunction with pre-*Miranda* decisions' assertions that excluding unreliable confessions was one of the goals of the voluntariness test,[31] *Connelly*'s refusal to consider a confession's apparent lack of reliability perhaps seems anomalous. A distinction should be drawn, however, between assessing the reliability of a particular confession and determining whether an interrogation method is likely to produce an untrustworthy confession. As the Court indicated in *Miller v. Fenton*,[32] the focus of the due process test has always been on the methods employed by the police and their probable effect on the suspect.[33] Although the pre-*Miranda* due process test was designed to discourage interrogation methods likely to produce untrustworthy confessions, the cases applying that test never assessed the actual trustworthiness of particular confessions. Thus *Connelly*'s dictum is consistent with these cases. Although a confession's lack of trustworthiness will not tend to establish that it is involuntary, an interrogation method that is substantially likely to induce an untrustworthy statement should still be impermissible under the due process test.

Indeed, the post-*Miranda* due process cases offer no reason to indicate that this principle has been discarded. In *Arizona v. Fulminante*,[34] a case in which an undercover government agent employed an interrogation method that was likely to elicit an untrustworthy statement,[35] the confession was held involuntary.[36] Moreover, both *Fulminante* and *Connelly* purported to apply the same totality-of-circumstances test that was applied in pre-*Miranda* cases.[37] *Connelly*'s conclusion that the voluntariness test should take into account suspects' mental disabilities only when they are known to the interrogating officers does seem inconsistent with pre-*Miranda* voluntariness cases that took such vulnerabilities into account whether or not they were known to the police.[38] Nevertheless, *Connelly* should not be read as changing the voluntariness test's prohibition on interrogation methods substantially likely to produce untrustworthy statements. As under the pre-*Miranda* test, that prohibition should be viewed as a core principle of the post-*Miranda* due process test.*

---

* Consistent with this principle, state cases applying the post-*Miranda* due process test have continued to hold that interrogation methods likely to produce untrustworthy statements are impermissible. *See* State v. Kelekolio, 849 P.2d 58, 73 (Haw. 1993) ("[D]eliberate falsehoods . . . which are of a type reasonably likely to procure an untrue statement or to influence an accused to make a confession regardless of guilt, will be regarded as coercive *per se*, thus obviating the need for a 'totality of circumstances' analysis of voluntariness"); State v. Stevenson, 264 N.W.2d 848, 851 (Neb. 1978) ("Police deception is not sufficient to make an otherwise valid confession inadmissible, unless it is such as to produce a false or untrustworthy confession."); State v. Glover, 343 So. 2d 118, 131 (La. 1977) (holding confession of mentally ill defendant involuntary because "the probable testimonial trustworthiness of a confession still is and ought to be established as a necessary antecedent to its introduction in evidence").

Reviving the Voluntariness Test to Prohibit
Interrogation Practices Substantially Likely to Produce
Untrustworthy Statements

Based on recent empirical evidence relating to false confessions, it is possible to identify at least some of the interrogation methods that are substantially likely to produce untrustworthy confessions. Leo and Ofshe's examination of sixty known and probable false confession cases shows that two interrogation practices—employing standard interrogation methods on mentally handicapped suspects and conducting lengthy interrogations, both of which were used in a substantial proportion of Leo and Ofshe's sample of sixty cases[39]—appear to play a major part in precipitating untrustworthy confessions. When either of these practices is employed, there is a very substantial likelihood that suspects will provide the answers sought by their interrogators, regardless of their own belief in the truth of those answers. In addition, Ofshe and Leo's analysis of the interrogation process indicates that certain interrogation tactics— especially certain types of threats, promises of leniency, and misrepresentations relating to the evidence establishing the suspect's guilt—may also be substantially likely to produce untrustworthy confessions.

The data revealed by Leo and Ofshe's study would not be enough by itself to mandate the imposition of new constitutional protections. If Leo and Ofshe had been the only commentators to conclude that lengthy interrogations are likely to produce false or untrustworthy confessions, for example, their presentation of several cases in which probably false confessions occurred after lengthy interrogations would not be sufficient to require new constitutional protections. With respect to both lengthy interrogations and the interrogation of mentally handicapped suspects, however, Leo and Ofshe's conclusions are supported not only by a wealth of previous data but also by intuition. Informed observers have long been aware that prolonged interrogation sometimes wears down a suspect's resistance to the point where he will say whatever he believes his interrogators want him to say and that mentally handicapped suspects are the population that is most likely to confess falsely in response to standard interrogation methods. As a result, the due process voluntariness test already provides protections in both these areas. Prolonged interrogation at some point becomes inherently coercive. And in determining the voluntariness of a mentally handicapped suspect's confession, the suspect's mental condition has generally been taken into account.

The data emanating from recent interrogation cases, such as those collected by Leo and Ofshe, is useful in that it enables courts to refine the constitutional principles in light of the most up-to-date information. In determining when confessions produced by lengthy interrogations should be excluded as involuntary, recent cases in which lengthy interrogations produced probably false confessions provide a basis for intelligent line-drawing, identifying the approximate point at which confessions produced by lengthy interrogations appear to become untrustworthy. And the recent data documenting instances in which mentally handicapped suspects were persuaded to confess falsely indicates that *Connelly's* holding should be modified so that courts will be able to determine the voluntariness of mentally handicapped suspects' confessions through an approach that takes into account the suspect's mental infirmity. In both instances, my argument is not that new constitutional principles should be developed as a result of new empirical data; rather, existing constitutional principles should be altered in light of new evidence suggesting that the existing principles need to be strengthened.

In dealing with interrogation tactics involving promises of leniency or misrepresenting the strength of the evidence against the suspect, the law is less clear. Based on recent Supreme Court precedent, such interrogation tactics are not prohibited.[40] In some due process cases, however, the Court has unfavorably viewed interrogation tactics involving promises,[41] threats,[42] and certain types of or trickery.[43] Empirical data relating to the circumstances under which these kinds of interrogation tactics are likely to produce false confessions provides a basis for charting this still murky area of law, defining more precisely the circumstances under which threats, promises of leniency, or misrepresentation as to the strength of the government's case will be impermissible.

Confessions Given by Mentally Handicapped Defendants

Leo and Ofshe's study of false confession cases provides ample support for their conclusion that mentally handicapped suspects are "especially vulnerable to the pressures of accusatorial interrogation."[44] Their examination of sixty proven or probable false confessions included at least seventeen by mentally handicapped suspects.[45] Their conclusion that mentally handicapped suspects are especially vulnerable to police interrogation techniques, moreover, is not new. More than thirty years ago, the President's Commission on Law Enforcement explained why this population is particularly at risk.[46] And more than ten years ago, Professor Fred E. Inbau, the senior author of the *Inbau Manual*, maintained that "special protections must be afforded to juveniles and to all other persons of below-average intelligence, to minimize the risk of untruthful admissions due to their vulnerability to suggestive questioning."[47] Thus, in order to reduce the likelihood that interrogation methods will produce untrustworthy confessions, mentally handicapped suspects' special vulnerability to the pressures exerted by police interrogation methods should be taken into consideration.

In applying the pre-*Miranda* voluntariness test, the Court routinely took into account the particular weaknesses of the suspect being interrogated.[48] In cases decided during the 1950s and 1960s, it weighed such factors as the suspect's mental retardation,[49] emotional instability,[50] schizophrenia[51] and insanity.[52] Moreover, notwithstanding *Connelly*'s intimation to the contrary,[53] the Court did not suggest that it was weighing these suspects' individual characteristics only because they were known to the police at the time of the interrogation. On the contrary, the Court's analysis suggested that the suspects' weaknesses were considered because their weaknesses made them more susceptible to the pressures exerted by police interrogation.

In order to protect a population as to which standard interrogation methods are substantially likely to produce untrustworthy confessions, the Court should return to this approach. In determining whether interrogation methods employed by the police exerted unfair or coercive pressure on the suspect, the voluntariness test should take into account the suspect's special vulnerabilities, weighing the extent to which these vulnerabilities might make the suspect prone to respond to interrogation methods by providing statements sought by the interrogator regardless of his or her initial belief in the truth of those statements. In applying this approach, moreover, weight should be given to the empirical evidence indicating that for mentally handicapped suspects, "even the average level of stress built into an interrogation can be excessive and overbearing."[54]

This approach is admittedly inconsistent with *Connelly*'s dictum intimating that an interrogated suspect's mental problems are constitutionally irrelevant unless the interrogating officer is or should be aware of them. As I have indicated, however, *Connelly*'s dictum is inconsistent with the Court's approach in pre-*Miranda* due process cases. Moreover, determining the legitimacy of an interrogation method on the basis of what an officer knew or should have known about the suspect's mental weaknesses is not administratively feasible. Interrogating officers could often plausibly assert that they were not in fact aware and had no reason to be aware of a suspect's particular weakness, such as mental retardation.* Reviving the pre-*Miranda* due process test's approach of considering the individual characteristics of suspects subjected to interrogation is thus the only viable means of providing mentally handicapped suspects with protection from interrogation methods substantially likely to produce untrustworthy confessions.

Lengthy Interrogations

Empirical data provides ample support for the conclusion that lengthy interrogations are substantially likely to produce untrustworthy confessions. In fifteen of the sixteen cases in which Leo and Ofshe specify the time of the interrogation, the interrogation's length exceeded six hours.[55] In some of these cases, moreover, suspects attributed their confessions solely to the length of their interrogation. Richard LaPointe, a suspect who confessed after being questioned for nine hours, explained his confession by stating, "I just wanted to leave the police station. I was there long enough."[56] And Leo Bruce, who falsely confessed after almost thirteen hours of intermittent interrogation, did so because he "'just wanted it to end right there. I wanted to sleep. I was exhausted.'"[57]

The Crowe and Treadway confessions, which were too recent to be included in Leo and Ofshe's collection, provide further support for the conclusion that lengthy interrogations are substantially likely to produce untrustworthy confessions. After interrogations exceeding ten hours, both of the youthful suspects became increasingly willing to accept their interrogators' suggestions. Intuitively, it seems obvious that virtually continuous interrogation will at some point overbear a suspect's ability to resist the interrogator's suggestions. Empirical evidence relating to false confessions produced by protracted interrogation helps to establish the typical suspect's likely breaking point.

In *Ashcraft v. Tennessee*,[58] the Court dealt with a situation in which the suspect was subjected to thirty-six hours of virtually continuous interrogation.[59] In holding the suspect's confession involuntary, the majority stated that the interrogation was "inherently coercive,"[60] thus establishing that a continuous interrogation of some undetermined length will automatically render a confession involuntary. No matter

---

* Mentally impaired individuals are often extremely adept at hiding their mental problems. Masking mental impairment may be a mentally handicapped individual's most effective skill, developed as a result of the natural inclination to avoid derision or abuse from others. See James W. Ellis & Ruth A. Luckasson, *Symposium on the ABA Criminal Justice Mental Health Standards: Mentally Retarded Defendants*, 53 GEO. WASH. L. REV. 414, 430–31 (1986).

how benign the process, virtually continuous questioning by the police will at some point be unfair because it exerts too much pressure on the suspect. If this is a proper perspective, some effort must be made to determine how long it takes for custodial interrogation to exert unfair or coercive pressure on the typical suspect.

The empirical data showing a relationship between lengthy interrogation and false or untrustworthy confessions substantiates the conclusion that lengthy interrogation exerts unfair or coercive pressure on suspects and provides a legitimate basis for line drawing. From Leo and Ofshe's sample of cases, it appears that when the total length of an interrogation exceeds six hours, the chances of a false or untrustworthy confession increase substantially. Thus in determining the point at which a lengthy interrogation is "inherently coercive," a reasonable benchmark would be to hold that confessions obtained after more than six hours of interrogation are automatically involuntary.*

Confessions Induced by Threats of Punishment or Promises of Leniency

At common law, confessions induced by any threat or promise were excluded as unreliable.[61] This exclusionary principle was adopted in America during the nineteenth century. In 1896, *Russell on Crimes*, a leading criminal law treatise, asserted that in order to be admissible, a confession could not be obtained by any direct or implied promise.[62] One year later, in *Bram v. United States*,[63] the Supreme Court adopted this rule as a matter of constitutional law, holding that the admission of a confession induced by "any direct or implied promise, however slight,"[64] violated the Fifth Amendment privilege.

Over the next century, *Bram* exerted only limited influence. In applying the pre-*Miranda* voluntariness test, the Court never rigorously applied *Bram's* prohibition. In one case, it held that a confession that occurred after the defendant negotiated "a bargain with the police and parole officers" was valid;[65] in two others, it held that confessions induced by threats of harsh punishment and express or implied

---

* Drawing from *Ashcraft's* holding that thirty-six hours of virtually continuous interrogation was "inherently coercive," *see* 322 U.S. at 153–54, the prohibition should apply whenever a suspect is subjected to relatively uninterrupted police interrogation for more than six hours. If there is a substantial break in the interrogation (for instance, so that the suspect is allowed to rest or to meet with members of his family), the prohibition should not apply. On the other hand, short interruptions in police questioning or momentary respites for the suspect should not be sufficient to extend the six-hour prohibition.

promises of significant leniency were involuntary,[66] but did not specify that the threats or promises were sufficient in themselves to dictate either result.[67] In the post-*Miranda* case of *Arizona v. Fulminante*,[68] the Court expressly repudiated *Bram*'s holding prohibiting confessions induced by all promises, stating that that rule "does not state the standard for determining the voluntariness of a confession."[69]

Fulminante's repudiation of *Bram* nevertheless leaves open the possibility of barring confessions induced by promises that are substantially likely to produce untrustworthy confessions. As Wigmore observed,[70] the premise that a confession produced by any promise is untrustworthy was probably never correct. If the inducement to confess is relatively slight—a promise that the officer will testify that the suspect cooperated, for example[71]—there is little reason to believe that a suspect will respond with a false confession.

When an interrogator promises a suspect that in exchange for a confession, he will not be charged at all or will be granted leniency, however, the chances that the promise will produce a false confession are substantially greater. Based on the advice provided in the leading interrogation manual,[72] one of the interrogator's goals is to convince the suspect that the police either already have or will be able to obtain evidence that establishes the suspect's guilt. After hearing the police repeatedly state that they have or will have evidence establishing his guilt, an innocent suspect might believe that if he does not confess, the police intend either to frame him for a crime he did not commit or to present genuine evidence that could result in conviction despite his innocence. An innocent suspect might thus rationally conclude that a false confession in exchange for leniency is his best alternative.

Leo and Ofshe's data support the conclusion that threats of punishment and promises of leniency are sometimes substantially likely to produce untrustworthy confessions. In their analysis of sixty proven or probable false confession cases, Leo and Ofshe identified this tactic as one that played a major role in precipitating false confessions in several cases. In one case, for example, a seventeen-year-old suspect falsely confessed to stabbing her mother after an interrogator told her she would die in the electric chair if she maintained her innocence;[73] in another, a young woman falsely confessed to shoving her boyfriend off a cliff 320 feet above the Oregon coast after the police "created the impression that her admission . . . carried no punishment."[74]

Empirical data as well as precedent thus support imposing some kind of prohibition on inducing confessions through threats or promises. Since the prohibition's underlying purpose is to bar threats or promises that are substantially likely to produce untrustworthy confessions, the focus should be on the way in which the suspect would interpret the interrogator's words rather than on whether the interrogator's words constitute an explicit threat or a binding promise. When the suspect would be likely to interpret the interrogator's words as constituting a threat of serious adverse consequences if he does not confess or a promise of significant leniency if he does, empirical data as well as intuition indicate that even an innocent suspect will be quite likely to confess rather than risk the consequences of maintaining his innocence. In order to provide a restriction that will provide adequate protection against inducements likely to produce untrustworthy confessions, interrogators should thus be prohibited from making statements (or engaging in conduct) that would be likely to lead the suspect to believe that he will suffer serious adverse consequences if he does not confess or be granted significant leniency if he does.

Applying this test will often be difficult. As Professor Philip Johnson has said, "[T]he difference between expressions of compassionate understanding on the one hand, and implied promises of leniency on the other, is at the margins sometimes a matter of emphasis and nuance."[75] Similarly, a fine line will sometimes exist between implied threats and statements that merely suggest the possibility of adverse consequences. In determining whether an interrogator's statements are impermissible, an objective standard—which considers the probable perceptions of both the interrogator and the suspect subjected to interrogation—should be adopted. If the interrogator should be aware that either the suspect or a reasonable person in the suspect's position would perceive that the interrogator's statements indicated that the suspect would be likely to receive significant leniency if he did confess or significant adverse consequences if he did not, then the interrogator's statements should be viewed as improper and a confession occurring as a result of such statements should be excluded as involuntary.

Examples drawn from two cases illustrate how the test should be applied. In *Miller v. Fenton*,[76] Detective Boyce, who was investigating the murder of seventeen-year-old Deborah Margolin, interrogated Frank Miller for approximately one hour. During the course of the interrogation, Boyce repeatedly indicated to Miller that he was someone who needed help and that, if he confessed, Boyce would help him. At one point, for example, Boyce told Miller that the person responsible for the killing was "not a criminal."[77] He went on to say that the perpetrator had a "problem, and a good thing about that, Frank, is a problem can be rectified."[78] After

Miller agreed, Boyce developed his implicit proposal to Miller as follows: "I want to help you. I mean I really want to help you, but you know what they say, God helps those who help themselves, Frank."[79]

Boyce was never explicit about the kind of "help" that he hoped to provide for Miller. At one point, however, he asked Miller, "If I promise to, you know, do all I can with the psychiatrist and everything, and we get the proper help for you, . . . will you talk to me about it?"[80] Miller never answered this question,[81] and at least one of his responses to Boyce indicated that, despite Boyce's statements, he believed he would be treated as a criminal if he confessed.[82] Nevertheless, Miller eventually confessed to the killing.[83]

Under the proposed approach, the first question is whether Boyce should be aware that a reasonable person in Miller's position would believe that, if he confessed, he would be likely to receive significant leniency. Although Boyce never explicitly promised Miller leniency in exchange for a confession, his statements taken as a whole would certainly suggest to a reasonable person that if he "helped" Boyce by confessing to the crime, he would not be treated as a criminal, but rather would receive the psychiatric help he needed. The promise of receiving psychiatric help (presumably at a mental hospital) rather than being punished as a criminal certainly constitutes a promise of significant leniency. Boyce's statements to Miller thus constituted an improper promise.

Should Miller's confession following Boyce's promise be excluded as involuntary? Based on one of the statements he made to Boyce, Miller did not appear to believe that he would receive psychiatric treatment rather than being treated as a "criminal" if he confessed.[84] The government might thus claim that, even if Boyce made an improper promise, Miller's confession should not be excluded as involuntary because Boyce's promise did not induce the confession.

In determining whether a promise induced a confession, the focus should be on whether the promise played any part in precipitating the confession. If Miller did not believe that Boyce had made a promise or was certain that whatever promise Boyce made would not be kept, Miller's confession should be admitted. Miller's skepticism as to Boyce's intentions should not be sufficient, however, to negate a finding that the promise induced the confession. Even if Miller believed that Boyce was unlikely to honor his implied promise, he might have been induced by the promise to believe there was "a small open window at the top of [a] long wall"[85] through which he could miraculously escape the possibility of punishment. In the context of custodial interrogation, a suspect can be induced to confess by a promise even when he believes there is only a remote chance that the terms of the promise will be fulfilled.

Indeed, when a suspect's confession follows a promise of leniency, the conclusion that the promise did not induce the confession is generally implausible. Even if the suspect is aware that he is grasping at straws, the promise probably played some part in precipitating the confession. Barring unusual circumstances such as an explicit clarification of the officer's authority to make promises,[86] a confession following such a promise should be viewed as induced by the promise and, therefore, involuntary.[87] Since Miller's confession followed Boyce's implied promise of leniency, his confession should be excluded.

As a second example, consider the interrogation of Leo Bruce (discussed in chapter 12), who was suspected of murdering nine people at a Thai Buddhist temple west of Phoenix. After his arrest, Bruce was questioned by several officers, including FBI Agent Casey.[88] Near the beginning of the interrogation, Casey falsely told Bruce that the police had evidence showing that he was at the temple on the night of the killings. After Bruce denied ever being there, Casey said to him, "The best thing to do is to cooperate now . . . Don't you think it's smart to get your version of the story down . . . before everyone else gives theirs?"[89] When Bruce continued to deny he had been at the temple, Casey told Bruce that, if he stuck with that story, he was "gonna end up being sorry, I think."[90] He added, "You're making a mistake by not cooperating at this point."[91] Bruce continued to deny his involvement. After thirteen hours of intermittent interrogation, however, he confessed to the killings.[92]

In this case, the critical question is whether Casey should be aware that a reasonable person in Bruce's situation would believe that he was being threatened with significant adverse consequences if he did not confess. Casey's comments suggesting that it would be "smart" for Bruce to get his story down before other suspects gave theirs could not reasonably be interpreted as communicating such a threat. The comments do, of course, suggest that Bruce will obtain some advantage by admitting his involvement so that he can get his "version of the story down" first. But there is no suggestion that getting his version down first will lead to any concrete benefit relating to the disposition of his case. At most, Casey's comments seem to suggest that if Bruce gets his story down before the others tell theirs, the authorities will be more likely to believe his story, thus making it less likely that other suspects will later be able to convince the authorities that Bruce is more blameworthy than his statement indicates.

Casey's additional statement to the effect that Bruce "will end up being sorry" if he does not cooperate obviously comes closer to articulating a threat. Arguably, a reasonable person might take this language to mean that serious adverse consequences would accrue to him if he failed to comply with the agent's suggestion that he "cooperate" through making a statement admitting his involvement. On the other hand, when considered in the context of Casey's other statements, the suggestion that Bruce would be "sorry" if he did not make a statement might more reasonably be interpreted as merely reinforcing the suggestion contained in the earlier statements: if Bruce did not provide the police with his own inculpatory statement, he might later regret his failure to cooperate because the police would then be more inclined to believe other suspects' statements incriminating Bruce. Even though the words, "You'll end up being sorry," have an ominous ring, they are not on the same order as, "You'll lose your chance for being treated as a lesser offender," or other words that might suggest that the failure to cooperate would lead to tangible consequences relating to sentencing or disposition of the case.

Although the question is close, Agent Casey's statements to Bruce should not be interpreted as communicating a threat that his failure to confess would lead to significant adverse consequences. Accordingly, Bruce's confession should not be involuntary on the ground that it was induced by an improper threat or promise.

Threats of Adverse Consequences to a Friend or Loved One

In pre-*Miranda* due process cases, the Court's view of police trickery was ambivalent. In a few cases—most notably, *Spano v. New York*[93]—the Court indicated that police trickery was a factor contributing to its conclusion that the suspect's confession was involuntary.[94] The Court never indicated, however, that any particular sort of police trickery would be sufficient by itself to render a confession involuntary. Indeed, in *Frazier v. Cupp*,[95] the Court held that a confession induced by trickery that both misrepresented the strength of the evidence against the suspect[96] and minimized the suspect's culpability for the offense[97] was voluntary.[98] While stating that the interrogating officer's trickery was "relevant" under the due process test, it concluded that the trickery was insufficient to render the confession involuntary.[99]

Although the Court's dictum in *Spano*—which strongly condemned the deceptive tactics employed in that case[100]—seemed to suggest that some types of police trickery are worse than others, the Court has never articulated any basis for evaluating the propriety of particular types of interrogators' trickery. Based on the concern for prohibiting interrogation tactics that are substantially likely to produce untrustworthy statements, the Court should distinguish between different forms of trickery on the basis of whether or not the trickery has the potential for producing a false confession. This approach is consistent with *Spano* because, as lower courts have pointed out,[101] the type of trickery employed in that case does have the potential for precipitating a false confession.

In *Spano*, Bruno, the defendant's childhood friend and a "fledgling" police officer, falsely told the defendant that the defendant's failure to confess would cause him to lose his job as a police officer, resulting in dire consequences not only for himself but also his wife and children. Bruno's trickery could be classified as informing the suspect that a friend or loved one will suffer adverse consequences unless the suspect confesses. Both intuition and empirical data[102] suggest that this type of trickery does have substantial potential for precipitating false confessions. In the context of a police interrogation, a suspect might easily be led to feel that protecting his friend or loved one from harm is more important than avoiding the consequences of confessing. Based on an appropriate reading of *Spano*, interrogators should thus be prohibited from informing a suspect that his failure to confess will lead to adverse consequences for a friend or loved one.

If this prohibition is adopted, how should a court determine whether an interrogator is making a prohibited threat? Since the prohibition is designed to prohibit a pernicious interrogation practice, the court's ultimate focus should be on the situation as it reasonably appeared to the interrogator.[103] In assessing particular inducements, a reasonable interrogator's perception of how the suspect would be likely to view the inducement would, of course, be critical. If a reasonable interrogator would believe that the suspect would be likely to perceive that the interrogator was indicating that his failure to confess would result in adverse consequences for a friend or loved one, a confession given in response to this inducement should be involuntary.

If an interrogator tells the suspect, for example, that the police will take his wife or friend into custody if he does not confess, the question whether this constitutes a threat of adverse consequences to the suspect's wife or friend should be determined on the basis of the interrogator's perception of how the suspect would be likely to view this statement. If the interrogator knows that the suspect's wife suffers from arthritis,[104] then the interrogator should certainly be aware that the suspect would be likely to believe that the interrogator was trying to induce a confession by threatening his wife with adverse consequences. Similarly, if the interrogator had reason to believe that the suspect would be likely to believe that taking a person into custody amounts to an arrest or other serious curtailment of liberty, then the statement that the suspect's wife or a friend is going to be taken into custody should qualify as an impermissible threat regardless of his wife or friend's physical condition.

Since the interrogation tactic is problematic because of its potential for producing untrustworthy statements, in theory it should not matter whether the interrogator is misrepresenting his intentions when he tells a suspect that his failure to confess will lead to consequences for a third party. In practice, however, it seems likely that when the interrogator is lying to the suspect, there is a much greater likelihood that the interrogator believes that a reasonable person in the suspect's position would be likely to perceive that the interrogator is threatening a friend or loved one with adverse consequences. In most instances, therefore, the interrogator's misrepresentation as to the effect that a suspect's failure to confess will have for a third party should be strong evidence that the interrogator is employing an impermissible interrogation practice.

Misrepresenting the Evidence against the Suspect

Misrepresenting the evidence against the suspect is another interrogation tactic that has the potential for producing false confessions. When confronted with an interrogator's claim that the evidence overwhelmingly establishes his guilt, some suspects will be inclined to believe either that continued resistance is futile (because the police have evidence that will convict him despite his innocence) or that he is in fact guilty. Not every form of this misrepresentation is substantially likely to produce untrustworthy statements, however. If the police tell a suspect that they are confident that they will find evidence establishing his guilt or even that they have witnesses who will testify against him, an innocent suspect would be unlikely to confess because, even assuming he credits the interrogator's statements, he would be inclined to believe that the police or the witnesses are simply mistaken. On the other hand, if the interrogator shows the suspect a fabricated laboratory report indicating that the suspect's semen stains were found on the victim's underwear,[105] an innocent suspect might rationally conclude that the government's irrefutable proof of his guilt mandated his confession.

When should the tactic of misrepresenting the evidence against the suspect be impermissible? In view of the concern for prohibiting interrogation tactics substantially likely to produce untrustworthy statements, the test should be whether the interrogators employed a tactic that would be likely to suggest to the suspect that the evidence against him is so overwhelming that continued resistance is futile. When this test is met, there is a substantial risk that the suspect will simply make the statements sought by the interrogator, regardless of whether those statements are true. In determining whether this test is met, the type of evidence misrepresented, the nature and quality of the misrepresentation, the extent to which the misrepresented evidence seems to establish the suspect's guilt, and the suspect's apparent vulnerability should all be taken into consideration.

Misrepresentations relating to forensic or scientific evidence are particularly likely to convince suspects that further resistance is futile. Most people believe that evidence obtained through accepted scientific procedures—fingerprints, ballistic reports, or DNA evidence, for example—are likely to be not only reliable, but irrefutable. Moreover, based on their examination of false confession cases, Ofshe and Leo report that "false evidence ploys based on scientific procedures" are more likely than "[f]alse evidence ploys based on eyewitness reports" to induce a false confession.[106] Both intuition and the available empirical data thus suggest that misrepresenting the forensic or scientific evidence against the suspect should in some circumstances be an impermissible interrogation tactic because of its potential for producing untrustworthy statements.

Because scientific evidence has an inordinate potential for convincing a suspect that continued resistance is futile, misrepresenting the scientific evidence against the suspect should be impermissible whenever the misrepresented evidence would be sufficient to establish the suspect's guilt. Under this test, interrogators should certainly be barred from fabricating laboratory reports indicating that semen stains on the victim's underwear came from the suspect.[107] Since in most cases, manufacturing a false report would not be necessary to convince a suspect of the scientific evidence's authenticity,[108] falsely informing the suspect of scientific evidence sufficient to establish his guilt—telling him, for example, that his fingerprints were found at the scene of the crime or that his shoes matched tracks left by the perpetrator[109]—should also be impermissible.

The tactic of falsely informing a suspect that he failed a polygraph test presents a more difficult issue. An interrogator employing this tactic is misrepresenting scientific evidence; but the deception does not suggest to the suspect that the police will be able to present irrefutable proof of the suspect's guilt. A knowledgeable suspect would presumably be aware that polygraph results can be mistaken and that they are not admissible in court. Nevertheless, empirical data indicates that this form of deception can have a powerful impact on innocent suspects. Leo and Ofshe's study of false confession cases indicates that in at least two cases[110] misrepresenting polygraph results played a major part not only in precipitating an innocent suspect's confession but also in leading the suspect to believe, at least temporarily, that he was in fact guilty.[111] In Michael Crowe's case, moreover, the tactic seems to have at least played a major role in precipitating a false confession.[112]

Since the constitutional prohibition should only apply to prohibit interrogation tactics *substantially* likely to produce untrustworthy statements, the tactic of misrepresenting polygraph results should not be absolutely prohibited. As this example indicates, however, any tactic that distorts the suspect's perception of the scientific or forensic evidence relating to his participation in the crime does have some tendency to precipitate an untrustworthy statement. When such a tactic is employed, courts should at least closely scrutinize both the circumstances of the interrogation and the apparent vulnerability of the suspect, examining the extent to which the misrepresentation would be likely to precipitate an untrustworthy confession. When the tactic is employed on a youthful or mentally handicapped suspect, for example, a court should conclude that the interrogator's use of the tactic rendered the suspect's confession involuntary.

In determining whether a particular misrepresentation of government evidence will be impermissible, the extent and nature of the misrepresentation will also be significant. In *Miranda,* the Court expressed disapproval of the tactic of using a "reverse line-up" under which the "accused is placed in a line-up" and then "identified by several fictitious witnesses or victims who associated him with different offenses."[113] When the police employ this tactic, there is obviously a concern that even an innocent suspect "will become desperate and confess to the offense under investigation in order to escape from the false accusations."[114]

If, rather than conducting a reverse lineup, the police simply arranged to have a number of fictitious witnesses dramatically identify the suspect as the perpetrator of the crime under investigation, the tactic should still be impermissible. Even though suspects know that witnesses can be mistaken, the false evidence's power—in terms of both its apparent value to the prosecution and its vivid communication to the suspect—would be very likely to convince an innocent suspect that continued resistance would be futile.

As with other prohibitions on interrogators' trickery, it would often be difficult for a court to determine whether a particular misrepresentation of the government's evidence would be impermissible. In Leo

Bruce's interrogation, for example, the police took Bruce to a property room, showing him "photographs of enlarged fingerprints and other items of trace evidence, a floor plan of the temple, and a chart listing the names of Bruce's alleged associates."[115] If Bruce's interrogators falsely indicated that Bruce's fingerprints were found at the crime scene, then the interrogation tactic should be impermissible. If, on the other hand, they falsely indicated only that the forensic evidence, such as finger-prints, established the guilt of Bruce's alleged associates, the tactic should not be impermissible.

If they indicated that the forensic evidence established the guilt of Bruce's alleged associates and also stated (or intimated) that those asso-ciates were incriminating Bruce, the case would fall in the gray area. In determining whether this type of misrepresentation would be likely to convince an innocent suspect that further resistance was futile, a court would have to assess not only the exact nature of the misrepresentation but also other factors—including the vividness with which the misrepre-sentation was made and the suspect's apparent powers of resistance. If, during the course of a lengthy interrogation, the interrogator repeatedly falsely indicated to the suspect that others whose guilt was established were unequivocally implicating him, the court should probably hold that the interrogation tactic was impermissible on the ground that it would be likely to convince even an innocent suspect that further resis-tance to the interrogator was futile.

Conclusion

In arguing that the Supreme Court should impose constitutional restric-tions designed to reduce the admission into evidence of police-induced false confessions, I am not seeking to break new constitutional ground. On the contrary, I accept the present Court's interpretation of the con-trolling constitutional principles. Under the due process voluntariness test, confessions are involuntary when they are produced by interroga-tion techniques that either in general or in a particular context violate principles of fundamental fairness. Based on this principle, confessions are involuntary when they are produced by interrogation methods sub-stantially likely to produce untrustworthy confessions.

In applying the pre-*Miranda* due process test, the Court implicitly accepted this principle. In deciding which interrogation methods were substantially likely to produce untrustworthy confessions, however, it was forced to rely primarily on intuition or common-law precedents;

empirical evidence relating to the circumstances under which police-induced false confessions were likely to occur was lacking. In view of new empirical data showing the circumstances under which modern interrogation techniques have produced false confessions, the Court now has a sounder basis for determining which interrogation methods are likely to produce untrustworthy confessions and the circumstances under which such confessions are most likely to occur. Based on this data, I have identified some of the specific ways in which the Court should refurbish the due process voluntariness test so that it will provide significant restrictions on police interrogation methods that are substantially likely to produce untrustworthy confessions.

NOTES

1. See Manson v. Brathwaite, 432 U.S. 98 (1977); Stovall v. Denno, 388 U.S. 293 (1967).
2. See United States v. Bagley, 473 U.S. 667 (1985); Brady v. Maryland, 373 U.S. 83 (1963).
3. See Wardius v. Oregon, 412 U.S. 470 (1973).
4. See *supra* chapter 9, note 45.
5. See *supra* chapter 4.
6. KAMISAR, ESSAYS, *supra* chapter 1, note 24, at 20–21.
7. 437 U.S. 385 (1978).
8. 499 U.S. 279 (1991).
9. 479 U.S. 157 (1986).
10. *Fulminante*, 499 U.S. at 285–86; *Connelly*, 479 U.S. at 163–64; *Mincey*, 437 U.S. at 401.
11. See *Connelly*, 479 U.S. at 160.
12. *See id.*
13. *See id.*
14. *See id.* at 161.
15. *See id.*
16. *See id.* at 162 (citing State v. Connelly, 702 P.2d 722 (Colo. 1985)).
17. *See id.* at 163–64.
18. *Id.* at 163 (quoting Miller v. Fenton, 474 U.S. 104, 109 (1985)).
19. *Id.* at 165.

20. *See id.* at 161.
21. *See id.* at 164–65 (distinguishing Blackburn v. Alabama, 361 U.S. 199 (1960)).
22. *See id.* (distinguishing Townsend v. Sain, 372 U.S. 293 (1963)).
23. *See id.* at 165.
24. *See id.*
25. *Id.* at 167.
26. Based on this language, Professor George Dix has observed that the most surprising aspect of *Connelly* is its "rejection of reliability as a relevant primary consideration" for determining the admissibility of a confession under the due process test. George Dix, *Federal Constitutional Confession Law: The 1986 and 1987 Supreme Court Terms*, 67 TEX. L. REV. 231, 272 (1988). Emphasizing *Connelly*'s disregard of the defendant's mental disabilities, other commentators have interpreted the case as changing the nature of the voluntariness test so that it permits the police to employ the same

interrogation methods when dealing with vulnerable suspects as they do when dealing with normal ones. *See* Laurence Benner, *Requiem for Miranda: The Rehnquist Court's Voluntariness Doctrine in Historical Perspective,* 67 WASH. U. L.Q. 59, 124–26 (1989); Alfredo Garcia, *Mental Sanity and Confessions: The Supreme Court's New Version of the Old "Voluntariness" Standard,* 21 AKRON L. REV. 275, 280–81 (1988).

27. *Connelly,* 479 U.S. at 163 (quoting Miller v. Fenton, 474 U.S. 104, 109 (1985)).
28. *Id.* at 160.
29. *Id.*
30. *Id.* at 161.
31. See *Jackson,* 378 U.S. at 385–86 (referring to "complex of values," which includes protecting against the introduction of unreliable confessions); *Blackburn,* 361 U.S. at 206 (referring to "abhorrence" of unreliable confessions).
32. 474 U.S. 104 (1985).
33. *See id.* at 116.
34. 499 U.S. 279 (1991).
35. In *Fulminante,* the undercover government agent told the suspect that he would provide him with protection only if the suspect told "the truth" about his stepdaughter's death. Since the suspect had already denied any involvement in his stepdaughter's death, he might reasonably interpret the agent's offer as demanding an admission of guilt in exchange for the proffered protection.
36. See *Fulminante,* 499 U.S. at 287.
37. *Fulminante,* 499 U.S. at 287–88;

Connelly, 479 U.S. at 164–65.
38. *See, e.g.,* Townsend v. Sain, 372 U.S. 293, 307 (1963) (observing that "a drug-induced statement" is involuntary regardless of whether the "drug may have been administered and the questions asked by persons unfamiliar with [the administered substance's] properties").
39. As the authors acknowledge, *see* Leo & Ofshe, *Consequences, supra* chapter 11, note 3, at 435–36, the sixty known or suspected false confessions discussed in their article do not necessarily constitute a representative sample of the universe of known or suspected false confessions. Since the cases were identified from database searches, secondary sources, and case files to which the authors had access, they might be expected to overrepresent high-profile cases or at least those that had a substantial degree of notoriety.
40. See *Fulminante,* 499 U.S. at 285 (dictum stating confessions induced by promises of leniency are not automatically involuntary); Frazier v. Cupp, 394 U.S. 731 (1969) (confessions induced by police trickery are not automatically inadmissible).
41. *See, e.g.,* Leyra v. Denno, 347 U.S. 556 (1954).
42. See Rogers v. Richmond, 365 U.S. 534 (1961); Leyra v. Denno, 347 U.S. at 556.
43. See Spano v. New York, 360 U.S. 315 (1959).
44. Ofshe & Leo, *Social Psychology, supra* chapter 11, note 8, at 212.
45. Leo & Ofshe, *Consequences, supra* chapter 11, note 3, at 444–72.

Nine of these suspects are referred to as mentally handicapped adults, *see id.* at 446–49 (Case Identification #'s 26, 32, 44–46, 50, 54–55, 60), four as mentally retarded adults, *see id.* at 445–48 (Case Identification #'s 19, 43, 44, 52), two as mentally handicapped teenagers, *see id.* at 446–47 (Case Identification #'s 27, 38), one as a mentally ill adult, *see id.* at 445 (Case Identification #19), and one as mentally handicapped with AIDS, *see id.* at 446 (Case Identification #30). Examination of the secondary sources cited by Leo and Ofshe indicates that among their sixty proven and probable false confession cases, several additional suspects had serious mental problems. *See, e.g.,* Jolayne Houlz, *Murder Confessions False: Man Released,* SEATTLE TIMES, Apr. 23, 1991, at B1 (describing how Charles Lawson, a man with a history of psychological problems, falsely confessed to two murders in order to be imprisoned as a way to avoid people he feared); Matt Lait & Michael Granberry, *Charges Dropped in Laguna Arson When "Confession" Is Proved Bogus: Courts, Orange County Prosecutors Admit They Were Duped, Verify Suspect Was in Mexican Jail during Last Year's Firestorm,* L.A. TIMES, Oct. 6, 1994, at A1 (noting that Jose Soto Martinez was delusional at the time of his interrogation, in which he confessed to a crime committed while he was incarcerated); Joseph Shapiro, *Innocent, but behind Bars,* U.S. NEWS

& WORLD REP., Sept. 19, 1994, p. 36 (recounting the story of Johnny Lee Wilson, a mildly retarded twenty-six-year-old who falsely confessed to a murder and spent several years in jail although someone else later confessed to the crime).

46. See *supra* chapter 11.

47. Fred E. Inbau, *Miranda's Immunization of Low Intelligence Offenders,* 24 PROSECUTOR: J. NAT'L DISTRICT ATT'YS ASS'N, at 9–10 (spring 1991).

48. As Kamisar pointed out, the pre-*Miranda* cases considered suspect's personal characteristics only for the purpose of imposing greater restrictions on interrogation methods: "'Strong' personal characteristics rarely, if ever, 'cure' forbidden police methods; but 'weak' ones may invalidate what are generally permissible methods." KAMISAR, ESSAYS, *supra* chapter 1, note 24, at 24.

49. *See* Culombe v. Connecticut, 367 U.S. 620, 624–25 (1961).

50. *See* Spano v. New York, 360 U.S. 315, 321–22 (1959).

51. *See* Fikes v. Alabama, 352 U.S. 191, 193 (1957).

52. *See* Blackburn v. Alabama, 361 U.S. 199, 207 (1960).

53. *See* text accompanying notes 20–23.

54. Ofshe & Leo, *Social Psychology, supra* chapter 11, note 8, at 212. *See generally* James W. Ellis & Ruth A. Luckasson, *Symposium on the ABA Criminal Justice Mental Health Standards: Mentally Retarded Defendants,* 53 GEO. WASH. L. REV. 414, 445–52 (1986).

55. *See* Leo & Ofshe, *Consequences, supra* chapter 11, note 3. In the majority of these cases, the interrogation was virtually continuous. *See, e.g., id.* at 459 (Richard LaPointe confessed after being interrogated at the police station for more than nine hours); *id.* at 476 (George Abney confessed after being interrogated for ten hours). In other cases, however, the interrogation was spread over a period of time. *See, e.g., id.* at 490 (Juan Rivera confessed after being interrogated for thirty-three hours over a period of four days); *id.* at 452 (Robert Moore confessed after being subjected to several interrogation sessions lasting a total of twenty-five hours). Examination of the secondary sources cited by Leo and Ofshe indicates, moreover, that several other suspects who, according to Leo and Ofshe, gave proven or probable false confessions were interrogated for more than six hours. *See, e.g.,* MELANIE THERNSTROM, THE DEAD GIRL (1990) (noting that Bradley Page was interrogated for sixteen hours over five interrogation sessions); Richard Ofshe, *Coerced Confessions: The Logic of Seemingly Irrational Actions,* 6 CULTIC STUDIES J. 1, 6–12 (1989) (Tom Sawyer was interrogated nearly continuously for sixteen hours).

56. *60 Minutes: Did He Do It?* (CBS television broadcast, June 30, 1996), *available in* 1996 WL 80964916.

57. Parloff, *False Confessions, supra* chapter 12, note 59, at 60.

58. 322 U.S. 143 (1944).

59. *See id.* at 149, 153.

60. *Id.* at 154.

61. See 3 WIGMORE ON EVIDENCE, *supra* chapter 1, note 14, § 820, at 238.

62. 3 RUSSELL ON CRIMES 478 (6th ed. 1896).

63. 168 U.S. 532 (1897).

64. 168 U.S. at 543.

65. Stein v. New York, 346 U.S. 156, 185 (1953).

66. Lynumn v. Illinois, 372 U.S. 528 (1963); Leyra v. Denno, 347 U.S. 556 (1954).

67. In *Leyra,* the interrogator stated to the suspect that he would have "a much better chance" if he "play[ed] ball with the interrogators," and that "[t]hese people are going to throw the book at you unless you can show that in a fit of temper, you got so angry that you did it. Otherwise they toss premeditation in and it's premeditation. See?" *Leyra,* 347 U.S. at 583–84 (Appendix to Opinion of the Court). In holding the defendant's confession involuntary, the Court referred to the interrogator's "threat[s]" and "promise[s] of leniency." *Id.* at 559. In *Lynumn,* the interrogator told the defendant that if she did not confess she could get ten years and her children would be taken away and that if she did confess the interrogator would recommend mercy and see that she kept her children. 372 U.S. at 531–32. In a terse opinion, the Court held that the interrogator's statements to the defendant rendered her confession involuntary. *Id.* at 534.

68. 499 U.S. 279 (1991).

69. 499 U.S. at 285.

70. *See* 3 WIGMORE ON EVIDENCE,

supra chapter 1, note 14, § 836, at 238.

71. *See, e.g.,* State v. Fuqua, 152 S.E.2d 68, 72 (N.C. 1967) (excluding confession because officer told suspect he would testify that the suspect cooperated with the investigation).

72. INBAU ET AL., *supra* chapter 1, note 23, at 131.

73. See Leo & Ofshe, *Consequences, supra* chapter 11, note 3, at 466 (confession of Tammy Lynn Harrison).

74. *Id.* at 470–71 (confession of Linda Stangel).

75. Philip E. Johnson, *A Statutory Replacement for the Miranda Doctrine,* 24 AM. CRIM. L. REV. 303, 310–11 (1987).

76. 796 F.2d 598 (3d Cir. 1986), *cert. denied,* 479 U.S. 989 (1986).

77. 796 F.2d at 618 (Gibbons, J., dissenting).

78. *Id.*

79. *Id.*

80. *Id.* at 622.

81. His immediate response, "I can't talk to you about something I'm not . . ." was interrupted by Boyce. *Id.*

82. After Boyce at one point said, "I don't think you're a criminal, Frank," Miller responded, "No, but you're trying to make me one." *Id.* at 618.

83. *Id.* at 624–25.

84. *See infra* note 86.

85. *See* SIMON, HOMICIDE, *supra* chapter 3, note 52, at 197.

86. If, in response to a request for clarification, Boyce told Miller that he had no authority to make a promise that would be binding on the prosecutor, it could be found either that Boyce made no implied promises of

leniency or that the promises he did make did not induce Miller's confession.

87. For a similar view, *see* George E. Dix, *Confessions, and Wayne LaFave's Bright Line Analysis,* 1993 U. ILL. L. REV. 207, 259 (advocating "prophylactic promise rule requiring exclusion of a confession given after officers or prosecutors made a promise of leniency to the suspect").

88. See Parloff, *False Confessions, supra* chapter 12, note 59, at 58.

89. *Id.* at 59.

90. *Id.*

91. *Id.*

92. *Id.* Bruce was never brought to trial, however, because subsequently discovered evidence established that his confession was false. *Id. See supra* chapter 12.

93. 360 U.S. 315 (1959).

94. *See* 360 U.S. at 322–23.

95. 394 U.S. 731 (1969).

96. The interrogating officer falsely told the defendant that his confederate had confessed. *See* 394 U.S. at 737.

97. The officer also "sympathetically suggested that the victim had started a fight by making homosexual advances." *Id.* at 738.

98. *See id.* at 739.

99. *See id.*

100. *See Spano,* 360 U.S. at 323.

101. *See, e.g.,* Commonwealth v. DuPree, 275 A.2d 326, 327 (Pa. 1971) (citing *Spano* as an example in which "police employ threats likely to produce a false, involuntary confession").

102. For an account of the Dante Parker case in which this tactic

apparently played a significant part in precipitating a false confession, see *supra* chapter 12.

103. Adopting an objective focus for the purpose of determining whether an interrogation practice is impermissible is consistent with the Court's approach in dealing with other interrogation issues. *See, e.g.,* Berkemer v. McCarty, 468 U.S. 420, 442 (1984) (whether suspect in custody within the meaning of *Miranda* must be determined by assessing "how a reasonable man in the suspect's position would have understood his situation"); Rhode Island v. Innis, 446 U.S. 291, 301 (1980) (interrogation includes "words or actions on the part of the police . . . that the police should know are reasonably likely to elicit an incriminating response from the suspect").

104. *See Rogers,* 365 U.S. at 536 (1961) (referring to defendant's testimony that police chief threatened to bring defendant's wife, who suffered from arthritis, "in for questioning . . . unless he confessed").

105. See State v. Cayward, 552 So. 2d 971 (Fla. Dist. Ct. App. 1989) (excluding confession).

106. Ofshe & Leo, *Social Psychology, supra* chapter 11, note 8, at 202. As the authors state, "False scientific evidence can be presented so as to leave little opportunity for counters. Interrogators represent positive results of fingerprint, hair or DNA tests as error free and therefore unimpeachable." *Id.* Effective use of this ploy thus diminishes the suspect's ability to resist the interrogator's insistence on his guilt.

107. *See* State v. Cayward, 552 So. 2d 971 (Fla. Dist. Ct. App. 1989) (excluding confession).

108. In *Cayward,* the court distinguished between verbal misrepresentations and "manufacturing false documents" for the purpose of misrepresenting the strength of the government's case, stating that neither the suspect's nor the public's expectations "encompass the notion that the police will knowingly fabricate tangible documentation or physical evidence against an individual." 552 So. 2d at 974. In particular, the court expressed concern that "[a] report falsified for interrogation purposes might well be retained and filed in police paperwork," with the result that they might unintentionally "be admitted as substantive evidence against the defendant." *Id.* at 974–75.

109. *But see* Beasley v. United States, 512 A.2d 1007, 1010 (D.C. 1986) (admitting confession).

110. *But see* State v. Jackson, 304 S.E.2d 134, 144 (N.C. 1983) (admitting confession).

111. For a discussion of these cases, *see* White, *False Confessions, supra* chapter 1, note 40, at 128.

112. See *supra* chapter 12.

113. 384 U.S. at 453 (quoting from O'Hara, Fundamentals of Criminal Investigation 106 (1953)).

114. *Id.,* quoting O'Hara, *supra* note 113, at 106.

115. Parloff, *False Confessions, supra* chapter 12, note 59, at 60.

CHAPTER 15

Conclusion

Over the past two-thirds of a century, the Supreme Court has struggled to find some means of accommodating law enforcement's interest in obtaining reliable confessions and the individual's interest in not being subjected to overreaching interrogation practices. What judgment should we make of the Court's most recent efforts to accommodate these conflicting interests? Specifically, is there merit to Cassell's argument that *Miranda* has unnecessarily burdened law enforcement's ability to obtain reliable statements from suspects? And, from the opposite perspective, have the Court's decisions provided adequate safeguards for individuals subjected to police interrogation?

When *Miranda* was decided, the Warren Court undoubtedly believed that its safeguards would provide significant protection for suspects subjected to custodial interrogation, with the result that interrogators would obtain significantly fewer incriminating statements. During the thirty-five years that *Miranda* has been in effect, however, the post-*Miranda* Court has weakened *Miranda*'s safeguards. And as *Miranda*'s safeguards have become weaker, interrogators have become increasingly sophisticated in developing strategies designed to overcome *Miranda*'s remaining obstacles. As a result, interrogators are able to induce suspects to waive their *Miranda* rights in the great majority of cases; and even when they cannot so induce them, they are still sometimes able to obtain admissible incriminating statements.

In view of the way interrogators have adapted to *Miranda*, Cassell's concerns seem misplaced. In comparison to a system under which the due process voluntariness test provides the only protections for suspects subjected to custodial interrogation, *Miranda*'s safeguards have led to the loss of some incriminating statements. Given interrogators' ability to surmount the obstacles posed by *Miranda*, however, the burden that the loss of these statements imposes on law enforcement is undoubtedly small. In cases where the police are most eager to obtain incriminating statements, interrogators are generally able to employ strategies that enable them to surmount the obstacles posed by *Miranda*.

In assessing *Miranda*, moreover, we should consider its efficacy in providing protections for suspects as well as the burdens it imposes on law enforcement. *Miranda*'s safeguards provide both symbolic and actual protection for suspects. Symbolically, *Miranda*'s warnings represent the government's commitment to respecting the autonomy of even its most marginal citizens. In essence, the warnings inform suspects subjected to custodial interrogation that they have the right to remain silent and, if they do submit to interrogation, they can protect themselves through demanding the presence of an attorney or halting the interrogation. The warnings thus symbolize the government's recognition of rights that should be afforded to all individuals, including those suspected of crimes.

In the real world, of course, the great majority of suspects fail to take advantage of the rights afforded by *Miranda*. Nevertheless, in comparison to the protections afforded by the due process voluntariness test, *Miranda*'s safeguards provide practical as well as symbolic protection. Under the due process test, an interrogator only needed to be concerned about a court's after-the-fact evaluation of the tactics she employed during the interrogation. The suspect's statements would be excluded only if a court concluded that the interrogator's tactics were sufficiently offensive to render the statements involuntary. Under *Miranda*, however, the interrogator must also be concerned about the suspect's reaction to her tactics. In at least some cases, the interrogator's knowledge that the suspect can respond to her questions by invoking his rights—and thereby halting the interrogation—will incline her toward employing less intimidating interrogation techniques, producing a system under which confessions are more likely to occur as the "result of persuasion and the suspect's overconfidence" rather than "pressure and fear."[1]

But do *Miranda*'s safeguards go far enough? Does the combination of these safeguards and the protections afforded by the due process voluntariness test provide adequate protection for suspects subjected to custodial interrogation? Neither the frequency with which modern interrogators are able to obtain incriminating statements nor the examples of cases in which interrogators employ abusive interrogation practices demonstrate that the Court's restrictions on interrogators are inadequate. In accommodating law enforcement and individual interests, the Court may have developed a set of restrictions that enable interrogators to be extremely successful in obtaining incriminating statements while still prohibiting them from employing interrogation tactics that would be viewed as pernicious when measured against contemporary standards of fairness. Evidence that interrogators sometimes employ clearly pernicious interrogation practices, moreover, does not establish that the Court's constitutional restrictions are inadequate. Since we live in an imperfect world, the Court's restrictions' failure to deter prohibited interrogation practices in some cases is inevitable. In evaluating the adequacy of the Court's restrictions, the focus should be on whether they are generally effective in restraining the police from engaging in pernicious interrogation practices. So long as police interrogation is tolerated, no set of constitutional restrictions can be expected to eliminate *all* improper interrogation practices.

A careful examination of both modern interrogation practices and the Court's role in monitoring them indicates, however, that the safeguards provided by *Miranda* and the post-*Miranda* due process voluntariness test do not adequately restrain the police from employing interrogation practices that should properly be viewed as pernicious. Based on both long-standing and contemporary societal norms, interrogation practices that are substantially likely to produce untrustworthy statements should be viewed as pernicious. If this benchmark is accepted, the inadequacy of the Court's current constitutional restrictions becomes clear.

It is not just that a substantial number of police-induced false confessions have been shown to exist or even that the frequency with which modern interrogation practices produce such confessions—at least in high-profile cases—appears surprisingly high. Rather, a particularized examination of interrogations resulting in probably false confessions indicates that widely employed interrogation practices have considerable potential for producing false confessions; and analysis of controlling Supreme Court doctrine indicates that neither *Miranda* nor the post-*Miranda* voluntariness test has any significant potential for restraining the police from employing these practices. It thus appears that the Court's current constitutional restrictions not only fail in fact to restrain, but are not even effectively designed to restrain, interrogation practices that should be recognized as pernicious.

Miranda's safeguards clearly do not restrain the police from employing such practices. Once a suspect waives his *Miranda* rights, *Miranda,* as interpreted by the Burger and Rehnquist Courts, provides no restrictions on interrogation practices. The due process voluntariness test, moreover, does not effectively fill this gap. Although the pre-*Miranda* due process test was designed to prohibit pernicious interrogation practices, one of the problems with that test was that, with the exception of extremely abusive practices, it generally failed to identify the specific interrogation practices that should be prohibited. Although the post-*Miranda* due process voluntariness test is ostensibly the same as the pre-*Miranda* test, in practice the latter test provides even fewer restrictions than the former. Indeed, one of *Miranda*'s most unfortunate consequences is that it has had the effect of weakening the due process voluntariness test. Once a court finds that a suspect has waived his *Miranda* rights, establishing that the suspect's confession was involuntary is extremely difficult in practice. As a result, the Court's current constitutional protections do not provide adequate safeguards for suspects subjected to custodial interrogation.

In order to address this problem, the Court needs to refurbish the due process voluntariness test so that it will be more effective in restraining the police from employing interrogation practices that are substantially likely to produce untrustworthy statements. Toward this end, the Court should mandate a mechanism that will enable lower courts to make more accurate findings of fact in police interrogation cases. In the absence of unusual circumstances, police conducting an interrogation should be required to electronically record the interrogation so that a reviewing court will have a full record of the interrogation techniques employed and their apparent effect on the suspect.

In addition, the Court should refine the due process test so that it prohibits specific interrogation practices that are substantially likely to produce untrustworthy statements. In identifying such practices, the Court should draw from empirical data as well as intuition and precedent. At a minimum, the Court should impose more stringent restrictions on interrogation of mentally handicapped suspects, shorten interrogations' permissible length, and prohibit or closely monitor tactics, such as threats, promises, and certain types of deception, that are particularly likely to induce untrustworthy statements.

As Kamisar's writings on police interrogation have demonstrated,[2] our simultaneous commitments to promoting law enforcement's interest in obtaining confessions and to protecting individuals from overreaching interrogation practices have created a nearly irreconcilable tension. If the police must be granted authority to engage in effective questioning of suspects, it will obviously be difficult to insure that "the terrible engine of the criminal law . . . not be used to overreach individuals who stand helpless against it."[3] If we are in fact committed to accommodating these conflicting interests, however, some means must be found for imposing appropriate restraints on the police when they engage in interrogation. Through refurbishing the due process in the ways I have specified, the Court will at least come closer to imposing appropriate restraints on police interrogators and thereby reducing the likelihood that "the terrible engine of the criminal law . . . not be used to overreach individuals who stand helpless against it."[4]

NOTES

1. Stephen J. Schulhofer, *Reconsidering Miranda*, 54 U. CHI. L. REV. 435, 461 (1987).
2. KAMISAR, ESSAYS, *supra* chapter 1, note 24, at 728, 732.
3. See Culombe v. Connecticut, 367 U.S. 568, 581–82 (1961) (plurality opinion of Frankfurter, J.), quoted in KAMISAR, ESSAYS, *supra* chapter 1, note 24, at 13.
4. *Id.*

Table of Cases

Index